STEPPING STONES to an ABUNDANT LIFE

STEPPING STONES
to an
ABUNDANT LIFE

David O. McKay

Compiled by
Llewelyn R. McKay

Published by Deseret Book Company Salt Lake City, Utah 1971

Library of Congress Catalog Card No. 77-158727

SBN No. 87747-442-7

Copyright 1971
by
Deseret Book Co.

President David O. McKay

The life of President David O. McKay is distinguished by a singular embodiment of the highest ideals—both spiritual and educational—which are espoused by The Church of Jesus Christ of Latter-day Saints and its people.

He was born September 8, 1873 at Huntsville, Utah, the first son of David and Jennette Evans McKay, and through them received the rich cultural heritage of his Scottish and Welsh forebears. His early life was spent on the family farm in Huntsville where he developed a love of the outdoors, of animals and of sports which always characterized him.

In 1897 he was graduated from the University of Utah as president and valedictorian of his class, and entered directly upon a two-year mission in Great Britain. On his return he became a member of the faculty of Weber Stake Academy at Ogden (later Weber College), and less than three years later, at the age of 29, he became its principal. There his rich talents as teacher and administrator enriched the lives of the many students and associates who came under his influence.

Four years later, in 1906, he was ordained a member of the Quorum of the Twelve and became also a member of the General Superintendency of the Deseret Sunday School Union and a member of the Church Board of Education. He continued as a member of the Board of Trustees of Weber Academy, and later served as Church Commissioner of Education.

President McKay was one of the greatest missionaries of the Church. In 1920-21 he made a world tour of Church missions, during which he dedicated the land of China for the preaching of the Gospel. The following year he became president of the European Mission, and opened the Armenian Mission in 1924. In later years he also visited missions of the Church in Europe, South America and South Africa.

In 1934 he was sustained as second counselor to President Heber J. Grant in the First Presidency of the Church, and served in this position for eleven years. He served also in the same capacity during the presidency of George Albert Smith from 1945 to 1951. On April 9, 1951 he was sustained as President of the Church.

President McKay was an inspiring leader in education throughout his life. In addition to his service on the Church Board of Education and as Church Commissioner of Education from 1919 to 1921, he served as a member of the Board of Regents of the University of Utah, as president of the Board of Trustees of Utah State Agricultural College, and as a member and president of the Board of Trustees of Brigham Young University. In recognition of his great service and leadership there have been conferred upon him honorary doctorate degrees from Brigham Young University, Utah State Agricultural College, University of Utah and Temple University.

President McKay married Emma Ray Riggs on January 2, 1901. They have four sons and two daughters.

He died January 18, 1970, and she died a few months later on November 14.

Preface

President David O. McKay endeared himself to all
people with whom he met because of his universality and
his sincerity. He possessed an eminent degree of communi-
cation to men, women and children from all walks of life.
His knowledge of literature and his own ability in writing
gave force and power to influence countless individuals.
He had the charm and versatility to be at ease among rulers
and leaders of the world, as well as being a potent force to
the lowly.

During his long and brilliant career as a religious
leader, the world gained in material things, in science and
invention. He was cognizant of the marvelous progress of
man, yet at the same time he spoke and wrote of our
need to recognize the true and lasting values of life—belief
in and reverence for Deity—Peace—and the Brotherhood
of Man.

He awakened anew the hope in the philosophy found
in the principles of Christianity as opposed to agnostic
thinking. The ultimate goal is a good character. All mankind has the capacity to reach for something higher and
finer by mastering his baser impulses.

The pages of this book are to help us re-live and understand the messages he imparted to us and to inspire us with
hope for today and the years ahead. He has given to us a

profound analysis of his attitudes toward the spiritual state of mankind. His life, his works, reflect a deep respect and love for the goodness of his fellowman. Happiness, he believed is to be found in the family relationships as they reflect the eternal principles of love for one another.

Henry A. Smith travelled extensively with father and reported his messages to the press. I am grateful to him for reading the proofs of this manuscript and for his valuable suggestions. I am also deeply indebted to my wife, Alice, for her encouragement and help.

Llewelyn R. McKay

Contents

Section One —

Gospel Principles
and the Community

The Abundant Life in a Selfish World

I approach this subject with the belief that young people would like to live the abundant life. You want to live and have a good time, and not be deceived by an improper way of getting that good time. Is that not true?

> And now I am no more in the world, but these are in the world, and I come to thee . . .
>
> I have given them thy word; and the world hath hated them, because they are not of the world, even as I am not of the world.
>
> I pray not that thou shouldst take them out of the world, but that thou shouldst keep them from the evil.
>
> (John 17:11-14-15.)

You may add the phrase, "of the world," or take the revised interpretation— "that thou shouldst keep them from the evil one."

Thus, in perhaps the most impressive prayer ever offered, Jesus prayed for his disciples on the night that he faced Gethsemane. Nor did he plead for his disciples alone, but, as he said, "I pray not for these alone, but for them also which shall believe on me through their (the disciples') word." (John 17:2.)

There is our first point tonight. In this text is a clear implication of the divine purpose for man's being in this mortal probation. This purpose is expressly stated in the Book of Abraham by the eternal Father to his fellow intelligences as follows: ". . . We will make an earth whereon these (organized intelligences) may dwell. And we will prove them herewith, to see if they will do all things whatsoever the Lord their God shall command them." (Abraham 3:24-25.)

And so our place in this world is divinely appointed. We are not to be out of it. Christ himself prayed that we should not be taken out of it. Remember the phrase "but that thou shouldst keep them from the evil."

Tonight we have listened to some of the problems which young men and young women face while sojourning in this state of mortality. Let me summarize them:

First: Church ideals and Sunday sports;
Second: Choosing companions;
Third: Observing the Word of Wisdom;
Fourth: Does active membership in the Church inhibit or enhance one's freedom in development?
Fifth: The value of chastity in a world of lowering moral standards;
Sixth: "In the world but not of the world;"
Seventh: The value of doing right "though none might see me;"
Eighth: Getting back on the moral and spiritual highway.

Now, before commenting upon each of these specifically, I think it is well to consider some basic facts of life, which, when more clearly understood, may prove helpful directives in these and other difficulties which we meet in daily vicissitudes. There will be no time tonight to elaborate on these. I am going to give them to you because I think you will accept them, but we want those who are skeptical also to accept them. If you doubt them, go to your teachers, and they will prove that they are right.

I. Man a Dual Being

First, man is a dual being, and his life a plan of God. That is the first fundamental fact to keep in mind. Man has a *natural* body and a *spiritual* body. In declaring this fact the scriptures are very explicit: "And the Gods formed man from the dust of the ground, and took his spirit (that is, man's spirit), and put it into him; and breathed into his nostrils the breath of life, and man became a living soul." (Abraham 5:7.)

Man's body, therefore, is but the tabernacle in which his spirit dwells. *Too many, far too many, are prone to regard the body as the man, and consequently direct their efforts to the gratifying of the body's pleasures, its appetites, its whims, its desires, its passions.* Too few recognize that *the real man is an immortal spirit,* which "intelligence or the light of truth," animated as an individual entity before the body was begotten, and that *this spiritual entity with all its distinguishing traits will continue after the body ceases to respond to its earthly environment.* Said the Savior: "I came forth from the Father, and am come into the world; again, I leave the world, and go to my Father. (John 16:28.)

As Christ's pre-existent spirit animated a body of flesh and bones, so does the pre-existent spirit of every human being born into this world. Will you keep that in mind as the first basic truth of life.

The question, then, is: which will give the more abundant life—pampering our physical nature, or developing our spiritual selves? Is not that the real problem?

II. Man Has His Free Agency

The second fundamental fact is that man has his free agency. "For the power is in men wherein they are agents unto themselves." (D&C 58:28.)

All truth is independent in that sphere in which God has placed it, to act for itself, as all intelligences also; otherwise there is no existence.

Behold, here is the agency of man, and here is the condemnation of man; because that which was from the beginning is plainly manifest unto them, and they receive not the light.

And every man whose spirit receiveth not the light is under condemnation.

For man is spirit. The elements are eternal and spirit and element, inseparably connected, receive a fulness of joy;

And when separated, man cannot receive a fulness of joy.

The elements are the tabernacle of God; yea, man is the tabernacle of God, even temples; and whatsoever temple is defiled, God shall destroy that temple."

(D&C 93:30-35.)

I will conclude that thought by quoting the following:

> You are the person that has to decide
> Whether you'll do it or toss it aside.
> You are the person who makes up your mind
> Whether you'll lead or will linger behind.
> Whether you'll try for the goal that's far
> Or just be contented to stay where you are.
> Take it or leave it. Here's something to do!
> Just think it over—It's all up to you!
>
> Nobody here will compel you to rise;
> No one will force you to open your eyes;
> No one will answer for you yes or no,
> Whether to stay there or whether to go;
> Life is a game, but it's you who must say,
> Whether as cheat or as sportsman you'll play.
> Fate may betray you, but you settle first
> Whether to live to your best or your worst.
>
> So, whatever it is you are wanting to be,
> Remember, to fashion the choice you are free.
> Kindly or selfish, or gentle or strong,
> Keeping the right way or taking the wrong,
> Careless of honor or guarding your pride,

All these are questions which you must decide.
Yours the selection, whichever you do;
The thing men call character's all up to you.

III. Indulgence

The third basic fact to keep in mind is *indulgence,* and
I think there is not one of you here who can accept this
from experience. *Indulgence in appetites and desires of
the physical man satisfy but for the moment, and may lead
to unhappiness, misery, and possible degradation; spiritual
achievements give "joy not to be repented of."*

In his epistle to the Galatians, Paul specifically
enumerates the "works of the flesh," as he calls them, and
the "fruits of the spirit." Note this classification: The
works of the flesh are manifest as these: "Adultery, fornication, uncleanness, lasciviousness, idolatry, witchcraft,
enmity, strife, jealousies, factions, divisions, heresies, en-
vyings, drunkenness, revellings, and such like: of the which
I tell you before, as I have also told you in time past, that
they which do such things shall not inherit the kingdom of
God. *But the fruit of the Spirit* is love, joy, peace, long-
suffering, kindness, goodness, faithfulness, meekness, temperance; against such there is no law. And they that are
Christ's have crucified the flesh with the passions and
lusts. If we live in the Spirit, let us also walk in the Spirit."
(Galatians 5:19-25.)

IV. Spiritual Progress Demands Effort

From the forty days' fast on the Mount of Temptation to the moment on the cross when he cried in triumph:
"It is finished!", Christ's life was a divine example of subduing and overcoming. Full of significance are his words
spoken in his farewell address to his disciples: "These
things I have spoken unto you, that in me ye might have
peace. In the world ye shall have tribulation: but be of
good cheer; I have overcome the world." (John 16:33.)

"Moral law"—I am quoting now from a scientist who
has glimpsed these eternal truths I have named—just

glimpsed them, I think,—but on this he is right—"Moral
law imposes disinterestedness; it orders that which is dis-
agreeable, hard, and painful. Its requirements often revolt
the flesh whose sole ambition is to persist and to enjoy.
It demands the throttling of selfish sentiments for the sake
of something which is still obscure to those who do not
have faith, but which is even more powerful than the instinct of self-preservation: human dignity. The profound
awareness of this dignity poses a highly moral existence
and paves the way to spirituality. And the greatest miracle
is that this cruel law has won the universal respect of man
who sometimes uses his intelligence to combat it, thus
affirming its reality.

"The joys it procures compensate for the sacrifices it
demands. The sentiment of duty accomplished is accompanied by a kind of total satisfaction which alone gives
true peace of soul. The moral man—in olden days one
would have said the virtuous man—spreads happiness and
good will around him, or, if happiness is impossible, the
resignation which takes its place."

There are thousands, millions of men and women who
have high standards, and we do not have to yield to the
few who fail.

Now, having in mind these four fundamental facts of
life—the dual nature of man—his freedom of choice and his
responsibility therefor—indulgence contrary to one's conscience leaves heaviness of heart and unhappiness while
spiritual achievements always give joy—spiritual progress
demands effort—let us consider these eight difficulties:

First Problem: The Sabbath Day. Is it better to
cherish Church ideals on Sunday, or indulge in Sunday
sports? This is simply a question of *physical pleasure* or
spiritual development, and in that we should keep in mind
the following: first, it is a day of rest, essential to the true
development and strength of the body, and that is a
principle which we should publish more generally abroad
and practice. A second purpose for keeping holy the Sab-

bath Day is mentioned in the first sentence of modern revelation: *"That thou mayest more fully keep thyself unspotted from the world."* That is a glorious sentence. You will find it in the Doctrine and Covenants.

Third, keeping the Sabbath Day holy is a law of God, resounding through the ages from Mount Sinai. You cannot transgress the law of God without circumscribing your spirit.

Finally, our sabbath, the first day of the week, commemorates the greatest event in all history—Christ's resurrection, and his visit as a resurrected being to his assembled apostles.

Now if you want to indulge in bodily exercises and amusements, you cannot do it on the Sabbath Day with impunity.

The Second Problem: Choosing Companions. Having in mind our basic truths, this question is a simple one— Whether you will choose companions who appeal to your baser nature, or those who inspire you always to be at your best.

Recently, I was thrilled and thankful when I heard one of your number say that she felt she would have to give up her sweetheart. She likes him, and he likes her, but lately he has chosen the way of the world. He likes a cigaret; he speaks disparagingly of the ideals of the Church. Fortunately, she is wise enough to observe that tendency, and she has "given him up." I say with all my heart: God bless her, because she knows that companionship leads to love. It is from such companionship that you find your companion for the future. If she joins her life with his, her ideals are going to be lowered; and she would rather take a little suffering now than much suffering later.

Choose good companions, and find among them those with whom you would like to go through life and eternity.

Third Problem: Observing the Word of Wisdom. Obedience to the Word of Wisdom develops greater spiritual power, that spiritual power which comes from resistance.   Of the virtue of self-control, consider the following:

> The soul that is worth the honor of earth,
> Is the soul that resists desire.

And this for you students:

> What tho on campus I excell
>   A champ in meet and fight,
> If trained, efficient, still I can't
>   Control an appetite.
>
> What tho exemptions write my name
>   High on the honor-roll,
> Electives, solids fail me if
>   I learn no self-control.
>
> What tho I graduate and soar
>   And life is good to me,
> My heart shall write me failure 'till
>   I learn SELF MASTERY.

It is better for you in youth to say, "No, thank you," when invited to indulge in things which create an appetite for themselves.   Be master, not a slave.   Look around you and you will see the slaves to appetite—unfortunately now, largely among women—slaves!   Where is the spiritual power in these future mothers?

Fourth Problem: Does Active Membership in the Church Inhibit or Enhance One's Freedom and Development?   Can you think of any organization in the world in which you can serve more effectively in an organized way than in the Church of Jesus Christ?   Now I mention service and character because those are the only two things which we can take with us in a few years when we leave this world.

The question is: what have you made of yourself—your character; and what service have you rendered to others?   Do you remember that question given by some man whom I cannot name?

Supposing today were your last day on earth,
The last mile of the journey you've trod;
After all of your struggles how much are you worth
How much can you take home to God?
Don't count as possessions your silver and gold,
Tomorrow you leave these behind,
And all that is yours to have and to hold;
Is the service you've given mankind.

Fifth Problem: Chastity. The dominant evil in the world today is unchastity. I repeat what appeared over the signature of President Joseph F. Smith while he was living: "No more loathsome cancer disfigures the body and soul of society today than the frightful affliction of sexual sin. It vitiates the very fountains of life and bequeaths its foul effects to the yet unborn as a legacy of death."

He who is unchaste in young manhood is untrue to a trust given to him by the parents of the girl, and she who is unchaste in maidenhood is untrue to her future husband, and lays the foundation of unhappiness in the home, suspicion, and discord. Do not worry about these teachers who say something about inhibitions. Just keep in mind this eternal truth that chastity is a virtue to be prized as one of life's noblest achievements. It contributes to the virility of manhood. It is the crowning virtue of womanhood, and every red-blooded man knows that is true. It is a chief contributing factor to a happy home; it is the source of strength and perpetuity of the nation.

Sixth Problem: In the World but not of the World. There is no loss of prestige in maintaining in a dignified way your standards. I thought of a great illustration in literature wherein a Jewish maiden won the respect even of a profligate.

Read the story of Rebecca, that beautiful character in Sir Walter Scott's "Ivanhoe," who was the prisoner of Brian de Bois-Guilbert. He had chosen her for base reasons. Others of his crowd chose the old father to rob him of his wealth. When Brian de Bois-Guilbert came in to take charge of his prize, Rebecca "had already unclasped two costly bracelets and a collar, which she hastened to proffer to the supposed outlaw, concluding naturally to gratify his avarice was to bespeak his favor." "Take these," she said, "and be merciful to me and my aged father! These ornaments are of value, yet they are trifling to what he would bestow, to obtain our dismissal from this castle, free and uninjured."

"Fair flower," replied the outlaw, "These pearls are orient, but they yield in whiteness to your teeth; the diamonds are brilliant, but they cannot match your eyes; and ever since I have taken up this wild trade, I have made a vow to prefer beauty to wealth."

"Thou art no outlaw," said Rebecca; "No outlaw had refused such offers. . . . Thou art a Norman—a Norman, noble perhaps in birth—Oh be so in thy actions, and cast off this fearful masque of outrage and violence!"

"I am not an outlaw, then, fair rose of Sharon . . . And I am one who will be more prompt to hang thy neck and arms with pearls and diamonds, which so well become them, than to deprive thee of these ornaments."

"What would'st thou have of me," said Rebecca, "if not my wealth?—We can have nought in common between us—you are a Christian—I am a Jewess—our union were contrary to the laws alike of the church and the synagogue."

"It were so, indeed," replied Brian de Bois-Guilbert, laughing: "wed with a Jewess?—not if she were the Queen of Sheba!"

And then Rebecca knew his purpose. She threw open the latticed window, and an instant later stood on the verge of the parapet, with not the slightest screen between her and the tremendous depth below, and exclaimed: "Remain where thou art, proud Templar, or at thy choice, advance!—one foot nearer, and I plunge myself from the precipice; my body shall be crushed out of the very form of humanity upon the stones of that court-yard, ere it become the victim of thy brutality!"

As she spoke this, she clasped her hands and extended them towards Heaven, as if imploring mercy on her soul before she made the final plunge. The Templar hesitated, and a resolution which had never yielded to pity or disgrace, gave way to his admiration of her fortitude. "Come down," he said, "Rash girl—I swear by earth, and sea, and sky, I will offer thee no offence."

And the reprobate for the first time in his life was taught respect for womanhood.

You can be in this world and "not of the world." Keep your chastity above everything else.

Seventh Problem: The Value of Doing Right though None Might See Me. I will conclude with this addition:

> Sow a thought, reap an act
> Sow an act, reap a habit
> Sow a habit, reap a character,
> Sow a character, reap an eternal destiny.

"Tell me what you think about when you do not have to think and I will tell you what you are."

Temptation does not come to those who have not thought of it before. Keep your thoughts clean, and it will be easy to resist temptations as they come.

Eighth Problem: Getting Back on the Moral and Spiritual Highway. I, too, have mentioned the prodigal son who first "came to himself" before he turned his face homeward. Come back home, back to the path of virtue, but sense your own evil, and remember that there might be many who have been hurt on your way down.

When a man was asked how he could help those he had injured, particularly in slander, a good, wise old man took a sack of feathers, scattered them, and then he said: "Now, try to gather them up."

He said: "Oh, I cannot!"

That is just it.   Let us be careful that we have not wounded people, and hurt them as we have been going down selfishly on the road of indulgence.

Young people: Is it the body you are going to serve and be a slave, or is it the spirit you are going to develop, and live happily in this life and in the world to come?

"I pray not that thou shouldst take them out of the world, but that thou shouldst keep them from the evil."

One Safe Guide for Humanity

This is the stone which was set at nought of you builders, which is become the head of the corner. Neither is there salvation in any other: for there is none other name under heaven given among men, whereby we must be saved. (Acts 4:11-12.)

In these sublime and impressive words, Peter, the chief Apostle of our Lord testified before the Sanhedrin and through these rulers to the entire nation that only in Jesus Christ lies the hope of men.

This testimony was given in the presence of Annas and Caiaphas, high priests, John and Alexander, and others who had shortly before that condemned Jesus to the cross. These rulers had admitted the reality of a great miracle. The important man whom Peter had healed through the power of Christ was standing before them. Said they, that indeed a notable miracle "hath been done by them is manifest for all them that dwell in Jerusalem, and we cannot deny it." "By what power, or by what name, have ye done this?" they demanded of the Apostles. Boldly Peter answered: "Be it known unto you all and to all the people of Israel, that by the name of Jesus Christ of Nazareth, whom ye crucified, whom God raised from the dead, even by him doth this man stand here before you whole."

Today, as never before, the purport of this message should be heeded.

We are living in one of the extraordinary periods of the world's history—perhaps the most epoch-making period of all times. There is ample evidence on every hand that we are witnessing one of those tidal waves of human thought and emotion which periodically sweep over the world and change the destiny of the human race. It is a time that demands clear thinking and sound judgment.

Whether we are willing to admit it or not this is a revolutionary period. There is social and political upheaval. Thoroughly tested, well-tried principles are being thrown into discard. "Long accepted social theories," writes Charles Foster Kent, "have suddenly been rejected, and new ones are being adopted. Many of the moral standards of our fathers are being set aside in theory as well as in practice. The rising generation has no fear and little respect for elders. The elders, recognizing what a wreck they have made of civilization, question their own infallibility. Religious dogmas long regarded as the cornerstones of religion and the Church are being disproved or supplanted by the discoveries of modern science.

"It is not strange that the majority of the men and women in this world are unhappy because they feel the foundations beneath them are tottering."

At a noon-day luncheon given in Salt Lake City recently, the president of a national organization spoke of liberties and rights already lost, and appealed to the people to preserve those remaining. An experienced United States Congressman, characterized as the best lawyer in Congress, recently said: "There isn't a sensible person in this room now who can be certain that he can leave to his children the heritage of the privilege of being free."

> The world needs men, true men
>   who cannot be bought or sold,
> Men who have scorned to violate
>   the truth—genuine gold.

Changes in Progress in Discovery of Science

Changes and advancement in scientific discovery and invention have been much more marked and rapid than in the political realm.

For example, "people among whom Jesus lived never dreamed of a railroad, of a steamboat, of an automobile; could not have pictured by the wildest stretch of imagination the airplane or the radio. People in that day never saw a factory, a drill or a sulky plow. The only combined harvester that garnered wheat then was a man and a sickle."

It is said that in "the democracy of ancient Greece, the *Stentor* had a voice "as powerful as fifty voices of other men" but in our modern democracy, the candidate for high office whose voice is amplified and broadcast by mechanical means, can pour his promises or persuasion into the ears of millions without troubling them to rise from their easy chairs." The printing press, the railway, the steamship, the airplane, the telegraph, the telephone, the radio, and now the atomic bomb have put a power in the hands of man more potent for his progress or for his destruction than imagination can conceive. This vast increase of physical power becomes sinister and evil when put in the hands of men actuated by low ideals and evil motives.

Notwithstanding all our achievements, social unrest was never more pronounced than it is today. The difficult problems that arise between capital and labor are still unsolved. The evils of the slum and of the brothel are still with us.

The burden of taxes and the proper distribution of wealth are questions perplexing the wisest minds. Truly, we are living in an age of shifting opinions, of swiftly changing human relations. Man's wisdom is baffled. Obviously, there never was a greater need for anchorage to fixed principles, and never-changing truths.

Men are in need of a safe pilot to serve as a guide over the troubled and turbulent waters through which we are now sailing.

Men Must Change Motives and Ideals

If we would have a better world, it is evident that men must change their motives. Hatred and jealousy, envy, and selfishness must be replaced by wholesome, kindly thoughts and emotions. "Right thoughts and feelings if persistently kept in the forefront inevitably lead to right actions."

Ideals are stimulants to progress. Without them man would degenerate, and civilization would "cream and mantle like a standing pool." Through hope, ideals, and aspirations, God inspires men to move upward and onward toward the higher and better life.

Moral Ideals and Spiritual Teachings

The world needs fundamentals, eternal verities that never change. It needs to adopt the teachings of the man into whose hands the soldiers drove the iron spikes, "the only world-conqueror who came with clean hands," from whom down through the centuries have come these assuring words: *"I am the light of the world; he that followeth me shall not walk in darkness, but shall have the light of life."*

In the words of J. William Hudson, Professor of Philosophy, University of Missouri, "If there is to be social and political regeneration in the republic and in the rest of the world, it must be by tremendous regeneration of moral ideals."

Faith in God and Reverence for Sacred Things

One of the fundamental conditions contributive to a person's right thinking and acting is a reverence for God. A growing disbelief among the masses of mankind in a Supreme Being is a principal source of crime.

When God becomes the center of our being, "we become conscious of a new aim in life." To nourish and delight the body, as all animals do, is no longer a chief end
of mortal existence. Spiritual attainment, not physical
possessions, becomes the chief goal. God is not viewed
from the standpoint of what we may get from him, but
what we may give to him. Man serves God best by serving his children.

In an address delivered to the medical graduates of
the Edinburgh University, Sir Alexander Ralph Simpson,
Dean of the Faculty of Medicine, said:

I do not know in what mood of pessimism I might have stood
before you today had it not been that ere the dew of youth had
dried from off me, I made friends with the sinless Son of Man who
is the world head and the stream that vitalizes all advance in civilization and who claims to be the first and the last and is the life
forever more and has the keys of death and the unseen. My experience compels me to own that claim for to me he has established
a vivid and vivifying correspondence with our supersensuous environment. He has made us see that at the heart of things there is
a Father's heart. He has made us know that in the complex play of
circumstances, the reins of progress are in the hands of a circum-
stant who makes all things work together for our good.

Recently I made the remark that never before in the
history of the world has there been such need as today of
spiritual awakening. Not that man is more depraved, not
that he is less religious, but that he has in his grasp such
seemingly unlimited mechanized power. If you put bombs
into the hands of an inexperienced child, he is likely to
blow himself to pieces. To a degree, that is just what we
are witnessing today in the world. In the hands of undeveloped, spiritually unresponsive people has been placed
the power of explosives, the radio, the airplane, the sub-
marine, all the concentrated power of electricity, and now
the breaking up of the atom. Unless there is a spiritual
awakening, civilization is threatened. The carnal-minded

in the world are causing heartaches and threatening the extinction of the race.

A spiritual awakening in the hearts of millions of men and women would bring about a changed world. I am hopeful that the dawning of that day is not far distant. My faith in the ultimate triumph of the Gospel of Jesus Christ assures me that a spiritual awakening must come. To bring this about is the responsibility of the youth of the Church in whom I have confidence and place my hope.

Sacredness of Personality

Central in Christ's teachings is the guiding principle of Love; and comprehended in it is the divine ideal of the sacredness of personality. A proper conception of this principle will ameliorate many of the present ills of society, and contribute to the benefit and happiness of all human beings. It would bring into active operation the Golden Rule—"Do unto others as you would have others do unto you."

Marriage

Another divine ideal included in His plan is the supreme importance of marriage in the development of the individual and of society. Commenting upon Jesus' teaching regarding this principle, Charles Kent declares:

The wisdom of his conclusion is confirmed by modern sociology, which recognizes in the family the historic and actual basis of all stable society. Today the prevailing disregard of the rights and duties of the family is demonstrating anew their supreme importance. Leaders in modern thought are beginning to see clearly that the only final solution of our greatest political, social and economic problems must come through the faithful and efficient training of the individual in the home. The shame of our divorce courts and of our modern social system is slowly but surely preparing the present generation to listen attentively to Jesus' strenuous teachings regarding marriage.

Unfortunately, modern life is disintegrating the very foundation of the home. Clubs, intemperance, birth-control are insidious but vicious enemies of congenial family life. The evil of divorce, particularly here in the United States, is rampant. According to latest statistics, one out of every three marriages is wrecked on the shoals of divorce. One nation has assumed the right to take complete charge of the children soon after they are born, with the idea that they belong to the State. The fathers and mothers are merely agents with little or no responsibility of rearing the children after they have been brought into the world.

> To build a happy fireside clime
> For weans and for wife
> That's the true pathos and
> Sublime o' human life.

It's a worthy ideal for every young man during his premarital life to be loyal to his future wife; and for every young woman to be worthy of pure motherhood.

Loyalty

An eternal principle associated with the home is loyalty. "A father who can be trusted, a husband who can be believed, a man who can be relied upon, a daughter who can be depended upon—these are the jewels of home."

A Sense of Obligation

"Live and let live" is an old adage. "Live and *help* live" is a better one.

Selfishness is a principal cause of all our troubles, and the chief instigator of war. A true sense of our relationship to others and even a faint willingness to contribute to their happiness will help to overcome this almost universal evil of selfishness and envy.

> Man cannot live by himself alone
> All that we send into the hearts of others
> Comes back into our own.

Noted men and women of the world who have lifted the world up and pushed it forward to higher ideals are those who are willing to sacrifice themselves for others and for principle.

The dominant motive in man and in nations is still self-preservation, self-advancement, self-comfort without consideration for the welfare of others, material achievements, accumulation of money, accentuation of power at the subjugation, even the enslavement of the individual. From the root of selfishness spring all the pestilential vices that disrupt the harmony of human relationships. Envy, hatred, greed, bigotry, the exercising of unrighteous dominion in governing men and crushing them, unrestrained passion, ungoverned appetites, drunkeness and debauchery are debasing evils that banish happiness and peace from the hearts of men and create disunity and strife in communities and nations throughout the world. These are enemies to be conquered in the better future. You may call it a Utopian dream, if you will, but selfishness must be subdued before mankind can experience peace. No peace or freedom can come to this world so long as men live only for themselves. Self-preservation is the first law of nature, but it is not a law of spiritual growth. He who lets selfishness and his passions rule him binds his soul in slavery, but he who, in the majesty of spiritual strength, uses his physical tendencies and yearnings, and his possessions to serve purposes higher than personal indulgence and comfort, takes the first step toward the happy and useful life. This truth was taught not only "in the beginning" when the Gospel was first revealed to man, but also when Jesus began his earthly ministry. On the Mount of Temptation was enacted the first scene in Christ's earthly drama of the abundant life. There he resisted the challenge to gratify his appetite; he turned aside the appeal to his vanity and pride; he scorned the bribe of worldly wealth and power as in spiritual victory he said to the Tempter: "Get thee hence!" Only thus by the brilliant triumph of the spirit over the flesh can we hope for a better world.

Human Nature Must Be Changed

Our young men accepted the challenge and met in deadly conflict dictatorship and inhuman aggression. They won a glorious victory, but many will fight no more. It is our task to carry on!

Down through the ages men have retreated before the formidable enemies we now face; and thinkers, and some philosophers declare hopelessly that these enemies cannot be conquered, except only by changing human nature, and that, they insist, cannot be done.

I believe with the English writer, Beverly Nichols, that it can be done, and that "human nature *can* be changed, here and now.

"Human nature *has* been changed in the past.

"Human nature *must* be changed on an enormous scale in the future, unless the world is to be drowned in its own blood.

"And only Christ can change it . . . .

"Twelve men did quite a lot to change the world nineteen hundred years ago. Twelve simple men, with only the wind to bear them over the seas, with only a few pence in their pockets, and a shining faith in their hearts. They fell far short of their ideal, their words were twisted and mocked, and false temples were built over their bones, in praise of a Christ they would have rejected. And yet, by the light of their inspiration, many of the world's loveliest things were created, and many of the world's finest minds inspired.

"If twelve men did that, nineteen hundred years ago, what might not twelve men do today? For God has now given us the power of whispering across the space, of transmitting our thoughts from one end of the earth to another. What shall we whisper— what shall we think? That is the question!"

Need of a Guiding Light

In the incident depicted by our text, Peter courageously declares what we shall think, what we shall declare:— that "There is none other name under heaven given among men, whereby we must be saved." Moulders of a better future need the assurance that Christ is the unfailing guide.

Summary and Conclusion

In the United Nations are assembled men of different political views and of varying opinions as to the best form of government. No matter what their political differences may be if they would but apply fundamental Christian principles the objectives of this great organization for peace would be attained. For example, consider how contributive to the ending of war would be the application of individuals and nations of just two of the divine injunctions relating to arbitration and mutual happiness. "Moreover if thy brother shall trespass against thee, go and tell him his fault between thee and him alone: if he shall hear thee, thou has gained thy brother.

"But if he will not hear thee, then take with thee one or two more, that in the mouth of two or three witnesses every word may be established." (Matthew 18:15, 16.)

Though man may not overcome selfishness entirely, if, as conflicts arise, he would but subdue it sufficiently to submit to Christ's principle of arbitration, brute force, as manifested in world conflict would cease.

Again, Jesus taught that men and women fail to live truly, and really amount to nothing unless they have spirituality. The spiritual force underlies everything, and without it nothing worthwhile can be accomplished.

Spiritual needs can be met only by spiritual means. All government, laws, methods and organizations are of no value unless men and women are filled with truth, righteousness, and mercy. Material things have no power to raise the sunken spirit. Gravitation, electricity, and steam are great forces, but they are all powerless to change the motives of men and women. The wealth of a Rockefeller cannot heal a broken heart, and the wisdom of all our universities cannot turn into the paths of righteousness a wayward soul. Men can be born again only through religion.

Whether it is better to walk along the easy road of selfishness and indulgence than to strive through self-mastery and service for the realm of spirituality you must decide. "Whether it is better to serve God than man, judge ye."

"But as for us we cannot but speak the things which we have seen and heard."

In the words of John Oxenham:

God grant us wisdom in these coming days,
  . . .
To pledge our souls with nobler, loftier life,
  To win the world to his fair sanctities,
To bind the nations in a pact of peace.
  And free the soul of life for finer loyalties.

Not since Christ died upon his lonely cross,
  Has time such prospect held of life's new birth;
Not since the world of chaos first was born
  Has man so clearly visaged hope of a new earth.

Not of our own might can we hope to rise
  Above the ruts and soilures of the past,
But, with his help who did the first earth build,
  With hearts courageous we may fairer build this last.

The All-Important Quest

And the two disciples heard him speak,
and they followed Jesus.
Then Jesus turned, and saw them following,
and saith unto them, What seek ye?
They said, Master, where dwellest thou?
(John 1:37, 38.)

These two disciples sought Jesus upon the testimony of John, the Baptist, who, the day before had said: "Behold the Lamb of God which taketh away the sin of the world."

We can only conjecture how clearly or deeply they sensed the fact that in thus seeking the Son of Man they were taking the first step toward eternal life, but this we do know, that the Savior has given the divine assurance that "This is life eternal that they might know thee the only true God and Jesus Christ whom thou hast sent."

Man's success or failure, happiness or misery depend upon what he seeks and what he chooses. What a man is, what a nation is, may largely be determined by his or its dominant quest. It is a tragic thing to carry through life a low concept of it.

The thing a man does practically believe, the thing a man does practically lay to heart, and know for certain concerning his vital relations to this mysterious Universe, and his duty and destiny there, that is in all cases the primary thing for him, and creatively

determines all the rest. This is his religion; or it may be his mere
skepticism and no religion: the manner it is in which he feels himself to be spiritually related to the Unseen World or No World;
and I say, if you tell me what that is, you tell me to a very great
extent what the man is what the kind of things he will do is!

(Carlyle.)

The disciples' answer to the question, "What seek ye?"
gives a key to man's highest and noblest quest: "Master,
where dwellest thou?" saying in effect,—we desire to know
thee, and thy teachings.   Later, Andrew testified to his
brother, Cephas: "We have found the Messias, which being interpreted is the Christ."

"If thou shalt seek the Lord thy God, thou shalt find
him, if thou seek him with all thy heart and with all thy
soul." (Deut. 4:29.)

This, then, is the all-important quest—to seek God and
Jesus Christ, to know whom is eternal life.

Life, and freedom to shape that life, are two of the
most precious gifts to man.   Most men cherish these gifts
and possess an innate longing to achieve higher and better
things—to rise above the sordid and the low, and through
obedience to divine law to experience the joys that come
with being in harmony with a Supreme Being.   True, there
are some who, because of despondency and failure, or because of sinful indulgence, seek in desperation to end their
earthly existence; but normal persons, who sense the value
of moral and spiritual laws, such as kindness, generosity,
consideration for others, reverence for all things sacred, and
other divine attributes which contribute to nobility of
character, with joy and gratitude can say with Coleridge,
"O God, how glorious it is to live."   With expanding vision
they realize the meaning of the divine saying, "This is my
work and my glory—to bring to pass the immortality and
eternal life of man." (P of GP 4:39.)

How May We Know Him?

The messages given in this conference have directly

and indirectly answered that question. Jesus expressed
it clearly when, on one occasion, while attending the Feast
of the Tabernacles, he declared to the Jews who marvelled
at his preaching, "My doctrine is not mine, but his that
sent me. *If any man will do his will, he shall know of the
doctrine, whether it be of God, or whether I speak of myself.*" (John 7:17.) In his sermon on the Mount he expressed the same thought in these words: "Not every one
that saith unto me, Lord, Lord, shall enter into the kingdom of heaven: but he that doeth the will of my Father
which is in heaven." (Matthew 7:21.)

His Will

These statements of the Savior lead us to the next
important step in knowing our Father in Heaven and his
Son. What *is* the Lord's will? His will is summarized in
the memorable reply that Christ gave to the lawyer who
asked him the question, which is the great commandment
in the law. "Thou shalt love the Lord thy God with all thy
heart, and with all thy soul, and with all thy mind. This
is the first and great commandment. And the second is
like unto it, thou shalt love thy neighbor as thyself. On
these two commandments hang all the law and the
prophets." (Matthew 22:37.) Regarding the will of God,
the apostle Peter particularized, when on the Day of Pentecost, with one accord the people asked him and the rest
of the apostles: "Men and brethren, what shall we do?"
"Repent," answered Peter, "and be baptized every one of
you in the name of Jesus Christ for the remission of sins,
and ye shall receive the gift of the Holy Ghost. For the
promise is unto you, and to your children, and to all that are
afar off, even as many as the Lord our God will call."
(Acts 2:37-39.)

Repent means to feel regret, contrition, or compunc-
tion for what one has done or omitted to do. It means to
change one's mind with regard to past or intended action
and conduct on account of regret or dissatisfaction. It

means to conquer selfishness, greed, jealousy, faultfinding, and slander; to control one's temper. It means to rise above the sordid things which pure nature would prompt us to do to gratify our appetites and passions, and to enter into the higher or spiritual realm. Thus we become, in the words of Peter, "Partakers of the divine nature, having escaped the corruption that is in the world through lust." Then, beside this, giving all diligence, Peter admonishes to add "to faith virtue; and to virtue knowledge; and to knowledge temperance; and to temperance patience; and to patience godliness; and to godliness brotherly kindness; and to brotherly kindness charity. For if these things be in you, and abound, they make you that ye shall neither be barren nor unfruitful in the knowledge of our Lord Jesus Christ." (II Peter 1:4-8.)

These, then, are the sign posts along life's highway, which if followed, will lead any man who will do the Lord's will to know his Son the Redeemer of the world, to know whom is eternal life. And while we are gaining this knowledge, which leads to immortality, we find the greatest joy in mortality that can be experienced by the human soul.

The best of all men are they who realize in daily life their luminous hours and transmute their ideals into conduct and character. These are the soul-architects who build their thoughts and deeds into a plan, who travel forward, not aimlessly but toward a destination, who sail not anywhither, but toward a port, who steer, not by the clouds, but by the fixed stars. High in the scale of manhood those who ceaselessly aspire toward life's great Exemplar.

This great Exemplar is Jesus Christ who among all leaders in history, has wielded the greatest influence upon the human family. Wherein lies his greatness—he defeated the lawyer in argument, healed the sick where medicine failed, inspired the greatest music ever written, filled hundreds of thousands of libraries with books, inspired missionaries to go to the darkest depths of Africa; yet, in none of the realms in which other men and women have won renown was he considered great. "In the realm of character, he was supreme."

Today the world's greatest need is for men of integrity, men of honor, men whose word is as good as their bond, leaders of Nations who will consider international agreements sacred. Men whose impelling desire is to know God and Jesus Christ whom he has sent. All the happiness that comes with spiritual gifts may be his—"love, joy, peace, longsuffering, gentleness, goodness, faith, meekness, temperance." Friendship, love, communion with the Infinite —all these, and a thousand other blessings, which God gives him free of charge, are his.

> Earth gets its price
> For what earth gives us, . . .
> 'Tis heaven alone that is given away
> 'Tis only God may be had for the asking.
> (Lowell)

The only thing which places man above the beasts of the field is his possession of spiritual gifts. Man's earthly existence is but a test as to whether he will concentrate his efforts, his mind, his soul upon things which contribute to the comfort and gratification of his physical instincts and passions, or whether he will make as his life's end and purpose the acquisition of spiritual qualities.

Willingness to Serve

Our lives are wrapped up with the lives of others, and we are happiest as we contribute to their happiness. "Whosoever will lose his life for my sake shall find it." (Matthew 16:25.) This paradoxical saying of the Savior contains the crowning element of the upright character. Here we touch the one important phase of true Christianity. Selfishness is subdued, in which greed and avarice must be subordinated to higher principles of helpfulness, or kindliness. "If any man will do his will, he shall know of the doctrine, whether it be of God, or whether I speak of myself."

Choosing the right with unwavering determination, resisting temptations "from within and from without," cheerfulness in the face of difficulties and perplexities, reverence for God and respect for your fellow-men, willingness to assist in the establishment of the Kingdom of God—these, though you might miss some of the emoluments of the world, will bring peace and happiness to your soul, and through obedience to the principles and ordinances of the Gospel, bring immortality and eternal life.

As sure as you can tune in on the radio and hear voices from afar, so sure am I that God is our Father, and that the soul of man can commune with him through the Holy Spirit. So sure am I that Jesus Christ is the Savior of the world, through whom and only through whom may mankind find happiness and peace. So sure am I that the Gospel of Jesus Christ has been restored through the Prophet Joseph Smith and the authority to represent God on earth is again given to men.

Home and Church as Factors in Character Building

With the importance in mind of training youth, I have chosen the theme, "The Home and the Church as Factors in Character Building." As a text I give you that old, old saying, "Train up a child in the way he should go: and when he is old, he will not depart from it." Train the child early in life the way he should go. It is the responsibility of parents and leaders to show youth that way.

We train by thoughts. There is no one great thing which we can give a child which will determine his future any more than there was any one great thing which the rich young ruler could do to obtain eternal life, but there are many little things. As a child grows physically by eating regularly at intervals, by breathing fresh air constantly, by resting at stated intervals, so character is built by little things, by daily contacts, by an influence here, a fact of truth there.

Youth! Young men and young women facing their eternal destiny! What can we do to make them happy? What can we say and do to make them worthy citizens of our republic, faithful members of the Church of Jesus Christ? That is the question.

"The world is passing through troublous times. The

young people today think of nothing but themselves. They
have no reverence for parents or old age. They talk as if
they alone know everything. As for girls, they are forward,
immodest, and unwomanly in speech, behavior, and dress."

Possibly some of you will say, or at least will think,
that that is a pretty severe arraignment of our young people
of today. Others of you will consider it a real denunciation. Well, all of you will be surprised when I tell you
that what I have just read was written about young people
who lived six hundred and seventy-two years ago! That
makes you feel better, doesn't it? It was written in the
year 1274 after Christ. I cited it merely to bring to our
attention the fact that we are prone to think that young
folks today are worse than they used to be and that they
are heading for perdition as never before.

Another purpose that I have in mind is that we might
look with charity upon our young folks, try to enter into
their lives and gain their confidence, then we shall find
they are not entirely bad. This is a fact to which we must
not close our eyes.

Destructive to character is the fact that there is rampant in the intellectual world a disregard for fundamentals,
particularly the truths of religion. Of course, people have
met such conditions before in the world, but if they exist
now we had better face them and see if we can remedy
them.

There appeared in the Sunday School Times an article
commenting upon the lawlessness in the United States
since 1850. The writer had in mind the fact that we have
digressed if not entirely departed from the religious ideals
as set forth in the Bible. He gives us his view as follows:

"In 1850 the character and culture of the American
people demanded the respect of the entire world. European parents sent their sons and daughters to our institutions that they might imbibe this holy atmosphere. The
Sabbath was nationally recognized and observed. The

churches were well attended. Divorces were rare. Juvenile courts were unknown.

"Today America is one of the most lawless of nations. . . .

"What has happened to change this Christian concord of 1850 into this criminal chaos?

"Eighty years ago Americans were still being reared in public schools that included religious instruction. The great "New England Primer," which for more than a hundred and fifty years had been the text book of the American schools, was just passing into discard. Eighty-seven percent of the contents of this remarkable book—which had built the sturdy character of fathers, grandfathers, and great-grandfathers—was Bible. But from that time on the book of books ceased to be an important factor in public instruction."

Then he treats historically the fight that was waged against teaching of the Bible in the public schools as a result of which the teaching of the Bible was eliminated.

"The result of this long, drawn-out school controversy was that both sides lost. Catholics lost their subsidies and were forced to support their own schools. Protestants lost the public teaching of their religion. Public school pupils lost the moral restraint that religion alone can impart. Churches lost many who would have become faithful members. The state found its tax burdens increased and its citizenship degenerating. The sad, sickening consequence of this Godless education can be studied today in the juvenile delinquents who throng our courts and fill our prisons."

"But the real tragedy in America is not that we have permitted the Bible to slip out of our public schools, but that we have so openly neglected to teach it in either the home or the Church. We lament the fact that Bolshevistic and Modernistic teachers have entered our colleges and other institutions of higher learning and misled our youth, when we should weep over our earlier failure to implant the word of God in the heads of our boys and girls. One of our leading educators recently said: 'That the Bible no longer holds the place it once did in the home is a proposition that hardly needs proof.' Even before the World War a prominent writer declared that family worship was so rare as to be almost phenomenal when found."

Recently I had great pleasure in training a well-bred colt. He has a good disposition, clean, well-rounded eye, was well proportioned, and all in all, a choice equine possession. Under the saddle he was as willing, responsive, and cooperative as a horse could be. He and my dog "Scotty" were real companions. I liked the way he would go up to something of which he was afraid. He had confidence that if he would do as I bade him he would not be injured.

But "Dandy" resented restraint. He was ill-contented when tied, and would nibble at the tie-rope until he was free. He would not run away, just wanted to be free. Thinking other horses felt the same, he would proceed to untie their ropes. He hated to be confined in the pasture, and if he could find a place in the fence where there was only smooth wire, he would paw the wire carefully with his feet until he could step over to freedom. More than once my neighbors were kind enough to put him back in the field. He learned even to push open the gate. Though his depredations were provoking and sometimes expensive, I admired his intelligence and ingenuity.

But his curiosity and desire to explore the neighborhood led him and me into trouble. Once on the highway he was hit by an automobile, resulting in a demolished machine, injury to the horse, and slight, though not serious, injury to the driver.

Recovering from that, and still impelled with a feeling of wanderlust, he inspected the fence throughout the entire boundary. He even found the gates wired. So, for a while we thought we had "Dandy" secure in the pasture.

One day, however, somebody left the gate unwired. Detecting this "Dandy" unlatched it, took "Nig," his com-

panion, with him, and together they visited the neighbor's
field. They went to an old house used for storage.
"Dandy's" curiosity prompted him to push open the door.
Just as he had surmised, there was a sack of grain. What a
find! Yes, and what a tragedy! The grain was poisoned
bait for rodents! In a few minutes "Dandy" and "Nig"
were in spasmodic pain, and shortly both were dead.

How like "Dandy" are many of our youth! They are
not bad: they do not even intend to do wrong, but they are
impulsive, full of life, full of curiosity, and long to do something. They, too, are restive under restraint, but if they
are kept busy, guided carefully and rightly, they prove to
be responsive and capable; but if left to wander unguided,
they all too frequently find themselves in the environment
of temptation and too often are entangled in the snares of
evil.

To change men and nations, we must change and direct their way of thinking. "Train up a child in the way
he should go." That is our duty. The home is the most
potent influence in this training. Sunday Schools, Mu-
tuals, Primaries, Relief Societies are only supplemental.
No social, educational or service group could effectively
supplant the home as an effective force in making men out
of boys and women out of girls. In the words of former
President Hoover: "After we have determined every
scientific fact, after we have erected every public safeguard, after we have constructed every edifice for education or training or hospitalization or play, yet all these
things are but a tithe of the physical, moral, and spiritual
gifts which motherhood gives and home confers. None of
these things carry that affection, that devotion of soul,
which is the greatest endowment from mothers."

I know what you are thinking now—that it is from the
broken homes that these wanderers come. I know. And
that they also come from homes in which motherhood has
been debased. I know that, too. The other day a welfare
worker brought a little boy and his sister into my home and

said the mother was down in Bingham. Two little waifs—
father in the army, and mother wallowing in the gutter.
I know when we are speaking of homes that there are
broken homes, but let us not magnify them. As Latter-day
Saints it is our duty to present homes that are ideal. That
is why I am mentioning this matter.

No man or child is happy in doing wrong. Nature
herself teaches us that our actions are bound within certain
limits. But, like the horse, we want to break away from
those limits and go to the dangers beyond them, and boys
and girls should sense that. Growth and happiness are
found within certain restricted areas, beyond which lie
dangerous and injurious indulgences. There is pleasure
and health in eating; but pain and sickness in gormandiz-
ing. There is pleasure in moderate exercise; pain in excessive exertion. In all things, nature says, "thus far shalt thou
go and no farther."

The home is the best place in the world to teach the
child self-restraint, to give him happiness in self-control,
and respect for the rights of others.

Unhappiness in the child's life, as in the adult life,
springs largely from non-conformity to natural and social
laws. The home is the best place in which to develop obedience, which nature and society will later demand. "A
person's individuality is best safe-guarded and developed
through conformity with social conventions; if he has
learned the rules of the same he may hope to modify them,
but until he has learned them his attempts at modification
will be amateurish. If these rules are never learned, then
personal individuality is cramped, and his happiness constricted."

So many of our youth today like to break away from
conventions. They think their parents are old-fashioned.
What a great lesson to learn that you are perfectly free to
do as you please so long as you do not please to trespass
upon the rights of somebody else. My heart aches this
morning because one who was pretty close to me failed—

violated conventions in childhood—later broke through the fence of consideration and decency—found the poison grain of unbelief, and now languishes in spiritual apathy and decay.

It is my opinion, and my opinion is confirmed by experience, that the best time for the child to learn these rules of conformity is between the ages of three and five. I made that statement on another occasion, and someone who reported it put it up between thirteen and fifteen. I mean three and five. If the mother does not get control of the child during those ages, she will find great difficulty in getting control later. It seems to me, then, easy to understand how the home contributes to the happiness of the child, first, by teaching obedience. I do not mean to push and drag or confine—just let the little child be perfectly free to develop until he goes beyond the bounds of safety. Then let him feel the gentle but firm hand of restraint.

Once Sister McKay and I saw this rule effectively illustrated in a zoo in Los Angeles. For the first time in our lives we saw a little baby monkey just learning to toddle. The mother was taking care of it and feeding it. We were interested first in seeing the mother pat the little babe, and try to get it to go to sleep. But the little fellow broke away from the mother and began to climb up the cage. The mother apparently paid no attention and let it climb until it got up to danger. Then she reached up, brought it back, and let it play within the bounds of safety. I thought from nature that was one of the best lessons in control of childhood I had ever seen—the little one was given freedom until the danger point was reached, and then he was gently restrained. Thus, we see the first contribution of the home to the happiness of the child is to impress him with the fact that there are bounds beyond which he cannot go with safety; second, to teach him to be considerate of the rights of others; third, to have him feel that home is a place where confidence and consolations are exchanged; and, fourth, to have him cherish the thought that home is a haven of seclusion and rest from the worries and perplexities of life.

Beaconsfield was right when he said: "The best security for civilization is the dwelling, and that upon properly appointed and becoming dwellings depends more than anything else the improvement of mankind. Such dwellings are the nursery of all domestic virtues, and without a becoming home, the exercise of those virtues is impossible."

But, as already intimated, there are broken homes from which children go rambling into strange fields and have no will power to resist the evil. And there are children from well-directed homes who break away—they find the gate unlocked and away they go to unrestrained indulgence. Many of these come to you Sunday School instructors, so you have to take the place of parent as well as teacher and guide.

The function of the Sunday School is to foster religious education. To inculcate moral and religious ideals in the lives of children was the dominant motive in the mind of Robert Raikes of Gloucester, England, when he organized the first Sunday School at the close of the year 1781, when he took boys and girls off the street ostensibly to teach them to read and write. The real purpose, however, was to let them see that there is a spiritual world in this old physical world; that there is a spiritual happiness that exceeds the pleasures of indulgence of appetites and passions.

The first Sunday School here in the West was held Sunday, December 9, 1859, in the home of Elder Richard Ballantyne. His motive for organizing it was to give the children the privilege of gospel teaching. There were 30 pupils enrolled and the number grew to 50 during the first year. Here is a glimpse of the virility of Mormonism. Many thousands of men and women devoting fifty-two Sundays every year, and hours of study during each week, for the betterment of children and youth, "training them to virtue; habituating them to industry, activity, and spiri-

tuality; making them consider every vice as shameful and
unmanly; firing them with ambition to be useful; making
them disdain to be destitute of any useful knowledge, and
leading them into the joy of the Christ-life, into the friendship of God and the guidance of his Holy Spirit."

There is not a home in the Church, not an individual
that may not and should not come within the radiance of
one or more of these unselfish teachers. But the dimness
or brightness, in other words, the worth of each school
upon the boys and girls and upon the community depends,
first, upon the character, preparation, and devotion of the
officers and teachers; and, secondly, upon the loyalty of
the members and their desire and ability to uphold the
standards and ideals of the school. These two efficiency-
determining elements are fostered by successful class work,
and successful class work is dependent upon personality,
preparation, presentation, and prayer.

Never before in the history of our country was the
state in greater need of young men and young women who
cherish the higher life in preference to the sordid, the selfish, and the obscene. What the opinions of the youth are
today regarding life and its objectives will determine what
the moral standard of the nation will be tomorrow. "The
coming generation," says Mr. Babson, the statistician, "can
see in a minute more than the former generation could see
in a week. The coming generation can out-hear and out-
travel the former generation. Horse-power is expanded
beyond all dreams, but what about manpower, what about
spiritual power, and the power of judgment, discretion and
self-control? Unless there is a development of character
equal to this enlargement of physical forces there is sure
trouble ahead. Years ago an intoxicated man might tip a
buggy over, but commonly the old horse would bring him
home. Today a driver under the influence of liquor maims
and kills; tomorrow, therefore, is something to ponder over.
Without moral progress in pace with physical progress the
airplane will merely make dissipation more disastrous, im-

morality more widespread, and crime more efficient. As one result has been to put hell on wheels, the airplane will put hell on wings unless righteousness too is speeded up. On the development of character depends whether the airplane shall bring prosperity or calamity." And that may be applied now to the splitting of the atom.

Schools and churches should radiate the fact that there are in life certain fundamentals which never change, and which are essential to the happiness of every human soul. Some of these fundamentals are:

1. Honor, integrity, fair-dealing.

2. Another fundamental that never changes is kindness—kindness to animals, to children, and to mankind generally.

> "He prayeth best who loveth best
> All things—both great and small—
> For the dear God who loveth us,
> He made and loveth all."

It is wicked to torment and torture a dumb thing.

3. Another fundamental that never changes is reverence. Profanity, particularly among Church members, is reprehensible. A parent may kneel in prayer, but if after he rises from his knees and in the presence of his children he profanes the name of God, I think he is wicked. Reverence is a high, substantial virtue. I place it next to love itself.

We should appeal to children in Sunday School and Primary, and to youth in Mutual to be reverent when they come into the house of God. We can ask them to speak of his name in reverence. When we pray we say, "Our Father which art in heaven, hallowed be thy name." That is a fundamental which we must not disregard.

If children have never prayed to God in their home, then the Sunday School has the responsibility to teach the existence of that Being; that he is near to us if we can approach him properly, and that there is a wall between us if we defy him and are irreverent. That is why our class room should be more orderly. Busy, humming with industry and thought, yes, but reverent.

It is a good thing for boys and girls to learn that they can go to God in prayer. You students in the university will learn, as students in every school should learn, when you have difficulties that you can receive help and guidance if you seek it in sincerity. Perhaps you will arise as some of us did in youth and feel that your prayers are not answered, but some day you will realize the fact that God did answer your prayers just as a wise parent would have done. That is one of the greatest possessions of youth to feel that you can go to our Father and pour out your heart to him. Associated with faith in a Father in heaven is the fundamental fact that God has revealed the Gospel of Jesus Christ in this day to the Prophet Joseph Smith.

4. Another fundamental is the value of the human soul—that every little ragged barefoot boy is precious in God's sight. Yes, and that poor, forsaken, despised woman is, too. The welfare of each concerns us all. No boy or girl can gratify his or her passions without affecting the entire social group.

"It is not the will of your Father that one of these little ones should perish."

5. Finally I name as among the greatest responsibilities of life, clean fatherhood, and pure motherhood.

Today, youth is prone to ignore conventions, and follow without restraint what the fiery blood of passion prompts. They must be taught that there comes a tomorrow in which the wild expenditures of youth must inevitably be paid. Love is a most vital factor in a man's or a woman's life. To trifle with it by forming philandering habits might contribute to unhappiness and tragedy in married life. It is unfortunate if a girl gets the reputation of being "everybody's sweetheart," or if a boy be looked upon as one who would disregardingly stain a woman's character to gratify his own passionate desires.

No doubt you are teaching this subject indirectly in your Sunday School classes. I think we shall have to teach it more personally. I have mentioned it here, because it is the duty of parents even more than the duty of teachers and officers to get the confidence of their boys and girls so that those boys and girls will give the teachers their confidence. And you will find that that which motivates them most effectively touches this spring of love. The boy will tell you what he heard in the public school by a teacher who himself is probably unchaste. If so, the teacher's mind is poisoned. From such a polluted source, too, often comes encouragement for boys to follow indulgence rather than restraint. Boys, it is not indulgence but morality while you are in your youthful period that will develop your manhood. Girls, it is not the loss of your virtue, but maidenly modesty that will win the love of a man whose love you prize. Young man, your greatest responsibility is to keep the spring of life unpolluted. Do not believe it when some rake tells you that you will weaken your character if you inhibit a desire. Wise teachers can and will explain how nature will take care of that surplus energy through the channels of intellectual and physical activity.

I mention this as one responsibility of the teacher, because sometimes we parents find difficulty in discussing these confidential problems with our boys. Parents should be sufficiently companionable with their boys and girls as to merit their children's confidence. Be companions with them. When parents shirk this duty perhaps you teachers can succeed where parents fail. Teach the boys that it is chastity during youth that gives vigor, strength, and virility of manhood. Teach the girls that chastity is the crown of beautiful womanhood. When young men and young women learn that, and join hands in holy matrimony with a love that entwines their hearts, it is the memory of a virtuous life that contributes to the happiness of the home —not the memory of philandering or the suspicions of one or the other's having been unfaithful in youth. Instead, a memory that they came together as God would have them, prepared to go through life as parents worthy of pure children. It is chastity, not prostitution that contributes to the perpetuity and virility of the race.

"Train a child in the way he should go"—a worthy admonition to parents and teachers for all time!

"One day Jean Val Jean saw some country folks very busy pulling up nettles; he looked at the heap of plants, uprooted, and already wilted, and said: 'This is dead; but it would be well if we knew how to put it to some use. When the nettle is young the leaves make excellent greens; when it is old it has filaments and fibers like hemp and flax. Cloth made from the nettle is worth as much as that made from hemp. Chopped up, the nettle is good for poultry; pounded, it is good for horned cattle. The seed of the nettle mixed with the fodder of animals gives a luster to their skin; the root mixed with salt produces a beautiful yellow dye. It makes, moreover, excellent hay, as it can be cut twice in a season. And what does the nettle need? Very little soil, no care, no culture, except that the seeds fall as fast as they ripen, and it is difficult to gather them; that is all. If we would take a little pain the nettle would be useful; we neglect it and it becomes harmful. Then we kill it. How much men are like the nettle!' After a short silence, he added: 'My friends, remember this, that there are no bad herbs, and no bad men; there are only bad cultivators!' "

I quote this from Les Miserables to impress us all with the responsibility of guiding children and youth. The Sunday School and other auxiliaries offer excellent opportunities so to do. A responsibility of parents is to see that the boys and girls are put in the environment of these meetings.

> "He stood at the cross-roads all alone
> The sunlight in his face;
> He had no thought for the world unknown
> He was set for a manly race,

But the roads stretched east and the roads
    stretched west,
And the lad knew not which road was best.
So he chose the road that led him down,
And he lost the race and the victor's crown,
He was caught at last in an angry snare;
Because no one stood at the cross-roads there
To show him the better road.

Another day at the self same place,
A boy with high hopes stood;
He, too, was set for a manly race,
He was seeking the things that were good;
But one was there who the roads did know
And that one showed him which way to go.
So he turned from the road that would lead
    him down,
And he won the race and the victor's crown.
He walks today the highway fair
Because one stood at the cross-roads there
To show him the better road."

God inspire us to stand at the cross roads and lead
youth onward and upward along the way of truth and
integrity into the presence of God, I pray.

Responsibility of Choice

We men are just a little neglectful in expressing appreciation of what our wives do. Nearly always trouble in the home stems from the man—not always, I find, in disappointment. I grew to manhood thinking that that was the case, and generally speaking, it is. Be that as it may, many of us are like the Scotchman who lost his wife. While he was mourning her departure, his neighbor came in and praised the virtues of the departed wife—a beautiful woman, her noble character, what a good wife and neighbor she was, etc. The bereaved husband listened, and finally said, "Aye, Tammas she was a noble woman. Janet was a guid neebor. She was aye a guid, true wifey tae me, and *I cam near tellin her sae aince or twice.*"

Now, I wish to leave a message, particularly for these young boys and girls. As preliminary to it, I shall read three passages as follows:

From the Book of Moses:

And I, the Lord God, spake unto Moses, saying: That Satan, whom thou hast commanded in the name of mine Only Begotten, is the same which was from the beginning, and he came before me, saying— Behold, here am I, send me, I will be thy son, and I will redeem all mankind, that one soul shall not be lost, and surely I will do it; wherefore give me thine honor . . .

Wherefore, because that Satan rebelled against me, and sought to destroy the agency of man, which I the Lord God, had given him, . . . I caused that he should be cast down.   (Moses 4:1, 3)

And the second is this:

And I, the Lord God, took the man, and put him into the Garden of Eden, to dress it, and to keep it.

And I, the Lord God, commanded the man, saying: Of every tree of the garden thou mayest freely eat,

But of the tree of knowledge of good and evil, thou shalt not eat of it, nevertheless, *thou mayest choose for thyself,* for *it is given unto thee;* but, remember that I forbid it, for in the day thou eatest thereof thou shalt surely die.   (Moses 3:15-17.)

Third:

And it came to pass that after I, the Lord God, had driven them out, that Adam began to till the earth, and to have dominion over all the beasts of the field, and to eat his bread by the sweat of his brow, as I the Lord had commanded him. And Eve, also, his wife, did labor with him.

And Adam knew his wife, and she bare unto him sons and daughters, and they began to multiply and to replenish the earth.

And from that time forth, the sons and daughters of Adam began to divide two and two in the land, and to till the land, to tend flocks, and they also begat sons and daughters.

And Adam and Eve, his wife, called upon the name of the Lord, and they heard the voice of the Lord from the way toward the Garden of Eden, speaking unto them, and they saw him not; for they were shut out from his presence.

And he gave them commandments, that they should worship the Lord their God, and should offer the firstlings of their flocks, for an offering unto the Lord. And Adam was obedient unto the commandments of the Lord.   (Moses 5:1-5.)

Our purpose of building this house is to aid these young men and young women and all who would enter here to make the proper choice in life. Those three passages demonstrate three fundamentals in life. First, *that the Lord considered man's free agency,* his right to choose, *so vital that he permitted what is referred to as a war in heaven;* so vital that those who were with him in the spirit world had their choice to follow the dictator, known as the Evil One.

The world today does not comprehend the significance of that divine gift to the individual. It is inherent as the intelligence which has never been created nor can be. That is fundamental, young men. Hold to it when you get distracted in school studying about the origin of humanity and other things.

The second was the privilege that those first parents had to take upon themselves mortality. You may choose, but remember, if you choose to take upon yourselves that mortality referred to as The Fall, then you shut yourselves out from his presence and you "shall surely die."

Adam and Eve chose to take upon themselves mortality, and they were banished from his presence. They were driven from the Garden, and in their "humiliation," their judgment, or their memory was taken from them.

Now, imagine, young men and young women, in what condition were those first people when they were placed upon this earth to gain their livelihood by the sweat of their brow, not remembering as the years passed, their spiritual state in the Garden. I picture them subject to the earth. If their bodies became cold, it was the sun that warmed them. If their throats became thirsty, it was a stream that quenched that thirst. If they wished to have a soft bed, it was a skin or the leaves of the trees that furnished it. They would hear the thunder and lightning. The most luscious piece of meat would come from the animals. In a word, the earth produced that which satisfied their wants and needs and the mysteries of nature would stir their souls.

They were, as other animals, subsisting upon what the earth gave them, and if, in that condition, 10, 15, 20, 100, 500 years passed, if no voice had come from "toward the garden," what condition would they have been in? They would naturally be grateful for the sun, for the moon and the stars that gave light by night: for the streams, and other gifts of nature. The Book of Moses says that under that condition some of them became "carnal, sensual, and devilish by nature."

There is a passage in the Bible which says, "By grace are ye saved through faith, and that not of yourselves. It is a gift of God."

There are several good explanations of that, but to me here is one of the best illustrations of the grace of God to man. Adam heard the voice of God "toward the garden." And the Lord gave him commandments, and said: "Offer unto me (unto God) the firstlings of your flocks," and by inference we conclude "the best that you raise in the garden and the field." See what that means in developing spirituality? The first of the flock is the most luscious, the most tender, the best fleece.

Selfishness, the animal nature, would say, "I want that," but God, knowing that the highest purpose of man is to develop the spirit within him, said, "Give the firstlings to God, thinking not of self, but of something higher." What a sublime purpose! What an essential purpose! It was as if the Lord said:

You who live in the earth need the experience to know good from evil, and to live not for yourself but for God. Whatever you do, do in his name. Therein is glimpsed the whole purpose of life.

Goethe, the great writer, says, "Life is a quarry, out of which we are to mold and chisel and complete a character."

Another writer says truly:

"If I could get the ear of every young man but for one word it would be this: *Make the most and best of yourself*. There is no tragedy like a wasted life, a life failing of its true end, and turned to a false end."

How great a pity that we should not feel for what end we were born into this world until just as we are about to leave it. The principle of choice comes to us in childhood.

We have it through young manhood and young womanhood. We have it through adulthood. We have it to the
end of our days—the principle of free agency, to choose
the right or to choose the wrong, and today many men and
women seeking happiness, which is a principal aim in life,
choose to remain in the animal world and suffer the conse-
quences.

The principle of choice came to Adam and Eve, and
to Cain and Abel. Let me refer to the account of those
first two boys. They too heard the doctrine, "you bring
for sacrifice the firstlings of your flock." They too heard
"Bring the best product the earth gives." And one of those
boys gave the firstlings of his flock, and gladly gave it.
But the other kept the best to himself.

When the Lord rewarded Abel, on natural principles,
Cain became jealous. He became so envious that in anger
he slew his brother. God asked Cain, "Where is thy brother" "Am I my brother's keeper?" answered the guilty man
sullenly. Said the Lord, "If thou doest well, wilt thou not
be accepted, and if thou doest not well, sin lieth at the
door."

Thus briefly were eternal principles, promulgated in
the first stages of man on earth, and applicable today.

The choice is given, whether we live in the physical
world as other animals, or whether we use what earth offers us as a means of living in the spiritual world that will
lead us back into the presence of God.

This means specifically:

Whether we choose selfishness, or whether we will
deny ourselves for the good of others. "For inasmuch as
ye do it unto the least of these, ye have done it unto me."

Whether we will cherish indulgence of appetite, passion, or whether we will develop restraint and self-control.

Whether we choose licentiousness, or chastity.

Whether we will encourage hate, or develop love.

Whether practice cruelty, or kindness.

Whether be cynical, or sanguine—hopeful.

Whether we be traitorous—disloyal to those who love us, to our country, to the Church or to God—or whether we will be loyal.

Whether we be deceitful, or honest, "Our word our bond."

Whether a slanderous or a controlled tongue.

You see something which you do not like. You can find fault if you wish, and have the satisfaction of feeling you have said something which makes you superior, or you can control your tongue and say nothing. If you would be happy, learn to think and to speak well of others among loved ones and close associates. Has somebody offended you in the Church? You may hold resentment if you wish, say nothing to him, and let resentment canker your soul. If you do, you will be the one who will be injured, not the one who you think has injured you. You will feel better and be far happier to follow the divine injunction: "If you have aught against your brother, go to him." No matter what problem you face in your daily life, always remember:

You are the person who has to decide
Whether you'll do it or toss it aside.
You are the person who makes up your mind
Whether you'll lead or will linger behind.
Whether you'll try for the goal that's far
Or just be contented to stay where you are.

Whatever it is you are wanting to be,
Remember, to fashion the choice you are free.
Kindly or selfish, or gentle or strong,
Keeping the right way or taking the wrong,
Careless of honor or guarding your pride,
All these are questions which you must decide.

Yours the selection, whichever you do;
The thing men call character's all up to you.

I mention this fundamental principle of choice which goes back to our pre-existent state because I think it is one of the most vital facing the world today, and particularly members of The Church of Jesus Christ.

I do not know that there was ever a time in the history of mankind when the evil one seemed so determined to strike at this fundamental virtue of free agency.

But thank heaven, there is innate in man a feeling that will rebel against tyranny. It has manifested itself throughout the ages. For example in the days of King John—men who resented dictatorship gathered at Runnymeade and made the king sign a paper that a man has the right to be tried by his peers, and that the individual is not a mere pawn in the hands of a dictator. A few hundred years afterward, came the Declaration of Independence, and then the Constitution of the United States, fundamental in which is the right of the individual to worship God, to speak as he feels, own his property, to take care of his family—his home, his castle.

I love the Gospel of Jesus Christ. I love the freedom it vouchsafes to the individual. I know that our Father in Heaven is just as close to us today as he was when his voice came out of the Garden to Adam and Eve and gave certain commandments by which Adam could come back into his presence. You and I are descendants of that first man, and the same principles that were taught to him are now taught to us.

> Know this that every soul is free,
> To choose his life, and what he'll be;
> For this eternal truth is given
> That God will force no man to Heaven.
> He'll call, persuade, direct aright,
> And bless with wisdom, love and light—
> In nameless ways be good and kind,
> But never force the human mind.
> Freedom and reason make us men;
> Take these away, what are we then?
> Mere animals and just as well
> The beasts may think of heaven or hell.

That is my message today, boys. The responsibility of choice. When you are tempted to drink spiritous liquor to have "a good time," remember that in such indulgence you are yielding to the baser part of yourself. Again some young men and young women think that indulgence in passion will give a good time. Pleasures yes, but not happiness. Fruit eaten before it is ripe will sour on the stomach. Some may think, "I can take advantage of that man. I will cheat him, and I will just add to my store." Well the man who robs is more greatly injured than the man who was robbed. It is an eternal law, for the law of compensation and retribution are eternally active in this world.

If you will be happy obey the principles of the Gospel. Let that happiness come from within. "Nae treasures, nor pleasures, could make us happy lang; the heart ay's the part ay that makes us right or wrang."

May the appreciation expressed be in each heart, but, above all, may we express gratitude today for the Gospel of Jesus Christ, and may each one feel as never before, to declare with Peter when he faced those dictators who wanted him to deny the Savior and his divinity, "For there is none other name under heaven given among men whereby we must be saved."

Though we are living in perilous times, you and I can rejoice, because the gospel is among men. The Church is established in this free country, never more to be thrown down or given to another people. Nations may rise, and nations may destroy each other in strife, but this gospel is here to stay, and we must preach it and proclaim it, that peace may come for it is only through obedience to the Gospel of Jesus Christ that peace will come permanently upon the earth.

Building of Character

Yes, I am indeed very happy. I am going to mention one or two things that have contributed to that happiness. First, I am glad to have the company of President (William H.) Reeder and President (Henry A.) Smith. President Reeder has been the president of a stake, president of the New England Mission; and President Smith is now in the presidency of the Pioneer Stake. The companionship of these two men with the two sisters made our drive up here most delightful. Coming up through the canyon and snow-capped hills on either side, the full moon made us all young again, until we reached Woodruff; then we encountered fog. It was not very thick, however, just about the same as it was a year ago when we came up; so we will have no trouble.

Then the welcome we got here from the president of your stake and President Johnson, and, as we entered the banquet hall, the hum of voices, six hundred young people, in cordiality and joviality, not in rudeness, but just the hum of voices of youth, pleased me most exceedingly.

But there was something that pleased me even more, and I am sure it did our companions. As soon as President Johnson moved down the aisle, all talking ceased, and there was perfect order. Perhaps many of you did not notice it, but that was very significant. It told us what your attitude is toward this gathering, and I was happy.

There is another thing that pleased me very much, and I should like to express it in the presence of your presidency, high council, bishopric of your wards and all others associated with them. I have learned through President Williams that there was a basketball practice tonight. That is pretty important when you are contesting with other schools or other counties and school districts, and that would take some of the young men away from this gathering. There was also a band practice in the public schools. That would have taken some others away, and those who have this gathering in charge were desirous of having present at least a majority of the young people of the stake.

I am informed that when President Williams approached your county superintendent, a nonmember of the Church, the latter replied: "President Williams, it isn't often you make a request of the directors of the school board and principal. Let me assure you that there will be no school activity tonight which will interfere with your assembly." I wish to thank that gentleman, in your presence, for his spirit of cordiality and support, which is most commendable.

But what pleases us most of all is the service rendered by your mothers, your sisters, in cooking those twenty-seven turkeys which were carved by President Peart, and so eagerly enjoyed by 600 of us, and served so carefully, expeditiously, by our mothers. We seldom tell them by words how much we love them. I think tonight it would be fitting for us, in appreciation of what they have done in serving that banquet, to rise and remain standing in quiet for about thirty seconds . . . Thank you. Mothers, that is for you.

I am happy now to have an opportunity to "How do you do," and to thank you for the tribute you paid to our party tonight. Nobody suggested that you rise when the

President of the Church was introduced, but you did it voluntarily. That was to the position, not to the man, and I hope you will always have that reverence of spirit for the priesthood throughout the Church. It means much.

Just what I can say to you tonight as a message that you will remember, I am not quite sure. I know what I have in mind, but just how to present it is the problem. May I continue to have your attention, your deferential attitude, for a few moments while I try to say what I believe will be a helpful suggestion to all.

Thirty years ago, President Hugh J. Cannon and I stood in the sculptor's yard in Florence, Italy. Around in that yard were unbroken, irregular pieces of granite from which the sculptor was going to cut out some vision which he saw in his mind. We did not pay much attention to those rude stones, scattered around in the yard, in the midst of which stood a magnificent figure, which is now famed in the world, and it was, of course, at that time.

That figure was carved over 400 years ago from pieces of stone which were just as crude as those which we saw around in the yard. Inside the museum were other carved statues. That huge statue was entitled "David," picturing David of old. It stands today in the Florence Museum, unfinished, but in our crude judgment we could not see but what it was perfectly finished.

I make that as a setting in your minds that you keep that in mind as I read these lines:

> Chisel in hand stood a sculptor boy,
> With his marble blocks before him,
> His eye lit up with a gleam of joy
> When his life dream passed before him.
> He carved it well on the shapeless stone
> With many a sharp incision.
> That angel dream he made his own,
> His own, that angel vision.
>
> Sculptors of life are we
> With our goals uncarved before us,

> Waiting the time when at God's command
> Our life dream shall pass o'er us.
> If we carve it well on the shapeless stone
> With many a sharp incision,
> That angel dream we make our own,
> Our own, that angel vision.

If you had stood, each or any of you, in that yard thirty years ago, and a man had placed in your hands a chisel and a hammer, would any of you have dared to take that shapeless block and carve a human image out of it? You could not do it. If he had placed before you a canvass and mixed the paints, and put in your hands a brush, would you have undertaken to paint on that canvass the picture of an ideal soul? No. You would say to the first, "I am not a sculptor." To the second, "I am not a painter. I cannot do it."

Well, each of you tonight is doing just that thing, everyone of us carving a soul. Is it going to be a deformed one, or is it going to be something admirable and beautiful for time and throughout eternity?

You answer. Yours is the responsibility. Nobody else can carve it for you. Your parents may guide, your teachers may help with suggestions, but each one of you has the responsibility to carve that ideal character, and your tools are ideas, what you are thinking about. The thought in your mind at this moment is shaping your character, contributing, almost indefinitely, it is true, to the lineaments of your face, so that those who can read character can see what the thoughts have shaped in you.

He was right who said:

> Sow a thought, reap an act;
> Sow an act, reap a habit;
> Sow a habit, reap a character;
> Sow a character, reap an eternal destiny.

With whatever thoughts you have, almost your outward expression will be shaped. Some or all of you girls wish to be beautiful, and we see a lot of beautiful girls here in this audience, and handsome young men. Some of you who wish you could be more beautiful, and, girl-like, feel regretful that you are not beautiful, should know this, that some of the most beautiful characters in the world have changed their very features by their inward thoughts. They have cherished noble ideals. They have cultivated cheerfulness. They radiate cheer wherever they go.

I recall now my youth, which is seemingly a long way off in years, but not very far in memory, the girls in our crowd; one particularly whom I remember with tender-ness, appreciation, had no beautiful features. You would not call her beautiful from the standpoint of her eyes, symmetry of features, but her radiance, her cheerfulness, made her beautiful, and we all sought her company.

Ideals are the tools by which you are going to shape your lives. What subordinate things one seeks will have less bearing upon the formation of one's character, and upon the direction of one's life than does the paramount thought of the mind, the dominant wish upon your heart.

With these few words of introduction I am going to tell you the story of three men. One cherished the ideas of pleasure. He did not care whether that pleasure was found by dancing, sleigh-riding, and all other legitimate pleasures of youth—and they are glorious—or whether he had to indulge in passion and stimulate his appetite with nicotine or strong drink.

He was a brilliant youth, not much older than some of you here tonight when he cherished those thoughts. He was a neat dresser, pleasant companion in society, a good dancer, but his thoughts went along that line toward the good time he was going to have. That was the dominant thought.

I think every young man should have a good time. I think every young girl is entitled to joy, and you get that in conference and association such as you have here to-night. May the Lord bless these brethren who have brought this about for your company, and our mothers, again. I believe in it. I believe in sociality. I believe in the drama, in the concert, in the dance hall, but not in the "honey-bug"—that is the extreme.

Well, this young man determined that if he could not get enough stimulant in the nicotine, he would take something else. The bishop thought he could go on a mission. You recognize that I am telling you a true story. His parents wanted him to go. They had been converts in England. This was an only son, and they were proud of him.

When the call came, he accepted it, and I first met him in Scotland when I was an unmarried man, presiding over the Scottish Conference. He came with a young man from Rock Springs, who later became a patriarch in this stake—John Young.

John Young was then a young man, and he was a bashful young man, as you who remember him know. This young man, whom I will call Jim, was not bashful. He was debonair and haughty. I heard of him from the president of the European Mission, who telephoned from Liverpool, saying: "We are sending this young man up to you. He doesn't seem to be missionary material. We are just leaving," said President Platte D. Lyman, "for Europe, but please take this young man and report when we come back."

Well, he did not enter into the spirit of the mission. He did not want to pray. He came to me and said, "Please do not call on me to pray." We went down to Sunday School the morning after he arrived, and he said, "Don't ask me to speak today." I promised that we would not. He was a problem.

Monday morning we asked him to say the prayer, and he stumbled for a few moments, then he said, "I can't do it." Unbelievable, almost! He said, "I am going home!"

I said, "Oh, well, you are homesick. We all felt that way when we came. You come with me. The other brethren can go out tracting, and you come with me."

I took him down to Sister Nelson's and Sister Lang's, good Scotch women who could drive the blues from any boy, but he was still despondent. He was as restless as, in the old familiar comparison, a fish out of water.

Then I took him down to the Arcade in Glasgow, where he could see almost everything. I thought we could get him interested in the business things—sightseeing. But when we came out of the Arcade he was still determined to go home. By that time, I turned to him and said, "Why do you want to go home?"

"Well, I'd rather go home than be sent home."

"What do you mean?"

Then he told me. He opened his heart and took me back to the little town here in Utah, back to the dance halls, back to the socials, in the saloons, and then made a confession.

I said, "How did you get to be called on a mission?"

"I lied to my bishop."

"Why did you do that?"

"Well, I thought I would come as far as Philadelphia, then go back home. When I got to Philadelphia, I thought I would cross the ocean, go to Liverpool, and then go home. But," he said, "I am out of my element. I am sure of it now more than ever."

I turned to him and said, "You may go home, and sail on the City of Rome next Friday. Go home. Ask your bishop's forgiveness. Marry the girl whom you have wronged, and give her an honorable name, and when you have made it right with your bishop and with that girl who trusted you, prove yourself worthy and come over and fulfill this mission, or you will never make a success."

He was on the City of Rome when she sailed from Glasgow the following Friday. I heard from one of the elders who returned home with him that he did not maintain the standards. He went to the bar and disgraced the other members of the Church by his drinking and his acting.

He was still the seeker of pleasure, nothing higher than the pleasure of a physical sensation, a pleasure which any beast of the field can enjoy. The high things in literature, the sacred things of religion did not appeal to him. Just the physical sensation. And when men or women, not only young people, but older men or women, are satisfied with that physical pleasure, they are on the low plane of the animal.

And when a nation rejects the things of God as one nation is doing today—several nations now—you may rest assured that that nation and the others are sinking down to the level of the animal world.

We advanced the money to take him home, of course, and he promised to return it. Eighteen months after that, when I was released, he had not returned it. So one day when they had an educational convention in that city, I went up to perform my part on the program, and, remembering that this was his town, that he had not paid back that sum, and the Church was held responsible for it, I thought I would call at his home.

A lovely woman answered the door, past middle age, but a motherly countenance, and somewhat bent. I said, "I have called to see Jim, whom I met in Scotland about eighteen months ago. My name is David O. McKay."

"Oh, come in!" She caught my hand. "Won't you please see him? He was always a good boy to me."

I said, "Is he married?"

"No."

Not enough honor to keep his promise! "Well, my train leaves at four o'clock. If you can reach him, will you please tell him that I would like to see him at the station?"

"Oh, I will try to get him. I want you to see him."

He did not come. He thought too much of what that road of pleasure would give to him. I could see from what that mother felt as the tears rolled down her cheeks, that he had not done a thing which we had asked him to do.

I did not hear any more about him until one day when I was teaching in the Academy, I read in the *Ogden Standard Examiner* an account of a saloon brawl up in that town, in which one man was seriously wounded, and he later died. The names were given, among which was this "Jim." Evidently he had not pulled the trigger that wounded the boy in the drunken brawl, but he was among those arrested for it.

I remember telling the students the story this far in our devotional exercises that morning. I said, "This is the story to date. He is up there in jail this morning. You may choose to go down that road of pleasure, and make it your dominant thought if you wish. You may violate the rules of morality, become unchaste as he if you wish, but that is where it leads.

So I thought I had closed the story, until one day, I am not sure whether it was after one of my visits up here to Evanston, or to Tooele, I do not know which it was, but I was walking from the station in Ogden where we then lived, up Twenty-fifth Street. The saloons were open, and the hangers-around were there—the saloons were not supposed to have been open, but those who had gone down that road were lounging around and could sneak in at the side door.

I thought I heard my name called. We had a fight on in temperance in Ogden at that time—Judge Reeder will remember. Heber Scowcroft was running for mayor, and some of those saloon hangers-on had threatened us for attempting to take away their liberty. That was before prohibition days. So I paid no attention to him. I thought it was one of those.

Then I heard footsteps behind me, and I turned and recognized him—his blood-shot eyes, slovenly suit, his pale, flushed face, not only flushed, but sallow, told the story, and he said, "Do you remember me?"

I said, "Yes, I remember you. Are you married?"

"Yes."

"Did you marry the girl you wronged?"

"No."

"Where is your mother?"

"She is dead."

I did not say it. I did not have heart enough. But I thought, "Yes, and you hastened her death." For I remembered the scene at her doorway several years before.

He said, "Can you give me fifty cents for a bed?"

I said, "No, but I'll go up here and speak to the owner, and tell him to make arrangements for you." I knew he would take that fifty cents for a drink.

The next day in school I said, "I have another chapter on the life of Jim, the pleasure seeker," and I thought that was the last. But one night when I came home, several months after that, Sister McKay handed me the paper, and I read of a man who had been taking a little three-year-old boy through the saloons in Ogden, and he was arrested and put in jail, and the wife was sent for to take the little boy home.

I said to Sister McKay, "I believe that is Jim." The name was wrong. "I am going to call up Chief Browning and see if I can have the privilege of going to the jail and check up."

Chief Browning did not hesitate. He took me in and unlocked the door, and there with two or three other prisoners sitting around what seemed to me a pipe up through the middle of the cell, sat Jim. I was right. I called him, and he came shamefacedly. I put my hand through the bars and shook his hand, and I said, "Well, it has come to this!"

He said, "Well, the paper was wrong, my boy is five years old."

"Oh," I said, "what does the age mean? Dragging a little boy through saloons!" I said, "Would you like to get out of this?"

"Yes, I would."

"Would you go home?"

"Yes, I would."

"Will you try to straighten up?"

"Yes," Oh, they will make any promise!

I said, "Well, we'll see." And the first thing I did was to call up his wife to see whether she wanted him home. I got on the long distance and called her. Her mother answered.

I said, "I just called up to see whether you want Jim to come home. I think Chief Browning will let him out on parole. I got permission for him to come home."

"Well, I will talk to Mary. But I wouldn't have him come home—the reprobate!" That was the wife's mother. Mary came, and I said:

"Would you like to have him come home?"

"Yes, please!"

Oh, these trusting wives! What they will endure for their babies' sake!

That is the last chapter, boys and girls, that I know of. What became of him I cannot tell. That was years ago. I have told you the story, illustrative of what one can carve if he cherishes as the dominant feature indulgence in appetite and passion. I have not exaggerated it, and it is not an exceptional case. For half a century I have watched it, since I taught the boys and girls in Weber Academy, and you can read the story every day in your own towns.

Choose it if you will, but you are carving your character as surely as that great artist, Michelangelo, chiseled out of that shapeless rock the statue which has become so famous.

The other story is not a personal one, but it is the story of one who turned his back on indulgence and pleasure and sin of physical nature, but who determined he would make his fortune in life in making money. It became his god— the dominant thought now, we are thinking, and this story is told by one of the master writers in English literature. I will have to just touch the high spots, and that is all that is necessary, because you students have already read the story of Silas Marner, a fine young man of noble character, and a lovely young girl, beautiful and trusting, for whom life seemed gloriously happy.

But some money was stolen, and in that day they drew lots to see whether a man was guilty or innocent. Silas Marner was innocent, but when they drew lots he was found guilty, though he knew in his heart he was innocent. His girl turned against him, and he turned his back upon the minister and upon society, and left town. His heart became bitter, but there was one thing he could do, though he was just a humble weaver. He could make his money and he could store it. So day by day he threw his shuttle, wove the rug, went out into the town and sold it, and came back with his schillings and his pounds, which he put in a sack and hid under a board in the floor.

He soon became rather ostracized from society. He was looked upon as a peculiar fellow—a miser. He would come home at night after peddling the products of his loom, and count his gold which he had accumulated, and feed upon it, taking only scanty meals, then hide it back and cover the board. Sometimes he would hide it under his pillow and sleep on it.

One afternoon he came back with added pounds and schillings, and after eating his scanty meal he lifted the board to glut once more in counting his gold, which had become his life. To his surprise, there was nothing but the dirt which met his hand. Eagerly he threw his hand in again, and then the other hand, pulling up the board, but the money was gone. He rushed over to his bed, lifted the pillow, threw down the blanket, but it was gone.

His life was gone. He had made it his life, and with a cry he rushed out, leaving the door open, rushed over to the Public House and said, "I've been robbed! I've been robbed!" The men became frightened. They thought he had gone mad. Of course, he was sort of a recluse anyhow. They laughed at him and scoffed at him, but the sheriff or constable followed him, and wanted to know why, and said, "I'll come over later. I'll be there in an hour."

Silas staggered back to his home. Then he realized that he had left the door open, and the light from the fireplace was glittering, and in front of it was a little child about three years old, a golden-haired girl. The story tells us how the mother had suffered just before she reached that house, and the little babe, after the mother had swooned, seeing the light, had crept in there and was sitting before the fire.

Silas, seeing the golden hair, almost clutched at it. It reminded him of his gold, though it was just a little living baby that had come into his life, the first time since he had turned his back upon society. He took the babe and called in a neighbor the next morning, who said, "Well, you can't keep it."

"Yes," he said, "I want to keep it."

She said, "I will come over and take care of it." But the neighbors said, "You can't. He is a wild man."

But the neighbor knew better, and Silas was permitted to keep that little girl. Day by day he continued to throw the shuttle of the loom. Day by day he took the product out into the town and sold it. He accumulated his schillings and his pounds, but this time he could use it for the benefit of another, a little child, who, with the assistance of a kind neighbor, grew and was taken into school. Silas paid for her education. She led him back to society, back to his friends, back to his God.

The dominant thought of acquiring wealth was supplanted by the dominant thought to use that which he had gained for the blessing of somebody else.

I have cited that second story to say that there are those in the world who make the dominant thought the acquisition of wealth, which is a noble purpose unless it is made a selfish one, when as the piles grow the character shrinks.

The third story you will find in the Bible. He was a student, a lawyer, an interpreter of the philosophies. As a young man he sat at the feet of Gamaliel, a noted philosopher in philosophic history. He graduated, and when he was still a young man, he heard about some Christians, about a Christ, who pretended to perform miracles, and he went to the chief priests in Jerusalem and said, "Authorize me to arrest every person in this city who believes that way." "That way" is the way he put it.

They deputized him, and he played havoc with the Church in Jerusalem until every member of the Church knew that Saul of Tarsus was their enemy. When they arrested Stephen and took him outside the wall—they will show you to this day where they stood him up against the wall outside of Jerusalem—and the Jews stoned him to death. Saul of Tarsus, though he did not throw stones, stood by and held the cloaks of those who stoned that humble man to death.

Then, after he played havoc with the Church in Jerusalem, he heard about an organization up in Damascus, and he started with his associates up there to destroy that. Just before they reached the city, they stopped for a noon siesta. If they had a camel, he was lying down chewing his cud, and there at the oasis they stood, when a light brighter than the sun appeared. Saul seemed to have been stricken blind by it, but he heard a voice saying: "Saul, Saul, why persecutest thou me?"

And he said, Who art thou, Lord? And the Lord said, I am Jesus whom thou persecutest: it is hard for thee to kick against the pricks.

And he trembling and astonished said, Lord, what wilt thou have me to do? And the Lord said unto him, Arise and go into the city, and it shall be told thee what thou must do.

A changed man, still a brilliant lawyer, still steeped in philosophy, but a vision had come to him, a new vision. The world needed a new ideal, not in philosophy, not

wealth, not passion, but a new vision, the development of
the spirit to come back into the presence of the Christ.

And later, though he was a Roman citizen, they put
him in stocks, which means, as you know, that they had
his arms and legs parallel. And in the darkness of the dungeon, he and Silas sang praises to God. No punishment
could deprive them of the happiness which that testimony
of the truth gave them. He was killed in Jerusalem, as you
will see in this great play that is coming here—"Quo Vad-
is"—a pretty good presentation. You should all see it. It
shows Peter and Paul, and the great power of Rome, the
greatest power on earth at the time, which was overthrown
by the truth that is in men's hearts.

I have not time to go further. There are your three
stories. I come back now to ask you, "Which are you going
to carve?" You are the carver. Will you have as your dominant thought indulgence in tobacco, whiskey, unchastity?
You know the road. You know what the statue is you are
going to carve. It will be your own. You will have chiseled
it.

Or are you going to be free and say, "I am going to
make money?" You can. In this great, free country, you
can make it. And he is worse than an infidel who does not
make and take care of his family. Note what I say, though
using it for the benefit of others. That is good. God help
you in that, but do not turn your back upon society nor
upon your Church when you are doing it. That is where
Silas Marner made his mistake, and he had to come back
into the church, and to the little ones, before he realized
happiness.

Or, finally, you can choose the ideal of the Christ, the
only name—boys and girls, remember this if you forget
everything else I have said—"the only name under heaven
given among men whereby we must be saved."

I bear you my testimony that that is the happy life.
I know it. Enjoy your sleigh-rides, surely. Enjoy your danc-
es within proper bounds, yes, and be happy in it. Enjoy

one another's company in socials, yes. Why, youth longs for
it. Youth is entitled to it.

You may think we are old fogies, but we are not very
far from youth when we enjoyed all these things, and we
enjoy them now. Like to ride horses? Yes. But, remember,
in all that pleasure, there are certain bounds. Within that
circle, that pleasure is legitimate. It is contributive to character building, but if you go beyond the bounds, it becomes
a scar, defacing the character you are forming. Study that
all through your lives, and you will see that most of your
problems are caused by going beyond the bounds of prudence.

If you love that sweet girl, then that is the most sacred
feeling in life; but if you prostitute it, it becomes the vilest
thing in life for her and you. Hunger is good—a legitimate
appetite—but if you gormandize, nature will punish you.
Do you see?

We have a long way to go tonight, so I will conclude
with just this statement:

> You are the person that has to decide
> Whether you'll do it or toss it aside.
> You are the person who makes up your mind
> Whether you'll lead or will linger behind.
> Whether you'll try for the goal that's afar
> Or just be contented to stay where you are.
> Take it or leave it. Here's something to do!
> Just think it over--It's all up to you!
>
> What do you wish? To be known as a shirk,
> Known as a good man who's willing to work,
> Scorned as a loafer, or praised by your chief,
> Rich man or poor man or beggar or thief?
> Eager or earnest or dull through the day?
> Honest or crooked? It's you who must say!
> You must decide in the face of the test
> Whether you'll shirk or give it your best.
>
> Nobody here will compel you to rise;
> No one will force you to open your eyes;

No one will answer for you, yes or no,
Whether to stay there or whether to go;
Life is a game, but it's you who must say
Whether as cheat or as sportsman you'll play.
Fate may betray you, but you settle first
Whether to live to your best or your worst.

So, whatever it is you are wanting to be,
Remember, to fashion the choice you are free.
Kindly or selfish, or gentle or strong,
Keeping the right way or taking the wrong,
Careless of honor or guarding your pride,
All these are questions which you must decide.
Yours the selection, whichever you do;
The thing men call character's all up to you.
                                        —Edgar A. Guest

Education

Now Morn, her rosy steps in the eastern clime
Advancing, sow'd the earth with orient pearl.
(Milton)

If I were to apply the entrance of graduates and of
well-trained youth into the streaming ranks of humanity to
that poetic picture of the breaking upon the world of the
effulgent light of morning, you would accuse me of making
a strained comparison, of attempting to give to education
an unmerited, over-estimated value.

Yet, as I face this class of approximately fourteen hundred graduates, and realize that they are but one group of
five hundred thousand others who will receive similar di-
plomas this year; when in imagination I see thirty-million
under-graduates and pupils in our public schools going
from school room into summer vacations, I can but think
that if every graduate and every child had been influenced
even in a slight degree to seek a higher and better life, the
moral tone of our nation would be improved, and the
foundations of our republican form of government made
more secure.

Of course, the annual influence of that army of young
people upon society is indeterminable, and some may claim
comparatively infinitesimal, but infinitesimal or not, it is
an influence which howsoever imperceptible, is constantly

raising or lowering the moral and intellectual standards of communities.

Who knows what earth needs from earth's lowest
                    creatures? No life
Can be pure in its purpose and strong in its strife
And all life not be purer and stronger thereby.
                              (Owen Meredity)

Education for a Livelihood

Students enter school primarily to gain economic or social advantage. But this aim is not always achieved, nor is it, nor should it be, the highest purpose of education. However, we must not underestimate the value of obtaining an education for a livelihood. Education for economic advancement is a good investment for the individual as well as for the state. The United States as a nation is still young, but its brief history is replete with striking examples of the value of its free public school system even as a financial investment.

Here, for instance, was a son of a slave entering Iowa State College, having worked his own way through the grades, high school, and three years at Simpson College. Four years later, he took his degree in agriculture. His work so impressed the authorities that they appointed him a member of the college faculty. Soon thereafter he refused a tempting offer of $100,000 a year. As a child, frail and undernourished, he earned a living by doing odd household chores. His adopted parents wanted him to get an education, but offered him no money. The handicapped boy's primary purpose was the same as that of every other child in America; namely to gain economic and social betterment —to broaden his means of gaining a livelihood. Experts say that this man (Dr. Carver) has done more than any other living man to rehabilitate agriculture in the South. Since 1898 the industry which he fostered has grown until it now runs into more than sixty million dollars a year.

No, I do not in the least disparage this aim, nor criticize our public school system for planning to make possible its realization. But education for a livelihood is not the highest purpose of education. "The fallacious belief," writes Dr. Robert M. Hutchins, Chancellor of the University of Chicago, "that education can in some way contribute to vocational and social success has done more than most things to disrupt American education. What education can do, and perhaps all it can do, is produce a trained mind.

"It is principles, and everlastingly principles, not data, not facts, not helpful hints, but *principles* which the rising generation requires if it is to find its way through the mazes of tomorrow. No man among us can tell what tomorrow will be like. All we know with certainty is that it will be different from today." (From "Ferment in Education," pages 34-35)

Patriotic citizens, clear-thinking men look with apprehension and foreboding upon this increasing tendency of youth toward delinquency and criminality, and with commendable zeal and enterprise put forth every effort to foster counteracting and uplifting organizations.

However, after all is said and done, the most potent force for training youth in the United States today is our public school system. But let us face clearly and forcefully the fact that the paramount ideal permeating all education in the grades, the high school, through college and the university, should be more spiritual than economic.

I am but repeating what we all know and feel when I say that our country's greatest asset is its manhood. Upon that depends not only the survival of the individual freedom vouchsafed by the Constitution and Bill of Rights, and all other ideals for which the founders of the republic fought and died, but the survival of the best that we cherish in present-day civilization throughout the world.

The preservation of these must come through education. Lest you think that I am merely an idealist, appealing for something which cannot be attained practically through the curriculum of our public schools, let me say that if the purpose be properly emphasized and the desire to achieve it be generally sensed, the coming generation and adults of the present time can be influenced within the next ten years. Still fresh in our memory is the fact that a paranoiac, with a native ability to influence the masses, demonstrated how, through concentrated, continued effort by specially-trained instructors and leaders, the minds of youth could be directed within two decades to accept even a perverted ideal. How near he came to the realization of his aim within a few short years is now a matter of history. If youth can be so influenced to degenerate to the jungle, it can also be trained by united purpose to ascend the path of spiritual attainment.

Only through proper education can these fundamental principles become fixed and guiding influences in the lives of human beings. Our educational system will radiate such principles just to the extent that we employ in our public schools, high schools, colleges and universities men and women who are not only eminent in their particular professions, but loyal to the Constitution of our land, influential as leaders, noble in character.

Imagine what it would mean to the national integrity of America if every one of the half million graduates, in addition to his diploma certifying to his having completed the specified requirements in his chosen profession, he could cherish the memory of a noble teacher of whom throughout the years he could say as a chief justice of the Supreme Court of the United States said of one who influenced his university career—"I admired him for his learning, loved him for his goodness, profited greatly from both. He believed that scholastic attainments were better than riches, but that better than either were faith, love, charity, clean living, clean thinking, loyalty, tolerance, and all the other attributes that combine to constitute that most precious of all possessions—good character."

In his appreciation of the instructor who wielded the most influence in his life, this leader of men is but echoing the sentiments expressed by Ralph Waldo Emerson, reputedly the wisest American—"Character is higher than intellect; a great soul will be fit to live as well as to think." The most potent influence in training our youth to cherish life, to keep their word of honor, to have increased respect for human kind and love of justice, is the life and personality of the teacher. If the people of the United States would have the highest returns for their financial investment in education, they must as a matter of sound business judgment have in all our schools teachers of outstanding leadership and wholesome influence. Dr. Ralph Macdonald rightly portrays as follows the high class of men and women whom youth should have as leaders and exemplars: "The teachers of our young must be strong and vigorous; keen of intellect, balanced in outlook, superior in personality traits, deep-rooted in their spiritual foundations. They must have a passionate devotion to human freedom, and be anchored to an abiding faith in the improvability of man. To such an outstanding personality must be added education and the heritage of the human race, with a loving understanding of human growth and development in the precepts of democracy, in the lure of the school, and in the skills of teaching."

Commenting upon this, Mr. Charles Luckman, president of Lever Brothers Company, writes: "I think it is an active portrayal of the kind of people most of us expect our children's teachers to be. It is not the job-description that is amazing; what is amazing is . . . that we are so naive that we actually expect to command the services of this type of intellect at an average salary which is lower than our starting-wage for the youngsters who are just beginning to work in our factories.

"No educational system in the world could be expected to survive in the face of such absurd economic thinking." He asserts that there are two hundred sixty-one thousand business men who today serve on school boards throughout the nation, constituting 76% of the total membership of these boards. What a mighty responsibility these business men have to remedy the bad economic thinking which now paralyzes our educational system!

The contribution of general education to the industrial and commercial greatness of the country is obvious on every hand—in research laboratories, in increased productivity of farms, in achievements of electrical, physical, chemical, engineering sciences, in harnessing either for the benefit or destruction of man the boundless force of atomic energy—but what true education has done, and may do to awaken in the human heart a sense of the end and aim of human existence on this earth, what it has done to raise the standard of citizenship, how it has helped to make living happier by contributing to the prosperity, peace and security of our country, are beyond evaluation!

Stockholders—the people of the United States—must make this greatest of industries in our Republic pay dividends in character and true citizenship or face inevitable failure and possible catastrophe.

Southey tells us that in his walks one stormy day, he met an old woman, to whom, by way of greeting, he made the rather obvious remark that it was dreadful weather. She answered philosophically that in her opinion "any weather is better than none!" So we may say that any education is better than none, but a free people to remain free must ever strive for the highest and best.

Conclusion

To you members of the graduating class, I extend sincere congratulations upon your having completed the prescribed courses of study in your respective chosen professions, but, more than that, upon your increased ability to preserve the liberties of your country, and to be of greater service to your fellow men—for whatever your future successes or seeming failures, I still look upon all recipients of true education as individuals and groups radiating an influence that makes less dense and ineffective the darkness of ignorance, of suspicion, of hatred, of bigotry, avarice and greed that continue to envelop in darkness the lives of men. Of course, to quote Newel Dwight Hillis: "Not all men are of equal value—not many Platos—only one, to whom a thousand lesser minds look up and learn and think. Not many Dantes: One, and a thousand poets tune their harps to his and repeat his notes. Not many Raphaels; one, and no second. But a thousand lesser artists looking up to him are lifted to his level. Not many royal hearts—great magazines of kindness. Happy the town blessed with a few great minds and a few great hearts. One such citizen will civilize an entire community."

May the inspiration of the Lord guide and keep you in all worthy endeavors!

Faith Triumphant

The most ominous threat to the peace and happiness of mankind in this the twentieth century is not the probable misuse of the atomic bomb, but the dwindling in men's hearts of faith in God. "Epochs of faith are epochs of fruitfulness; but epochs of unbelief, however glittering, are barren of all permanent good."

The scriptures tell us that "without faith it is impossible to please God," that through faith prophets and men of old "subdued kingdoms, wrought righteousness, obtained promises, stopped the mouths of lions, quenched the violence of fire, escaped the edge of the sword, out of weakness were made strong."

It was faith that braved Columbus to sail on and on into the unknown horizon until he discovered a new land. It was faith that brought to America the "Mayflower," freighted with the destinies of a continent. It was faith that impelled President Brigham Young and the Utah Pioneers to establish permanent settlements in an unforbidding, defiant western desert.

Faith is more potent in human endeavor even than judgment or experience. Let me illustrate: One hundred years ago today a group of men with a 900-mile prairie trail behind them, were hacking their way through underbrush on a mountain trail and prying loose boulders that rolled with an echoing crash into the bottom of the ravine below. Trudging slowly and wearily up this ravine moved a caravan of covered wagons. The advance company of Utah Pioneers were nearing the summit of "Big Mountain," from which they would obtain their first glimpse of the Great Salt Lake Basin. In the western fringe of that basin lay the "Dead Sea of America" shimmering in the sunlight more like a threatening omen than a promise of prosperity.

If that barren, seemingly unproductive valley could be made fruitful, could become the center of a western empire, it would most surely be one of the most striking examples in history of faith triumphant over human judgment and experience.

Of the great pioneers of history, Brigham Young is given place among the foremost. But suppose he had failed, as men who knew western America better than he thought he would. What a tragedy would have befallen thousands —what severe censure history would have heaped upon such a foolhardy leader!

Picture his situation a century ago. Upon him rested the responsibility to supply food and shelter for the 152 persons who composed that first company seeking a home in a desert land, and the season so far advanced that there was little or no hope that crops planted would mature. Besides these 152 persons, there were thousands of others who had left their homes in Nauvoo after the martyrdom of their prophet who were following their leader to this hoped-for place of refuge and peace. Approximately 2000 were at Mt. Pisgah (Union County) Iowa, 145 miles from the west bank of the Mississippi River.

There was another colony at Garden Grove (Decatur County), Iowa, 126 miles east of Council Bluffs.

Six thousand others were at Winter Quarters on the banks of the Missouri River, six miles from Omaha.

Ten thousand people already on the march towards the Great Basin, which gave scant assurance that even a small colony could gain subsistence. All told, there were 40,000 Mormons between the British Isles and Emigration Canyon, Utah who, with confidence in a great leader, were moving toward some unknown refuge yet to be designated.

The judgment of the scout and of the trapper regarding the chances of survival was against settlement. Major Morris Harris, for example, said, among other discouraging facts about the Great Salt Lake Valley: "It is sandy and destitute of timber and vegetation except for the wild sagebrush." Captain James Bridger thought it imprudent to bring a large population into the Great Basin until it was ascertained that grain could be raised. He offered to give a thousand dollars for the first ear of corn ripened in the basin. "I have been here 20 years," he said, "and have tried it in vain over and over again."

At Green River, Samuel Brannan, who established a colony where San Francisco now stands, met the pioneers and gave a glowing description of climate and productivity of the soil in sunny California.

Notwithstanding these warnings of the desolation of the country, and the plea to go on to more productive climes, there was that assurance in President Young's mind which had greater influence upon him than the trapper's experience of unproductivity and of monthly frosts, and more influential than the glowing description of the California coast.

Greater than human judgment, towering above man's experience, was the great leader's trust in God. In referring to this faith which had guided him, he said: "As I viewed a portion of Salt Lake Valley, the spirit of light rested upon me and moved over the valley, and I felt that there the Saints would find protection and safety," an apt illustration of the lines of Dryden—

"Dim as the borrowed rays of moon and stars too lonely, weary wandering travelers,
Is reason to the soul; and as on high those rolling fires discover but the sky,

Not light us here, so Reason's glimmering ray was lent not to assure
 our doubtful way,
But lead us upward to a brighter day.
And as those nightly tapers disappear,
When day's bright lord ascends our hemisphere,
So pale grows Reason at Religion's sight,
So dies and so dissolves in supernatural light."

The unwavering faith of that dauntless band in a
divine Providence—that invisible power which "makes the
discords of the present harmonies of the future," lives on
imperishably. Their undying fortitude and heroism have
been and will continue to be a guiding and an encouraging
light to all who read their simple but incomparable story.

Ideality, Faith an Impelling Force

I have made reference to this epoch in pioneer history
not only to pay slight deference to the brave men and
women whose migration westward contributed so much
to the development and progress of the western United
States, but also to emphasize the superior power of faith
as a motivating force in human endeavor. Men die, but
principles live on. Ideality is ever the true source of inspiration and progress.

Discouraging Trends in Modern Society

Anybody who thoughtfully observes the trend of this
modern world cannot fail to have noticed a revolt among
people generally against what they consider old-fashioned
conventions and moral standards, against restraints and
inhibitions. Modesty among women, for example, is almost a lost virtue; chivalry among men toward the opposite sex is seldom manifest. Marriage is looked upon by
too many not as a sacrament, but as a contract to be can-
celled at pleasure. The responsibility of family life, too
frequently shirked by parents, is ominously being shifted
to the state. Hitler's denunciation of the Ten Commandments, his reversion to the law of the jungle, the denial of

the existence of God by Russian leaders, the rejecting of Christ by Communists and other anti-Christians seem to justify the claim that there is a weakening of faith in God, in Jesus Christ, his Son, and in the moral order.

Faith Will Dispel Threatening Clouds

Faith is the eternal light that will dispel these threatening clouds. With all my soul I cry with Emerson:

O my brothers, God exists. There is a soul at the center of nature and over the will of every man, so that none of us can wrong the universe. It has so infused its strong enchantment into nature that we prosper when we accept its advice, and when we struggle to wound its creatures our hands are glued to our sides, or they beat our own breasts. The whole course of things goes to teach us faith. We need only obey. There is guidance for each of us and by lowly listening we shall hear the right word . . . Place yourself in the middle of the stream of power and wisdom which animates all whom it floats, and you are without effort impelled to truth, to right and a perfect contentment. Then you put all gainsayers in the wrong. Then you are the world, the measure of right, of truth, of beauty. If we would not be mar-plots with our miserable interferences, the work, the society, letters, arts, science, religion of men would go on far better than now, and the heaven predicted from the beginning of the world, and still predicted from the bottom of the heart, would organize itself, as do now the rose and the air and the sun.

And again this great thinker continues:

The end of all political struggle is to establish morality as the basis of all legislation. It is not free institutions, it is not a republic, it is not a democracy that is the end—no, but only the means. Morality is the object of government. We want a state of things in which crime shall not pay. This is the consolation on which we rest in the darkness of the future and the afflictions of today, that the government of the world is moral, and does forever destroy what is not.

The economic progress of our country during the past century has been phenomenal. So also has been her influence politically among the nations. Today America is reputedly the only nation in the world "capable of sustaining western civilization."

Opposed to her is Russia, which has renounced faith in God and in his overruling power in the universe.

The threatened impending clash between these two nations is more than a test of political supremacy, more than a fight between capitalism and communism—it is the ever-contending conflict between faith in God and in the Gospel of Jesus Christ, and disbelief in the philosophy of Christian ideals. Faith in man is the power that leads to brotherhood; faith in God, the ladder by which men climb toward perfection. Faith is strength; doubt, weakness and disintegration.

There can be no question about the outcome of the anticipated ominous clash, which we earnestly hope and pray will never come between these two great nations of conflicting ideals, if the inhabitants of America will but keep their faith in the Lord of heaven and earth, and in the principles of peace taught by his Son on the shores of Galilee two thousand years ago. Upon this is the promise of possession of this land and prosperity therein based:

"Behold," says the Prophet, "this is a choice land, and whatsoever nation shall possess it shall be free from bondage and from captivity, and from all other nations under heaven if they will but serve the God of the land, who is Jesus Christ."

The guiding light in our time, as in Pioneer days and always, is faith in God and in the ultimate establishment of the brotherhood of man through the Gospel of Jesus Christ.

> "God was and is and e'er shall be,
> Christ lived and loved—and loves us still
> And man goes forward, proud and free,
> God's present purposes to fulfill."

Free Agency and Its Implications

Remember, my brethren, . . . ye are free; ye are permitted to act for yourselves; for behold, God hath given unto you a knowledge and he hath made you free.

These words taken from the Book of Helaman indicate the purport of what I should like to say this afternoon.

Next to the bestowal of life itself, the right to direct that life is God's greatest gift to man. Among the obligations and duties resting upon members of the Church today, and one of the most urgent and pressing for attention and action of all liberty-loving people, is the preservation of individual liberty. Freedom of choice is more to be treasured than any possession earth can give. It is inherent in the spirit of man. It is a divine gift to every normal being. Whether born in abject poverty, or shackled at birth by inherent riches, everyone has this most precious of all life's endowments—the gift of free agency; man's inherited and inalienable right.

Free agency is the impelling source of the soul's progress. It is the purpose of the Lord that man become like him. In order for man to achieve this it was necessary for the Creator first to make him free. "Personal liberty," says Bulwer Lytton, "is the paramount essential to human dignity and human happiness."

The poet summarizes the value of this principle as follows:

> Know this, that every soul is free
> To choose his life and what he'll be,
> For this eternal truth is given
> That God will force no man to heaven.
>
> He'll call, persuade, direct aright—
> And bless with wisdom, love and light—
> In nameless ways be good and kind
> But never force the human mind.
>
> Freedom and reason make us men;
> Take these away, what are we then?
> Mere animals and just as well
> The beasts may think of heaven or hell.

Man Responsible For His Acts

With free agency, there comes responsibility. If man is to be rewarded for righteousness and punished for evil, then common justice demands that he be given the power of independent action. A knowledge of good and evil is essential to man's progress on earth. If he were coerced to do right at all times, or were helplessly enticed to commit sin, he would merit neither a blessing for the first nor punishment for the second.

"Wherefore," says the Prophet Lehi, "The Lord God gave unto man that he should act for himself. Wherefore, man could not act for himself save it should be that he was enticed by the one or the other.

". . . Wherefore men are free according to the flesh; and all things are given them which are expedient unto man. And they are free to choose liberty and eternal life, through the great mediation of all men, or to choose captivity and death, according to the captivity and power of the devil; for he seeketh that all men might be miserable like unto himself." (II Nephi 2:16-27.)

Thus we see that man's responsibility is corresponding-
ly operative with his free agency. Actions in harmony with
divine law, and the laws of nature will bring happiness,
and those in opposition to divine truth, misery. Man is
responsible not only for every deed, but for every idle
word and thought. Said the Savior: "Every idle word
that men shall speak, they shall give account thereof in
the day of judgment." (Matthew 12:36.)

As a boy I questioned that truth when I first heard it
expressed by my father. I remember saying to myself,
"Not even the Lord knows what I am thinking now." I
was very much surprised, therefore, when, later as a student in the University, I read the following in James'
psychology about the effect of thought and action on human character:

> We are spinning our own fates good or evil, and never to be
> undone. Every smallest stroke of virtue or of vice leaves its never
> so little scar. The drunken Rip Van Winkle, in Jefferson's play, ex-
> cuses himself for every fresh dereliction by saying, "I won't count
> this time!" Well! he may not count it, and a kind Heaven may not
> count it; but it is being counted nonetheless. Down among his
> nerve-cells and fibres the molecules are counting it, registering and
> storing it up to be used against him when the next temptation
> comes. Nothing we ever do is, in strict scientific literalness, wiped
> out. Of course, this has its good side as well as its bad one. As we
> become permanent drunkards by so many separate drinks, so we
> become saints in the moral, and authorities and experts in the prac-
> tical and scientific spheres, by so many separate acts and hours of
> work. Let no youth have anxiety about the upshot of his edu-
> cation whatever the line of it be: If he keep faithfully busy each
> hour of the working day, he may safely leave the final result to it-
> self. He can with perfect certainty count on waking up some fine
> morning to find himself one of the competent ones of his generation,
> in whatever pursuit he may have singled out. Silently, between all
> the details of his business, the power of judging in all that class
> of matter will have built itself up within him as a possession that
> will never pass away. Young people should know this truth in ad-
> vance. The ignorance of it has probably engendered more discour-
> agement and faint-heartedness in youth's embarking on arduous,
> careers than all other causes put together.

Responsibility Associated With Personal Influence

There is another responsibility correlated and even coexistent with free agency, which is too infrequently emphasized, and that is the effect not only of a person's actions, but of even his thoughts upon others. Man radiates what he is, and that radiation affects to a greater or less degree every person who comes within that radiation.

Of the power of this personal influence William George Jordan impressively writes:

Into the hands of every individual is given a marvelous power for good or for evil—the silent, unconscious, unseen influence of his life. This is simply the constant radiation of what man really *is*, not what he *pretends* to be. Every man, by his mere living, is radiating sympathy, or sorrow, or morbidity, or cynicism, or happiness, or hope, or any of a hundred other qualities. Life is a state of constant radiation and absorption; to exist is to radiate; to exist is to be the recipient of radiation. . . .

Man cannot escape for one moment from this radiation of his character, this constantly weakening or strengthening of others. He cannot evade the responsibility by saying it is an unconscious influence. He can select the qualities that he will permit to be radiated. He can cultivate sweetness, calmness, trust, generosity, truth, justice, loyalty, nobility—make them vitally active in his character—and by these qualities he will constantly affect the world.

Freedom Of Will Taught By Jesus

Freedom of the will and the responsibility associated with it are fundamental aspects of Jesus' teachings. Throughout his ministry he emphasized the worth of the individual, and exemplified what is now expressed in modern revelation as the work and glory of God—"To bring to pass the immortality and eternal life of man." Only through the divine gift of soul freedom is such progress possible.

Force of the Evil One

Force, on the other hand, emanates from Lucifer himself. Even in man's pre-existent state, Satan sought power to compel the human family to do his will by suggesting that the free agency of man be inoperative. If his plan had been accepted, human beings would have become mere puppets in the hands of a dictator, and the purpose of man's coming to earth would have been frustrated. Satan's proposed system of government, therefore, was rejected and the principle of free agency established in its place.

Force rules in the world to-day; consequently, our government must keep armies abroad, build navies and air squadrons, create atom bombs to protect itself from threatened aggression of a nation which seems to listen to no other appeal but compulsion.

Individual Freedom Threatened

Individual freedom is threatened by international rivalries, inter-racial animosities and false political ideals. Unwise legislation, prompted by political expediency, is periodically being enacted that seductively undermines man's right of free agency, robs him of his rightful liberties, and makes him but a cog in the crushing wheel of a regimentation, which, if persisted in, will end in dictatorship.

The Magna Carta, signed by King John at Runnymede June 15, 1215, was an expression of freedom-loving men against an usurping king. It was a guarantee of civil and personal liberty. These guarantees later found fuller and complete expression in the Constitution of the United States. Today, seven hundred years later, consider what is happening in Great Britain! With nationalization of industries, planned economy, control of all productive power, including persons and property, that country of liberty-loving people is on the verge of a totalitarian state as dictatorial as that which the feudal barons and the people wrested from King John. People are bargaining their liberty for a chimera of equality and security, not realizing that the more power you give the central government, the more you curtail your individual freedom. Governments are the *servants*, not the *masters* of the people. All who love the Constitution of the United States can vow with Thomas Jefferson, who, when he was president, said: "I have sworn upon the altar of God eternal hostility against every form of tyranny over the mind of men." He said further: "To preserve our independence, we must not let our rulers load us with perpetual debt. We must take our choice between economy and liberty, or profusion and servitude. If we run into such debts, we must be taxed in our meat and drink, in our necessities and in our comforts, in our labors and in our amusements. If we can prevent the government from wasting the labors of the people under pretense of caring for them, they will be happy. The same prudence which in private life would forbid our paying our money for unexplained projects, forbids it in the disposition of public money. We are endeavoring to reduce the government to the practice of rigid economy to avoid burdening the people and arming the magistrate with a patronage of money which might be used to corrupt the principles of our government."

Freedom of the Churches

This principle of free agency and the right of each individual to be free not only to think but to act within bounds that grant to every one else the same privilege, are sometimes violated even by churches that claim to teach the doctrines of Jesus Christ. The attitude of any organization toward this principle of freedom is a pretty good index to its nearness to the teachings of Christ or to those of the Evil One. For example, I read recently the statement of a leading clergyman who claimed the divine right of his church, wherever it was in power, to prohibit any other church from promulgating its doctrine. And, "if religious minorities actually exist, they shall have only de facto existence without opportunity to spread their beliefs."

He who tramples under foot one of God's greatest gifts to man, who would deny another the right to think and worship as he pleases, propagates error, and makes his own church in that regard a propagator of evil.

Contrast this unchristian-like stand with the statement of the Prophet Joseph Smith:

"We claim the privilege of worshiping Almighty God according to the dictates of our own conscience, and allow all men the same privilege, let them worship how, where, or what they may." And again, in one of the greatest revelations on government ever given, we read the following:

That the rights of the priesthood are inseparably connected with the powers of heaven, and that the powers of heaven cannot be controlled nor handled only upon the principles of righteousness.

That they may be conferred upon us, it is true; but when we undertake to cover our sins, or to gratify our pride, our vain ambition, or to exercise control or dominion or compulsion upon the souls of the children of men, in any degree of unrighteousness, behold, the heavens withdraw themselves; the Spirit of the Lord is grieved; and when it is withdrawn, Amen to the priesthood or the authority of that man. . . .

No power or influence can or ought to be maintained by virtue of the priesthood, only by persuasion, by long-suffering, by gentleness and meekness, and by love unfeigned;

By kindness, and pure knowledge; which shall greatly enlarge the soul without hypocrisy, and without guile—

Reproving betimes with sharpness, when moved upon by the Holy Ghost; and then showing forth afterwards an increase of love toward him whom thou hast reproved, lest he esteem thee to be his enemy;

That he may know that thy faithfulness is stronger than the cords of death.

Let thy bowels also be full of charity towards all men, and to the household of faith, and let virtue garnish thy thoughts unceasingly; then shall thy confidence wax strong in the presence of God; and the doctrine of the priesthood shall distill upon thy soul as the dews from heaven.

The Holy Ghost shall be thy constant companion, and thy scepter an unchanging scepter of righteousness and truth; and thy dominion shall be an everlasting dominion, and without compulsory means it shall flow unto thee forever and ever. (D&C 121:36-46.)

In conclusion, I repeat that no greater immediate responsibility rests upon members of the Church, upon all citizens of this republic and of neighboring republics than to protect the freedom vouchsafed by the Constitution of the United States.

Let us by exercising our privileges under the Constitution—

1. Preserve our right to worship God according to the dictates of our conscience;

2. Preserve the right to work when and where we choose. No free man should be compelled to pay tribute in order to realize this God-given privilege. "It is not right that any man should be in bondage to another."

3. To feel free to plant and to reap without the handicap of bureaucratic interference.

4. To devote our time, means, and life if necessary, to hold inviolate those laws which will secure to each individual the free exercise of conscience, the right and control of property, and the protection of life.

To sum up this whole question: in these days of uncertainty and unrest, liberty-loving people's greatest responsibility and paramount duty is to preserve and proclaim the freedom of the individual, his relationship to Deity, and the necessity of obedience to the principle of the Gospel of Jesus Christ—only thus will mankind find peace and happiness.

> If ye continue in my word, then are ye my disciples indeed;
> And ye shall know the truth, and the truth shall make you free.

The Folly of Following False Ideals

Choose you this day whom ye will serve; whether the gods which your fathers served that were on the other side of the flood, or the gods of the Amorites, in whose land ye dwell: but as for me and my house, we will serve the Lord. (Joshua 24:15.)

This scripture expresses the avowed and unalterable resolution of Joshua whose nobility of character and outstanding leadership won for him the title "the servant of the Lord." Just before his death he called upon Israel "to put away the strange Gods that were among them," and to be faithful and obedient to the God of Israel. The people in Joshua's day evidently made a wise choice, for, we are told, that Israel "served the Lord all the days of Joshua and all the days of the elders that overlived Joshua." To every normal person God has given "the freedom of choice." Our moral and spiritual progress depends upon the use we make of that freedom. God desires every man to become like him. In order for man so to advance, the Lord had first to make him free.

There are false gods in this day, even more real than those against whom Joshua warned ancient Israel. They are false ideals, which, when sought and indulged in, are even more destructive of spirituality than was the worship of the Amorite gods. Because of certain reports we receive of wild parties held by young people with consent of unwise parents; reports of objectionable, not to say lewd clubs, organized among a certain class; of reports of actions of girls whose parents permit them to come to the city unchaperoned to attend sport contests, there is reason to believe that not a few parents and some of our young people need to be warned against enticing evil practices, indulgence in which end only in disillusionment and sorrow.

There can be little doubt that war and a materialistic science have had a deadening effect upon the moral sensibilities of too many of our youth. One critic goes so far as to say: "Self-interest alone remains as a motive, and pleasure as the sole end of life."

It is the duty of parents and of the Church not only to teach but to demonstrate to young people that living a life of truth and moral purity brings joy and happiness, while violations of moral and social laws result only in dissatisfaction, sorrow, and, when carried to extremes, in degradation.

There is an old story told of the experience of a great artist who was engaged to paint a mural for the cathedral in a Sicilian town. The subject was the life of Christ. For many years the artist labored diligently, and finally the painting was finished except for the two most important figures: the Christ Child and Judas Iscariot. He searched far and wide for models for those two figures.

"One day while walking in an old part of the city he came upon some children playing in the street. Among them was a 12-year-old boy whose face stirred the painter's heart. It was the face of an angel—a very dirty one, perhaps, but the face he needed.

"The artist took the child home with him, and day after day the boy sat patiently until the face of the Christ Child was finished.

"But the painter still found no one to serve as model for the portrait of Judas. For years, haunted by the fear that his masterpiece would remain unfinished, he continued his search. . . .

. . . One afternoon, in a tavern, the painter saw a gaunt and tattered figure stagger across the threshold and fall to the floor, begging for a glass of wine. "The painter lifted him up, and looked into a face that startled him. It seemed to bear the marks of every sin of mankind."

"Come with me," the painter said: "I will give you wine, food, and clothing.

"Here at last was the model for Judas. For many days and parts of many nights the painter worked feverishly to complete his masterpiece.

"As the work went on a change came over the model. A strange tension replaced the stuporous languor, and his bloodshot eyes were fixed with horror on the painted likeness of himself. One day, perceiving his subject's agitation, the painter paused in his work. 'My son, I'd like to help you,' he said. 'What troubles you so?'

"The model sobbed and buried his face in his hands. After a long moment he lifted pleading eyes to the old painter's face.

"'Do you not then remember me? Years ago I was your model for the Christ child!'"

The story may be fact or fiction, but the lesson it teaches is true to life.

The dissipated man made a wrong choice in his youth, and in seeking gratification in indulgence sank ever lower and lower until he wallowed in the gutter.

Only recently I met this unfortunate man's counterpart—a man with bleary eyes and dissipated features whom I knew years ago as a brilliant open-countenanced youth with a promising future.

Man has a dual nature; one is related to the earthly or animal life; the other is akin to the divine. Whether a man remains in the animal world, yielding without effort to the whim of his appetites and passions and slipping farther and farther into the realm of indulgence, or whether, through self-mastery, he rises toward intellectual, moral, and spiritual enjoyments depends upon the kind of *choice* he makes every day, every hour of his earthly existence. "Man has two creators," says William George Jordan, "his God and himself. This first creator furnishes him the raw material of his life—the laws and conformity with which he can make that life what he will. The second creator—himself—has marvelous powers he rarely realizes. It is what a man makes of himself that counts."

We need not shut our eyes to the fact that too many of our young folk respond to the call of the physical, because it seems the easy and natural thing to do. Too many are vainly seeking short-cuts to happiness. It should always be kept in mind that that which is most worthwhile in life requires effort, strenuous effort. "Enter ye in at the straight gate: for wide is the gate, and broad is the way, that leadeth to destruction, and many there be which go in thereat. Because straight is the gate, and narrow is the way, which leadeth unto life, and few there be that find it."

As in days of old, so there are today some who prefer to revel in what I have heard President George Albert Smith designate as "the devil's territory" rather than to strive for the higher and better things of life. Persons who condemn their will to the service of their appetites, suffer the penalty. In the words of Charles Wagner:

Let your needs rule you, pamper them—you will see them multiply like insects in the sun. The more you give them, the more they demand. He is senseless who seeks for happiness in material prosperity alone. . . .

Our needs in place of the servants they should be, have become a turbulent and seditious crowd, a legion of tryants in miniature.

A man enslaved to his needs may best be compared to a bear with a ring in its nose, that is led about and made to dance at will. The likeness is not flattering, but you will grant that it is true.

It is said that one Roman emperor offered a reward to anybody who would invent a new pleasure. Nero set Rome on fire for the mere pleasure of a new form of diversion. Rome fell because of extravagance, luxury, and dissipation. In personal, as in national life, these are unfailing signs of decline and decay. Truly, "He that soweth to his flesh, shall of the flesh reap corruption. But he that soweth to the spirit shall of the spirit reap life everlasting."

In their yearning for a good time, young people are often tempted to indulge in things which appeal only to the baser side of humanity, five of the most common of which are:

1. Vulgarity and obscenity
2. Drinking and petting parties
3. Unchastity
4. Disloyalty
5. Irreverence

Vulgarity

Vulgarity is often the first step down the road of indulgence. To be vulgar is to give offense to good taste or refined feelings. A young man who would tell a vulgar joke in the presence of ladies discloses a nature leaning towards that which is low and coarse. A girl who would encourage it and laugh at it is taking a step toward that which is crude and unrefined. Most of you have read David Starr Jordan's denunciation of this vice.

Vulgarity weakens the mind, and thus brings all other weaknesses in its train. It is vulgar to wear dirty linen when one is not engaged in dirty work; it is vulgar to like poor music, to read weak books, to feed on sensational newspapers, to trust to patent medicines, to find amusement in trashy novels, to enjoy vulgar theatres, to find pleasure in cheap jokes, to tolerate coarseness and looseness in any of its myriad forms. We find the corrosion of vulgarity everywhere, and its poison enters every home. The billboards of our cities are covered with its evidence; our newspapers are redolent with it; our story books reek with it; our schools are tainted by it, and we cannot keep it out of our homes, or our churches, or our colleges.

It is only a step from vulgarity to obscenity. The executive secretary of a committee appointed to curtail the distribution of obscene literature put on my desk only recently a most vile plaque, covertly cast, reportedly here in our city, and sold to our young people at a nominal price. The best way to rid society of such baseness is for parents, business men, and especially every decent young person, to refuse to tolerate it and to report the vendors to the officers of the law.

Drinking and Petting Parties

It is right, indeed essential, to their happiness that young people meet in social parties, but it is an indication of low morals when for entertainment they must resort to physical stimulation and debasement. Such indulgence weakens your character; discredits your family name; robs your future wife or husband of a priceless treasure, and sows seed that may ripen into bitter fruit of marital suspicion, unhappiness, and divorce. A girl who sacrifices self-respect for social popularity debases true womanhood.

A spotless character, founded upon the ability to say no in the presence of those who mock and jeer, wins the respect and love of men and women whose opinion is most worth-while. Drinking and petting parties form an environment in which the moral sense becomes dulled, and unbridled passion holds sway. It then becomes easy to take the final step downward in moral disgrace.

Chastity

The test of true womanhood comes when woman stands innocent at the court of chastity. All qualities are crowned by this most precious virtue of beautiful womanhood. It is the most vital part of the foundation of a happy married life. It is a common saying throughout the world that young men may sow their wild oats, but that young women should be chaperoned and guarded. Even in the matter of chaperonage, there is too much laxity, if recent reports are to be relied upon, on the part of parents, and young women are given too free license.

In the Church of Jesus Christ there is but one standard of morality. No young man has any more right to sow his wild oats in youth than has a young girl. He who comes to his bishop to ask for a recommend to take a pure girl to the altar is expected to give the same purity that he expects to receive.

A woman crowned with virtue is the "highest, holiest, most precious gift to man." A woman who barters her virtue "is not one of the least of man's shames."

Disloyalty

When instead of high moral principles, a life of immoral indulgence is chosen, and man or woman gets far down in the scale of degeneracy, disloyalty is an inevitable part of his or her nature. Loyalty to parents becomes quenched; obedience to their teachings and ideals abandoned; loyalty to wife and children smothered in base gratification; loyalty to Church impossible, and is supplanted by a sneer at its teachings, and the perpetrator is left to himself to kick against the pricks and to fight against God.

Irreverence

At this stage, irreverence is an inevitable consequence, a pretty sure sign of moral weakness. No man will rise high who jeers at sacred things. It is said that when Mr. Landon Eli Perkins was preparing his volume on "Kings of the Platform and Pulpit," he wrote to Colonel Robert G. Ingersoll for a copy of his most famous lecture. In a letter which accompanied the manuscript, Mr. Ingersoll said: "Whatever you do, don't put anything into the book against Christ. I may have said silly things about him when a boy in Peoria, Illinois, but I now regard him as the one Perfect Man."

I said in the beginning that man is a dual being—a physical and spiritual entity, but his spiritual side is the all-important part. The real tragedy of following false ideals is that by so doing we stifle and sometimes choke out completely, spirituality. Rudolph Eucken truly asserts that without a consciousness of a spiritual relation to the infinite "no true civilization is possible. A civlization declining all contact with a super-natural life and refusing to establish those mysterious inner-relations, gradually degenerates into a mere human civilization, and becomes a parody of civilization."

The body with its five or more senses, with its appetite and passions is essential to life and happiness, but in the ultimate analysis it is only a means to a higher road. When man makes its gratification an end in itself, he frustrates the purpose and descends to sensuality. "Choose you this day whom ye will serve."

John P. Aligeld expresses more than mere imagination when he says:

> Young man, life is before you. Two voices are calling you— one coming out from the swamps of selfishness and force, where success means death; and the other from the hilltops of justice and progress, where even failure brings glory . . . . Two ways lie open for you—one leading to an even lower and lower plain, where are heard the cries of despair and the curses of the poor, where manhood shrivels and possession rots down the possessor; and the other leading to the highlands of the morning, where are heard the glad shouts of humanity and where honest effort is rewarded with immortality.

Spirituality is the consciousness of victory over self, and of communion with the infinite. Spirituality impels one to conquer difficulties and acquire more and more strength. To feel one's faculties unfolding and truth expanding the soul is one of life's sublimest experiences.

The real test of any religion is the kind of man it makes. Being "honest, true, chaste, benevolent, virtuous, and in doing good to all men," are virtues which contribute to spirituality, the highest acquisition of the soul. It is "the divine in man, the supreme, crowning gift that makes him king of all created things, the one final quality that makes him tower above all other animals."

Divine is that admonition and promise given to the Prophet Joseph Smith:

Let virtue garnish thy thoughts unceasingly; then shall thy confidence wax strong in the presence of God; and the doctrine of the priesthood shall distil upon thy soul as the dews from heaven. The Holy Ghost shall be thy constant companion and thy scepter an unchanging scepter of righteousness and truth; and thy dominion shall be an everlasting dominion, and without compulsory means it shall flow unto thee forever and ever. (D.&C. 121:45, 46.)

The Demands of Freedom

"Is life so dear, or peace so sweet as to be purchased at the price of chains and slavery?"

In so declaiming before the Continental Congress, Patrick Henry expressed the feelings of many colonists in whose breasts were arising feelings of revolt against the long series of oppressions that began when the British government passed and attempted to enforce the unfair Navigation Acts. When, in 1760, George the Third came to the throne "oppression followed oppression, insult was heaped upon insult, injustice was added to injustice, until the elemental power of intelligence, character, and feeling in the Americans was ready to burst forth like a volcano." This twenty-two-year-old King, "dull, uneducated, intolerant, bigoted, and finally crazy," arrogated to himself the thought that the common man existed only to contribute to his comfort, and that the American colonies could be used as a revenue-producing means to pay off his accumulated war debts.

In his arrogance, George the Third gave the world an excellent example of the evils of one man dictatorship.

The Continental Congress

In September, 1744, the Continental Congress was called to meet in Philadelphia "to deliberate upon wise and proper measures for the recovery of their just rights and liberties; and the restoration of union and harmony between Great Britain and the colonies, most ardently desired by all good men."

The Second Continental Congress met in May, 1775, within a month after the battles of Lexington and Concord. It was during the second Continental Congress that the Declaration of Independence was formulated and passed. The following are the circumstances:

June 11, 1776, a committee was appointed to prepare the Declaration of Independence. The members of this committee were Mr. Thomas Jefferson, Mr. J. Adams, Mr. Benjamin Franklin, Mr. Shearman, and Mr. R. R. Livingston. Of this committee (Thomas Jefferson writes in a letter to Mr. Madison): "The committee of five met. No such thing as a sub-committee was proposed, but they unanimously pressed on myself alone to undertake the draught. I consented; I drew it; but before I reported it to the committee I communicated it separately to Dr. Franklin and Mr. Adams requesting their corrections."

Thomas Jefferson was then a young man of thirty-three from Virginia. "He was a tall, charming, red-headed, lawyer; a horseman, a scientist, a philosopher, a man of wealth and social position; an aristocrat-democrat. He was one of America's truly great men—one of our greatest." John Adams said he was chosen to write the Declaration, because "he had a reputation for literature, science and a happy talent of composition. Writings of his were handed about remarkable for the peculiar felicity of expression."

Upon receiving his assignment, Jefferson retired to the second floor of his lodgings at the corner of Seventh and Market Streets, Philadelphia, and without consulting a book or pamphlet wrote, in a half day's time, our great national symbol. The rough draft may be seen now in the Library of Congress. There are many corrections in it, words crossed out, and words written in. It is filled with interlinings, and marginal notes. Most of these emendations are in the hand-writing of Jefferson himself. The draft was reported to Congress on June 28. It was laid on the table until July 1. On that day it was debated and adopted by the committee of the whole. On the 2nd of July the resolution that "These colonies are and of right ought to be free and independent states," was adopted by Congress, but not the declaration as drafted by Jefferson. Jefferson's draft was considered again on July 3, and finally adopted on July 4, 1776, and was signed later—56 names being appended.

The spirit pervading that old city, pending the adoption, is represented in the poem about the old liberty bell.

> There was tumult in the city
> In that quaint old quaker town.
> And the streets were rife with people
> Pacing restless up and down.
> People gathering at the corners
> Where they whispered each to each.
> And the sweat stood on their temples
> With the earnestness of speech.

The Declaration of Independence, A Summation of a Struggle Throughout the Ages

The inscription on the Liberty Bell itself "proclaim liberty throughout the land to all inhabitants thereof," is a biblical quotation, relating to the most extraordinary of all civil institutions, giving all prisoners and captives their liberties. Slaves were freed and debtors were absolved. Freedom is an essential element in happiness and rejoicing. This struggle seemed to achieve a high degree of success in the boasted democracy of Greece, and in the proud Roman Empire when "the masses in Rome had votes but lacked bread. It could be amused and distracted by shows and gladiatorial contests, and their cries stilled by the corn dole, but Caesar and Pompey saw to it that only those who voted as they directed should receive the dole."

The struggle gained impetus when King John in 1215 was compelled to sign the Magna Charta, but the complete flowering of this glorious plant of liberty occurred with the Declaration of Independence, followed by the establishment of the Constitution of the United States, the charter for the highest and best political government against which we find tirades and tempests raging.

Freedom Vouchsafed in These Two Noble Documents

Freedom of mind, freedom of soul, freedom of body, freedom from poverty, are vouchsafed to the individual. In other words, freedom to think and to speak as one desires; second, freedom to worship God according to the dictates of one's conscience; third, freedom from dominance of any man whether of wealth, political power, or religious. Fourth, the right to hold property.

Demands of Freedom

A few years ago these freedoms were challenged. A man in Europe, probably at first motivated by worthy ideals, had his ego inflated until he believed he would outdo Napoleon and become another world conquerer. He denounced democracy and individual liberty as a mockery and a failure. At terrific cost his madness was subdued, and in that subjection we see one of the first demands of freedom—loyalty, and self-sacrifice.

Illustration—A White House Garden Party

If you have been in Washington about five weeks ago, you might have beheld nearly a thousand disabled war veterans being entertained by the president of the United States. Some had arms and legs missing, some were walking on crutches and others moved about in wheelchairs. These were representatives of several hundred thousand others who five years ago were as sound and unmaimed as you and I.

Others Who Sleep in Foreign Soil

At that time fourteen hundred and fifty young men in Utah, filled with the animation of youth, looked with happy anticipation to a brilliant future. Our country, knowing that the liberties of mankind were threatened, called these young men to the colors. They answered, and gave their lives that freedom might survive. An honor list of the state's war dead and missing, published June 27, 1946, disclosed that Utah lost more than her share of armed personnel during World War II. Of the ten million men and women who saw army service during the conflict, three hundred and nine thousand paid the supreme sacrifice.

The New Age

The atomic bombs that burst over Hiroshima and Nagasaki and caused the death of 150,000 people, ushered in a new age, and loosed a force which, if improperly controlled, threatens civilization itself. Things are different from what they were five years ago. Conditions here in our own country seem to indicate to these returned veterans that some of the freedoms for which they have been fighting, and for which their comrades gave their lives, have already been lost. The bomb that burst over Hiroshima destroyed more than houses, land, and human lives—it shattered moorings of defense to which nations have clung for centuries, and ushered the world into a new era. Whether we are willing to admit it or not, this is a revolutionary period. There is social and political upheaval. Thoroughly tested, well-tried principles are being thrown into discard. "Long accepted social theories have suddenly been rejected, and new ones are being adopted," so writes Charles Foster Kent. Many of the moral standards of our fathers are being set aside in theory as well as in practice. The rising generation has no fear and little respect for elders. The elders, recognizing what a wreck they have made of civilization, question their own infallibility. Religious dogmas long regarded as the cornerstones of religion and the Church are being disproved or supplanted by the discoveries of modern science.

"It is not strange that the majority of the men and women in this war-shattered world are unhappy because they feel the foundations beneath them are tottering."

At a noon-day luncheon given in Salt Lake City recently the president of a national organization spoke of liberties and rights already lost, and appealed to the people to preserve those remaining. An experienced United States Congressman, characterized as the best lawyer in Congress, recently said: "There isn't a sensible person in this room now who can be certain that he can leave to his children the heritage and privilege of being free."

Democracy demands adherence to moral standards. Thomas Jefferson was right when he expressed the idea that "the moral sense is as much a part of our Constitution as that of feeling, seeing, or hearing, as a wise Creator must have seen to be necessary in an animal destined to live in society." "I sincerely believe," he continued, "in a general existence of a moral instinct. I think it is the brightest gem with which the human character is studded, and the want of it is more degrading than the most hideous of bodily deformities."

The father of our country, speaking upon this same theme, said: "There is no truth more thoroughly established than there exists in the economy and course of nature, an indissoluble union between virtue and happiness; between duty and advantage; between the genuine maxims of an honest and magnanimous policy and the sordid rewards of public prosperity and policy; since we ought to be no less persuaded that the propitious smiles of heaven can never be expected on a Nation that disregards the external rules of order and right which Heaven itself has ordained." (Inaug. Address 1789)

Self-government implies a sense of obligation to one's fellows. Today men face a vital issue on government. First, whether the interests of the State come before those of men; or, whether the State exists for the protection of the individual and for his welfare and happiness.

It is the individual who is happy, not the state; and freedom is a fundamental factor in the individual man's happiness.

I AM THE UNITED STATES
by Benjamin Decasseres

For 150 years all the peoples of the earth have held me as a hope in their eyes.

Every revolution in the last 150 years that had for its aim more freedom has modeled its law on my Constitution. From the four corners of the earth people of all colors, religions and races have set sail to make their home under the folds of Old Glory.

In 150 years I have raised the level of wages and living to the highest point ever attained in all historic time.

I have given more persons opportunities to raise themselves under my individualistic capitalistic-free enterprise system, from menial to commanding positions than any other nation in the world, past or present.

I have guaranteed to each and all, native and foreign, free speech, a free pen, freedom of religion, and trial by jury.

I have abolished slavery and succored the victims of flood, famine, and earthquake everywhere on earth.

I have given the world the greatest symbol for all time of revolt against oppression—George Washington.

I have given the world the greatest expounder of individualistic democracy and personal freedom in the history of mankind—Thomas Jefferson.

I have given the world the greatest symbol of a liberator of an enslaved people, and the most humane ruler in time of civil war that history records—Abraham Lincoln.

I have given the world in a Congress, a Supreme Court, and an Executive—the best-balanced governmental set-up in history.

I have made the words liberty and America synonymous.

No call from an oppressed people has ever gone unanswered by me.

When I have made mistakes—and I have made some great ones—I have admitted them finally and tried to rectify whatever injustice may have flowed from them.

My mighty rivers, my towering mountains, my prairies, my forests, and my oceans have been open to travel for all my people without police permits or a spy system.

I was born in Philadelphia on July 4, 1776.

I gave the world its model Constitution on September 17, 1787.

I froze, shoeless, in the snow at Valley Forge.

I hung on by a hair for my life at Gettysburg.

I freed Europe and myself from the deadly menace of Prussian Militarism in 1917-18.

Today I lift myself to my full proud height and proclaim that I who froze at Valley Forge and battled for my life at Gettysburg shall lay in the dust those enemies who again seek to enslave me.

For—I am Democracy in Action!

I AM THE UNITED STATES.

Conditions of Happiness

A number of years ago, a group of friends, and I were about to enter the temple at Cardston when an automobile stopped at the west gate. None of us recognized the travelers—a man, his wife, and two children, if I remember rightly. They came toward us, and then he introduced himself as a minister from Iowa.

He said, "We have just driven through Utah, and the first building that impressed us was the temple at St. George. We came north and we saw the Manti Temple, a beautiful structure. We continued further north, and visited the Temple Grounds and the Tabernacle in Salt Lake City. Everybody around there seemed to radiate joy, and we heard the congregation sing 'Come, Come Ye Saints.' Now in Canada we see this temple. There is something among the people whom we have met from St. George to Canada which has impressed us greatly. It is the happiness you seem to radiate. I am going to teach my congregation to sing that song, 'Come, Come ye Saints.' "

He was impressed with something which to him was indefinable. We are a happy people. "Man is that he might have joy," not what an enemy accused us of doing—living for physical comforts and pleasures. He is wide of the mark. That man had in mind *pleasure*, not *joy*. There is a difference between *pleasure* and *joy*. Any living thing in the animal world can experience pleasure, but that may be only temporary. A sensual or physical pleasure—may be experienced but for a moment and followed by pain. Not so with joy. Joy is an element of the soul. So is happiness.

The significance of pleasure is well expressed by the poet Burns in these words:

> Pleasures are like poppies spread,
> You seize the flower, its bloom is shed:
> Or like the snowfall in the river,
> A moment white—then melts forever;
> Or like the borealis race,
> That flits ere you can point their place;
> Or like the rainbow's lovely form,
> Evanishing amid the storm.

Pleasure is not the purpose of man's existence. Joy is. "Happiness," says the Prophet Joseph Smith, "is the object and design of our existence and will be the end thereof if we pursue the path that leads to it, and this path is virtue, uprightness, faithfulness, holiness, and keeping all the commandments of God. But we cannot keep all the commandments without first knowing them, and we cannot expect to know all or more than we now know unless we comply with or keep those we have already received."

In that statement there is found the first condition of happiness. Virtue, living righteously. Therein the prophet gives the very key of the soul in its enjoyment of happiness. Happiness is not something which comes from without. Generally speaking, this is a pleasure seeking, not a joy experiencing world. In that loneliness to which Sister McKay referred, the people sought pleasure in entertainment and outward things. With such, the soul is never satisfied. But one who forgets pleasure in seeking the good of others will find happiness, which must come from within.

The first condition of happiness is a clear conscience. No man who does wrong or who is unvirtuous will be happy. No unvirtuous woman can ever be happy unless she fully repents. Uprightness of character, honesty in dealing with our fellow men, honor bright, your word as good as your bond; then when your head touches your pillow at night and you contemplate your actions during the day you sleep with a good conscience.

Daniel Webster said, "Weighed against conscience, the world itself is but a bubble, for God himself is in conscience lending it authority."

Happiness is the end and design of life, for man is that he might have joy; but I repeat, it doesn't come from without.

> It's no in titles, nor in rank;
> It's no in wealth like London bank,
> To purchase peace and rest,
> It's no in makin' muckle mair;
> It's no in books, it's no in lear,
> To make you truly blest;
>
> If happiness hae not her seat
> And centre in the breast
> We maye be wise, or rich, or great
> But never can be blest:
> Nae treasures, nor pleasures,
> Could make us happy lang;
> The heart ay's the part ay
> That makes us right or wrang.

A Sense of Freedom

The second factor I name as contributing to happiness is a sense of freedom. It is sweet to contemplate that word. It is glorious to think of the liberties that we enjoy as citizens of this great republic. We love to look back to the heroes who offered their lives, their fortunes, and their sacred honor in defense of individual liberty. We like to repeat what Patrick Henry said, "Is life so dear or peace so sweet as to be purchased at the price of chains and slavery? Forbid it Almighty God. I know not what course others may take, but as for me, give me liberty or give me death."

We love to think of the heroes and the heroic actions of the pioneers who crossed the plains, the first group of which, on July 22, 1847, were camped in Emigration Canyon. On this day also, some of the Vanguard entered Salt Lake Valley. Forty thousand members of the Church between Great Britain and the barren waste that would someday be their home! What a mighty responsibility rested upon their leader, President Brigham Young! With a testimony in their hearts of the truth, they were inspired also with a sense of freedom to worship God according to the dictates of their conscience. A consciousness of individual initiative, the right to think, the right to plan without hinderance of anybody else as long as they did not interfere with that same right to others! Happiness? There is no happiness without it. There are men dying today in defense of it, and they will die in the future in defense of it, because it is a God-given gift. Cherish it and thwart the efforts of enemies in our midst who would deprive us of that individual liberty.

"God is endeavoring to make men like himself. To do this he must first make them free." The philosopher who wrote those words got a glimpse of an eternal gospel truth. Man can choose the highest good, or choose the lower good, and fall short of what he was intended to be.

> Know this that every soul is free,
> To choose his life, and what he'll be;
> For this eternal truth is given,
> That God will force no man to heaven.

I leave this second fundamental to happiness with the admonition to you men and women to be true to the Constitution of the United States, to the Bill of Rights. Do not let any theories of immigrants or misguided politicians induce you to do anything that will deprive us of our liberties as vouchsafed by that immortal document.

Confidence of Self-Mastery

A third contributing factor to happiness I name as, *The Confidence of Self-Mastery*. No one wishes to be a slave to other human beings, no one willingly bows down to a dictator. But some are slaves to themselves, to their appetites, and passions. They are not free. They have deprived themselves of freedom and of individual liberty. Instead of being kings and masters of self they are slaves.

That is one reason why the Lord has given us the Word of Wisdom, one reason why he has told us to control our passions, to control anger, not to speak evil of one another, but to control that tendency of human nature to slander, or to rejoice in a brother's faults.

Emerson touches that human frailty by saying, "an accident cannot happen in the street but the bystanders will be animated with the faint hope that the victim may die." Rise above that feeling. Control it.

Any physiology book will tell you how nicotine may harm the body, particularly how injurious is its effect upon the young. Science demonstrates that; but there is a greater reason why young people especially should not indulge in cigarette smoking or in habit forming drinks—because as children of God they should not be slaves to an appetite.

I heard today of a man who would like to join the Church and he is going to as soon as he can overcome that habit of smoking. Sure, he can overcome it. He can do as Brother Tracy did, the first man with whom I went teaching. I heard him tell Harvey Brown, "I put my pipe upon the shelf, and I said, 'I'll never touch it again.'" Then he added, "I never have."

From an excellent book written by Charles Wagner, author of "The Simple Life" I quote the following:

He who lives to eat, drink, sleep, dress, take his walk, in short, who lives to pamper himself all that he can, be it the courtier basking in the sun, the drunken laborer, the commoner serving his belly, the woman absorbed in her toilette, the profligate of low estate or high, or simply the ordinary pleasure-lover, be he obedient to material needs, that man or woman is on the downward way of desire, and the descent is fatal. Those who follow it obey the same law as a body on an inclined plane. Dupes of an illusion forever repeated, they think, "Oh, just a few steps more, the last, toward the thing down there that we covet. Then we'll halt." But the velocity they gain sweeps them on and the further they go the less able they are to resist it.

Here is the secret of the unrest, the madness of many of our contemporaries, having condemned their will to the service of their appetites, they suffer the penalty. They are delivered up to violent passions, which devour flesh, crush their bones, suck their blood, and can not be sated.

No, this is not a lofty moral denunciation. I have been listening to what life says, and have recorded as I have heard them, some of the truths that resound in every square.

Has drunkenness, inventive as it is of new drinks, found the means of quenching thirst? No, not at all. It might rather be called the art of making thirst inextinguishable.

Listen, young men and young women:

Frank libertinage—does it deaden the sting of the senses? No, it envenoms it, converts natural desire into a morbid obsession, and makes it a dominant passion. Let your needs rule you, pamper them, and you will see them multiply like insects in the sun. The more you give them, the more they demand. He is senseless who seeks for happiness in material prosperity alone.

Our needs, in place of the servants that they should be, have become a turbulent and seditious crowd, a legion of tyrants in miniature. A man enslaved to his needs may best be compared to a bear with a ring in its nose that is led about and made to dance at will. The likeness is not flattering, but you will grant that it is true.

Resist the devil and he will flee from you. Court him, and you will soon have shackles, not on your wrists, but on your soul.

Happiness consists in mastering evil tendencies, not in indulging them, and the gospel of Jesus Christ enables us to master those evil tendencies. I know that as I know that I am looking into your eyes tonight.

Health

A fourth condition of happiness is health. We may be comparatively happy about it. I have seen cheerful, radiant people who have not enjoyed good health, but their joy and radiance result from patient endurance. A kind Providence seems to reward them.

To most of us who must be actively performing our duties good health is essential to success and happiness. And thank heaven obedience to the gospel of Jesus Christ contributes to both. It is glorious, glorious, to have the body respond to what the active spirit within would like it to perform. Compliance with the Word of Wisdom, contribute to health and vigor of body and mind.

When Orlando, in "As You Like It," was banished by his unscrupulous brother, his old servant, Adam, who had attended him from babyhood, proffered to go with him, saying, "Let me be your servant: Though I look old, yet I am strong and lusty."

Then he gave as a reason, "For in my youth I never did apply hot and rebellious liquors in my blood, nor did not with unbashful forehead woo the means of weakness and debility; therefore, my age is as a lusty winter, frosty, but kindly."

Work

Next to health as a means of giving happiness I think I would name work. That is why Latter-day Saints are so happy. They have so much to do they have not time to think of their troubles, but better than that, they are thinking of others. They are not seeking happiness, but when they give others joy, happiness is their reward.

For example, I have seen young girls who have spent the entire day serving people on Old Folks' Day: seeking the comfort and happiness of somebody else. I remember on one occasion when one of those young ladies came home in the evening she suddenly realized she was weary, threw herself on the cot and said, "My, I am tired, but do you know this has been one of the happiest days of my life." She had found joy in work that gave joy to others.

Learn to like your work. Learn to say "This is my work, my glory, not my doom." God has blessed us with the privilege of working. When he said, "Earn thy bread by the sweat of thy brow," he gave a blessing. Men and women have so accepted it. Too much leisure is dangerous. Work is a divine gift.

Enjoyment of Nature

Another contributing factor to happiness is to be able to enjoy the gifts of nature. I saw that last evening when we were driven to an eminence from which we beheld the beauty of Hood River Valley—with Mt. Hood in the south and Mt. Adams one hundred miles toward the north. Extending toward the foothills were orchards so heavily laden with pears that the branches of the trees were sagging. Already orchardists are putting props under them to sustain the increasing weight of an abundant crop.

One of the brethren said, "In the springtime when you look over that valley and see the blossoms in pink and white it is an inspiration." Appreciation of the beauty of nature! The poorest man living can enjoy that because God gives all his blessings free. " 'Tis heaven alone can be had for the asking."

Everybody can enjoy a glorious sunset. You would have to pay a great sum for a painting by a skilled artist. Only the wealthy can afford it, but almost any evening we can look at a brilliant western sky and each one of us can say, "That's mine."

Too few of us appreciate what this means. Helen Keller, blind, deaf, speechless when she was a young girl up to seven years of age, has become reputedly one of the seven greatest women in the world. This is what she wrote about the glories and beauty of nature.

Recently I asked a friend who had just returned from a long walk in the woods what she had observed. "Oh, nothing in particular," was the reply. How is it possible, I asked myself, to walk for an hour through the woods and see nothing worthy of note? I who cannot see, find hundreds of things to interest me through mere touch. I feel the delicate symmetry of a leaf. I pass my hands lovingly about the smooth skin of a silver birch, or the rough shaggy bark of a pine. In the spring I touch the branches of trees hopefully in search of a bud, the first sign of awakening nature after her winter's sleep. Occasionally, if I am very fortunate, I place my hand gently upon a small tree and feel the happy quiver of a bird in full song. At times my heart cries out with longing to see all these things with physical eyes, but if I can get so much pleasure from mere touch, how much more beauty must be revealed by sight, and I have imagined what I should most like to see if I were granted the use of my eyes even for just three days.

On my first day I should want to see the people whose kindness and companionship have made my life worth living. Now I can only see through my fingertips the outline of a face. I can detect laughter, sorrow and many other obvious emotions. I know my friends from the feel of their faces, but their inner nature, revealed by the subtleties of expression, the quiver of a muscle, or the flutter of a hand I cannot know.

So many people, I fear, grasp only casually the outward features of a face as I can do and let it go at that.

On the first day, could I see with my physical eyes, I should call to me all my dear friends and look long into their faces, imprinting upon my mind the outward evidence of the beauty that is within them.

The next day I should arise with the dawn and see the thrilling miracles by which night is transformed into day.

I should behold the magnificent panorama of light with which the sun awakens the sleeping earth. The morning of the third day I should again greet the dawn, anxious to discover new delights, new revelations of beauty. Today, the business life, the city becomes my destination.

First I stand at a busy corner, merely looking at people, trying by sight of them to understand something of their daily lives. I see smiles and I am happy; I see serious determination, and I am proud; I see suffering, and I am compassionate.

I am sure if any of you face the fate of eternal darkness you would use your eyes as if never before. Everything you saw would become dear to you. Your eyes would touch and embrace every object that came within your range of vision. Then at last you would really see, and a new world of beauty would open itself to you.

I who am blind and deaf can give a word to those of you who can see: Use your eyes as if tomorrow you would be stricken blind. And hear the music of voices, the song of birds, the mighty strains of an orchestra, as if you would be stricken deaf tomorrow. Touch each object as if tomorrow your sense of touch would fail. Smell the perfume of flowers, taste with relish each morsel as if tomorrow you could never smell and taste again. Glory in all the facts of pleasure and beauty which the world reveals to you. But of all the senses, I am sure that sight is the most delightful.

In Serving Others We Best Serve the Lord

In conclusion, there is one more thing needful for joy to which man is entitled, and it is the greatest of all. It is the service we render mankind.

One writer confirms this thought as follows:

> Supposing today were your last day on earth,
> The last mile of the journey you've trod;
> After all of your struggles, how much are you worth?
> How much can you take home to God?
> Don't count as possessions your silver and gold,
> Tomorrow you leave these behind;
> And all that is yours, to have and to hold,
> Is the service you've rendered mankind.

Though those lines emphasize the value of service they do not tell all the truth. There is something else we can take home to God, in achieving which we find true happiness, and that is *character*—what you have made of yourself during this mortal existence. Character—it may be weak, it may be strong. You must decide, but whatever you make it during the 20, 30, 50, 70, 80, 100 years that you spend here will be what you take back there. Character and the service you have rendered will determine your position and place in the next world.

The poet Robert Browning has Paracelsus say to his old friend, "Festus, There was a time when I was happy; the secret of life was in that happiness." "When, when was that?" asks Festus, "All I hope that answer will decide." And the old dying philosopher answered, "When but the time I vowed myself to man." Festus murmured: "Great God, thy judgments are inscrutable." Paracelsus continued: "There is an answer to the passionate longings of the heart for fullness, and I knew it, and the answer is this: Live in all things outside yourself by love, and you will have joy. That is the life of God; It ought to be our life. In him it is accomplished and perfect; but in all created things it is a lesson learned slowly and through difficulty."

Let us in life distinguish between the *joy* that the Prophet had in mind when he said, "Man is that he might have joy," and the *pleasure* that the world is seeking by indulging in appetites and passions, vainly hoping to find happiness. Happiness springs from within.

"He that would save his life shall lose it, but he that will lose his life for my sake shall find it."

The Gospel—
The Source of Salvation

My mind has gone back many years to my first visit to the Emery Stake. I was driven over the same road on which we travelled today in about thirty-five minutes from Price. It took us over a day when the president of the stake, with a fine team of brown horses and a white-top, drove us from Price to Castle Dale. That was my first visit. I remember he had a long neck yoke, the first I had ever seen. I said, "What's the idea?" But I soon found out. It was so the horses could travel out of the beaten path, and keep the wheels out of the wagon rut.

When Paul wrote to the Romans, he said, among other things, "For I am not ashamed of the gospel of Christ; for it is the power of God unto salvation to every man that believeth; to the Jew first, and also to the Greek.

"For therein is the righteousness of God revealed from faith: as it is written, The just shall live by faith."

And so with you I say, "We are not ashamed of the gospel of Christ." I am looking upon a segment of the Church of Christ who share the responsibility of preaching this gospel to all the world, for we are part of a world-wide organization. This gospel is not confined to Utah, nor Idaho, nor Wyoming, nor California, nor the United States, nor just to Europe, but it is the power of God to salvation to all who believe, and you and I must share part of the responsibility of declaring it to all the world.

For a few moments I should like to call your attention to what the gospel is and why we have it, what its purpose is. Paul says that it is the power of God unto salvation. Salvation from what? Tell me, you young folks, from what does the world need to be saved?

For a few moments let us consider from what this old world should be saved.

I. From Dominating Animal Instincts.

The world needs to be saved first from the dominating influence of animal instincts, of passions, of appetites. Is it not true, after all, that men generally are pretty close to the animal world? What is the propelling influence of animal life? Self-preservation, the first law of nature!

Animals fight for existence. They will strike down any other animal that tries to take away from them any piece of food that they might have. You see the struggle throughout nature, the hawk chasing the robin, the magpie trying to rob the nest of a little bird. You see it even in the blades of grass—the weeds choking out the profitable grains and flowers, and in life you see man striking down his neighbor, prompted by that same law of nature.

In nations you see the same law in operation when one nation becomes overcrowded and desires to reach out and take possession of a weaker nation, as Mussolini did a few years ago, merely because he was strong enough to crush Ethiopia.

You see it in the communists, reaching out to take possession of the world and to crush what they call capitalism. And, mark my word, underneath the peace talks going on at this very moment, there will be dominant a desire to maintain national supremacy. The world needs saving from the dominance of selfishness, and individuals need saving from that same dominance of appetites and passions.

Homes today that are being broken by suits of divorce have at the base of their trouble the dominance, the enslaving power, if you wish, of individual passions. It may be anger, either the husband or wife flying into fits of rage because of some little insignificant thing instead of controlling his passion. Or it may be the dominance of the animal desire for gratification, causing perhaps unhappiness and misery.

What is your church doing toward remedying such conditions? Well, there are a few little simple rules. You call them simple, but at the base of those little simple principles lies the means of subduing and conquering these animal instincts.

Take, for example, the Word of Wisdom. Basic in that simple though sublime revelation are principles that apply directly to the theme to which I am referring this afternoon.

By indulging in nicotine, strong drinks or anything else that creates an appetite for itself, you are likely to become a slave to appetite. Do you want to be master of yourself, a free man, a free woman, or do you wish to be a slave?

In nature, animals are dominated by the physical desire of indulgence, of which man should be master.

Again consider the marriage covenant. Fundamental in the eternity of the marriage covenant you will find the principle of mastery over your baser instincts. No man who has felt the spirit of the gospel can violate his covenant with impunity. He recognizes as sacred those same ties in his neighbor's household, and he does not violate the sanctity of that household by yielding to any primitive yearnings.

Young men and young women, do you see something glorious in that? There is not a young man and there is not a young woman in this audience who is not looking forward to the building of a happy home. All right then, you choose a mate who is striving to save himself or herself through the power of Christ, the saving power of the gospel, from the dominant passion of animal life.

That is just one glimpse of what Paul had in mind when he said the gospel is the power of God unto salvation. He could say it is the power of God unto happiness, which the Prophet Joseph said is the purpose of our existence here on earth.

In the daily application of conquering animal instincts and passions, remember this:

> It is easy enough to be virtuous
> When nothing tempts you to stray,
> When without or within no voice of sin
> Is burning your soul away.
> But it's only a negative virtue
> Until it's tried by fire,
> And the soul that's worth the honor of earth
> Is the soul that resists desire.
>
> By the cynic the sad and the fallen.
> Who had no strength for the strife
> The world's highway is cumbered today
> They made up the item of life.
> But the virtue that conquers passion
> The sadness that rides in a smile
> It is these that are worth the honor of earth
> And you'll find them but once in a while.

You will all agree, I am sure, that the world needs to be saved from the dominance, the dictatorship of our inward passions.

II. Saved from Ignorance of Human and
      Divine Relationship

What is the second thing from which the world needs to be saved? It needs to saved from ignorance of its relationship to God. In their lack of knowledge of the existence of Deity, many men agnostically say, "I don't know." Others, and bombastically, say, "There is no God. Life came on earth by chance and developed man through evolutionary operations of ten or fifteen millions or billions of years." Paul, James, Cephas, and John, Joseph Smith and a host of others know and so have testified that we are sons and daughters of our father in heaven. He is our God, and Jesus Christ came to the world to prove that great truth.

From the very beginning he established our relationship with Deity, and we are his sons and daughters. Oh, what that truth means to young people, particularly, who in moments of discouragement wonder what they are going to do and how they are going to live, to be inspired with the idea that they are truly of divine origin. Being of divine heritage, there is no limit to their achievement.

Abraham Lincoln was inspired by that thought when lanky, poor, and motherless, a young boy, he read by the firelight the life of Washington and other books that were believed by him to be honest and honorable.

Joseph Smith, a humble boy, felt a divinity within him. And that is the inspiration that comes to any young man or young woman who senses his or her relation to our Father in heaven.

The Church is established to eradicate from the minds of men and women, in all the world, ignorance of their relationship to this divine Being. Mormonism declares that they are sons and daughters of our Father in heaven.

> Admire the goodness of Almighty God.
> He riches gave. the intellectual strength to few,
> Nor now commands to be nor rich nor learned,
> Nor promises reward of peace to these.
> On all he moral worth bestowed,
> And moral tribute asks from all,
> And who that could not pay,
> Who, born so poor, of intellect so mean as not to know
> What seemed the best and knowing might not do.

And he who acted thus (that is, chose what seemed right)
He who acted thus fulfilled the law eternal
And its promises reaped in peace.
Who sought else, (chose what didn't seem to be right)
Who sought else, sought mellow grapes beneath the icy Pole,
Sought blooming roses on the cheek of death,
Sought substance in a world of fleeting shades.

Are we agreed that the gospel is here to save men from that feeling that they are nothing, that they have come by chance, to teach to them the divinity of the human soul and its eternal nature?

III. Saved From Physical Suffering

The world needs saving from unnecessary hunger and suffering. There is no need of people to be hungry, of little children starving to death in a world of plenty. I say there is no need of it.

For example, in 1921 Brother Hugh J. Cannon and I, while traveling by train from Peiking, China, to Tientsin, saw little children at the stations pleading with the passengers for "baksheesh." Their little arms were just as thin, seemingly, as one of my fingers, their faces drawn and emaciated. You remember in 1921 there was a famine in China. In November of 1920 there appeared in our public press the statement that 40 million Chinese would starve to death.

We had called on the United States minister in Peiking, who said, "No, not forty million, but there will be fifteen million starve to death this year unless other nations cooperatively supply food for these starving people." At that time the nations did cooperate. Japan sent rice, United States shipped wheat, France cooperated and so did England. We saw carloads of wheat at stations, yet these little kiddies going hungry and pleading for a "baksheesh."

Something was lacking. What was it? As the train pulled out to go on to Shanghai we did a little figuring.

There were four hundred fifty million people in China, fifteen million hungry, starving. There was food, but not distributed. They lacked organization. We shall eliminate the 50—let us say if 400 million Chinese would observe one little principle, established and practiced in the Church of Jesus Christ, there would be enough food in China itself to have given two meals every day to those fifteen million starving Chinese.

You can figure that out yourselves. Three hundred fifty million going without two meals once a month, seven hundred million meals, give the value of those two meals in fast offerings to the proper source, and let it be distributed, and without France or Japan or the United States they would have had the means there, within themselves, of saving these hungry children from starving.

Ah, but they would have to have had the wards, stakes, bishops, teachers, and the central organization as the Lord has provided in his Church as a part of the gospel. There is a practical demonstration of the power of God unto physical salvation, and it is not just dreaming, because you and I know it can be carried out in practice.

IV. Saved from Moral Impurity

The world needs to be saved from immorality. God has spoken and explained how in truth young men and young women may protect themselves and grow up through their teens into young manhood and womanhood and, unpolluted, transmit to their children a kingly birth, queenly attributes. You who have travelled through the world know what that means, and you in the Church who have knelt at the altar and covenanted to rear a family in purity, know wherein lies the happiness here in this life.

The ideals of the gospel in regard to living in purity through your teens, are fundamental in character building, fundamental in establishing the virility of manhood, the crowning glory of young womanhood, the foundation of happiness in the home, and the source of the perpetuation of the human race. The gospel of Jesus Christ touches the heart life, the very existence, of the individual as an individual, and as a member of the home, and as a citizen in this great republic or in any other nation.

"The power of God unto salvation!" Somebody in the audience might say, as a man said to Beverly Nichols, the English writer, "Before the gospel could bring all this about you would have to change human nature."

Beverly Nichols wrote what I have given before in public, what I think is a good answer to that. You will find it in a book, "The Fool Hath Said."

If you deny the possibility of changing human nature you are saying to Christ by implication, "Go back. We don't want you." You are attempting the impossible.

Well, some brave men have said this, but it was the gray uniforms of the atheists that they were wearing and not the shining robes of the servants of Christ. You can change human nature. No man who has felt in him the Spirit of Christ even for half a minute can deny this truth, the one great truth in a world of little lies.

You do change human nature, your own human nature, if you surrender it to Christ. Human nature can be changed here and now. Human nature has been changed in the past. Human nature must be changed on an enormous scale in the future, unless the world is to be drowned in its own blood. And only Christ can change it.

Twelve men did quite a lot to change the world 100 years ago. Twelve simple men, with only the wind to bear them over the sea, and with only a few pence in their pockets, and a shining faith in their hearts They fell far short of their ideals. Their words were twisted and mocked, and false temples were built over their bones in praise of a Christ they would have rejected, and yet by the light of their inspiration many of the world's loveliest . . . were created, and many of the world's finest minds inspired.

If twelve men did that 100 years ago what might not twelve men do today? For God has now given us the power of whispering across space, of transmitting our thoughts from one end of the earth to the other. What shall we whisper? What shall we think? That is the question.

We will whisper that "the gospel is the power of God unto salvation to all them that believe, to the Jew first and also to the Greek, for therein is the righteousness of God revealed from faith to faith." We will whisper—not only whisper but proclaim—that the gospel of Jesus Christ has been restored by the visit of our Father in heaven and his Son Jesus Christ to the Prophet Joseph Smith; that man's spirit is just as eternal as is Christ's, who lived on this earth 2,000 years ago and who came back in this dispensation, a living Being.

That being true of him, it is true of you, my fellow men who hold the priesthood. It is true of you mother, wife, child, and we will whisper it to the world that the gospel of Jesus Christ is established and the power of the priesthood given to represent God on earth, and that the organization of this Church is so complete that these few things to which I have referred this afternoon may be made applicable to all the world.

Facing Another World Crisis

Jesus said on one occasion to his disciples who were somewhat worried and anxious because Jesus had told them he was going to leave them.

Let not your heart be troubled: ye believe in God believe also in me. (John 14:1)

In that one sentence, Jesus gives both a comforting admonition and a guide to contentment and peace.

We are living in a troublous age. Many people in the Church, as millions in the world, are stirred with anxiety; hearts are heavy with feelings of foreboding. For the third time in half a century lowering war clouds threaten world peace. O foolish man! Will he never profit by the experiences of the past! The responsibility of choice always rests upon each normal individual. Never was that responsibility greater than today. A former member of the Deseret Sunday School Union Board (author of an excellent little work, *Out of the Ashes*) expresses the thought succinctly thus:

What the people now think or do, or what they fail to think, or what they fail to do means which way to this generation, and means what chance to the generation next to come.

A leading businessman, Mr. W. T. Holiday, president of the Standard Oil Company of Ohio, in an article captioned, "Our Final Choice," declares that

. . . whenever a civilizaion is faced with a new and fundamental challenge, there is only one thing that can save it from decline and fall—its men and women must change their habits of thought to meet the challenge. Either they meet their new world with new thinking, or they go under.

Though with a different ideal in mind, that is the advice which Peter gave the multitude on the day of Pentecost, when in perplexity they cried: "Men and brethren, what shall we do?" His answer was:

Repent, and be baptized every one of you in the name of Jesus Christ for the remission of sins, and ye shall receive the gift of the Holy Ghost.

For the promise is unto you, and to your children, and to all that are afar off, even as many as the Lord our God shall call. (Acts 2:37-39.)

To repent is to change one's mind or one's heart with regard to past or intended action, conduct, etc., on account of regret or dissatisfaction.

Individuals, groups, and nations viewing with alarm the many critical national, industrial, and moral problems are hoping that "some means will be found to turn our misdirected powers into new channels, leading to the establishment of new and prosperous conditions."

Radio and press commentators, contributors to magazines, editorial writers and statesmen suggest various plans and policies as solutions of our difficulties and perplexities. One of the best is a plan for a world federation, supported by a sufficiently strong armament to enforce its laws and statutes.

One great objection to its adoption, however, is that

"human nature is not spiritually ready" for such a federation.

It is of this "spiritual readiness" I wish to speak.

It is the duty of the members of the Church to hold aloft true spiritual standards. Then we shall be better prepared for any eventuality brought about by pagan aggression. These principles have been proclaimed in all ages. They are simple, easily understood, but all too generally ignored.

Approximately thirty-five centuries ago Moses, "the human transmitter of the greatest human conduct code of all time," warned the people of Israel as follows:

Therefore thou shalt keep the commandments of the Lord thy God, to walk in his ways, and to fear him.

For the Lord thy God bringeth thee into a good land, a land of brooks of water, of fountains and depths that spring out of valleys and hills;

A land of wheat, and barley, and vines, and fig trees, and pomegranates; a land of oil olive, and honey;

A land wherein thou shalt eat bread without scarceness, thou shalt not lack any thing in it; a land whose stones are iron and out of whose hills thou mayest dig brass.

When thou has eaten and art full, then thou shalt bless the Lord thy God for the good land which he hath given thee.

Beware that thou forget not the Lord thy God, in not keeping his commandments and his judgments, and his statutes, which I command thee this day:

Lest when thou hast eaten and art full, and hast built goodly houses, and dwelt therein:

And when thy herds and thy flocks multiply, and thy silver and thy gold is multiplied, and all that thou hast is multiplied;

Then thine heart be lifted up, and thou forget the Lord thy God, which brought thee forth . . .

And thou say in thine heart, My power and the might of mine hand hath gotten me this wealth.

But thou shalt remember the Lord thy God: for it is he that giveth thee power to get wealth, that he may establish his covenant.

And it shall be if thou do at all forget the Lord thy God and walk after other gods and serve them and worship them I testify against you this day that ye shall surely perish. (Deut. 8:6-14 17-1.)

All that Moses wrote in praise of the richness and productivity of the promised land, and more than he wrote can be applied to this great land of America—a land of corn, wheat, barley, and all other kinds of grain—a land of milk and honey—a land where we eat bread without scarceness —a land whose stones are gold, silver, and iron, and out of whose hills we dig brass—a land aptly called the "granary of the world."

His words of admonition are equally applicable—

When thou hast eaten and art full, then thou shalt bless the Lord thy God for the good land which he hath given thee. (Ibid., 8:10)

That was the message to ancient Israel.

Fifteen hundred years later, a little group of men faced a future that was just as threatening and forboding to them as that which the world faces today. The men in that group were Simon Peter, Thomas, Nathanael of Cana in Galilee, James and John, sons of Zebedee, and two others of his disciples. A short time before that gloomy period Jesus had said to them:

Let not your hearts be troubled: ye believe in God, believe also in me. (John 14:1.)

He promised them the Comforter who would testify of the Christ, who would bring all things to their remembrance, who would show them things to come.

Notwithstanding all those promises and divine exhortations, the disciples, following the crucifixion of their Lord, were depressed in their feelings. Their hopes were shattered. Their future, so far as Christ's triumph on earth was concerned, seemed all but blighted. They had been called and set apart to be "fishers" of men, and to Peter had been given the keys of the kingdom. Notwithstanding all this, in that hour of despondency, Peter turned to his old vocation, and said: "I go a fishing," and the others replied, "We go also with thee." (See John 21:3, 15-18)

They were in that state of mind when the resurrected Christ said to the discouraged leader of the Twelve: "Simon, son of Jonas, lovest thou me more than these?" Peter answered, "Yea, Lord; thou knowest that I love thee." Said the Lord, "Feed my sheep." I have my own interpretation of what "these" means. Keep in mind, will you please, that it was his vocation—what he would get. He had there before him the products of his morning's fishing, for he had fished all night and had caught nothing. "Simon, son of Jonas, lovest thou me more than these?" "Yea, Lord, thou knowest, I love thee." "Feed my sheep."

On that occasion Peter became conscious of his responsibility not only as a fisher of men, but also as a shepherd of the flock. It was then that he sensed finally and completely the full meaning of the divine injunction, "Follow thou me."

With that never-failing light, those twelve humble men succeeded in changing the course of human relations.

The world wants peace, the winning of which seems to be more difficult than the winning of the war.

No peace, even though temporarily obtained,will be permanent unless it is built upon the solid foundation of eternal principles enunciated in the two incidents I have mentioned.

The first of these the Lord gave to Moses on Mount Sinai—"Thou shalt worship the Lord thy God." Consider what that means. When we sincerely accept God as our Father and make him the center of our being, we become conscious of a new aim in life. No longer is the chief end of daily life merely to nourish and to pamper the body as all animals do. Spiritual attainment, not physical indulgence, becomes the chief goal. God is not viewed from the standpoint of what we may get from him, but what we may give to him. Only in the complete surrender of our inner life may we rise above the selfish, sordid pull of nature. Divine and eternal as an element in the acquisition of peace is Christ's admonition.

> . . . seek ye first the kingdom of God and his righteousness.

Of equal importance is the acceptance of the Son of God as the Savior of mankind.

When Jesus was talking to his disciples, just immediately preceding his betrayal, explaining to them that he would have to leave them, he said: "ye believe in God, believe also in me." He desired them to understand, as he wants the whole world to know, that only through him can man find the life abundant. Those were not mere words of defiance which Peter uttered as he and John stood prisoners before the high priests. He proclaimed an eternal truth when he said:

> . . . for there is none other name under heaven given among men, whereby we must be saved. (Acts 4:12)

That truth is reiterated in the Doctrine and Covenants—

> . . . all men must repent and believe on the name of Jesus Christ, and worship the Father in his name, and endure in faith on his name to the end, or they cannot be saved in the kingdom of God. (D & C 20:29)

I like to associate with that word "saved" the power that man gets in this life to rise above his animal instincts and passions, power to overcome or resist social evils that blight men's and women's souls and shut them out not only from the peace of the world, but also from membership in the kingdom of God. Men may yearn for peace, cry for peace, and work for peace, but there will be no peace until they follow the path pointed out by the living Christ.

A third essential to our peace of mind, and eventually to the peace of nations, is to keep confidence in our fellow men. You say how can we keep confidence when men are so corrupt? I answer that even if two or three, or even a score of men prove themselves dishonest and wicked, we are not justified in losing confidence in all men. Most people are honorable and upright—I like to think that—and desirous to:

. . . do justly, and to love mercy, and to walk humbly with thy God. (Micah 6:8)

Even if international leaders of a nation or of five nations disavow their Creator, and that's what they are saying in their hearts, "my power and the might of mine hand have got me this wealth," and even deny the Christ who redeemed them, let us remember that ten times that number of nations still profess to believe in God and in individual freedom.

These three principles—faith in God—acceptance of Christ as the Savior of men—confidence in our fellow men—are summed up by the Savior as follows:

. . . Thou shalt love the Lord thy God with all thy heart, and with all thy soul, and with all thy mind.
This is the first and great commandment.
And the second is like unto it. Thou shalt love thy neighbor as thyself. (Matthew 22:37-39)

We learn from authentic sources that communistic countries operating from behind the "iron curtain" accuse democratic countries, and particularly the United States, of virtually every political and moral crime under the sun. Our democracy is described as an instrument to enslave people.

Such slander has been compared to slugs that crawl over our cabbages. You may kill them, but there is still the slime.

The surest method against such slander is to live it down by perseverance in well doing, and by prayer to God that he would cure the distempered mind of those who traduce and injure us.

To the Church today are applicable the words of the Savior:

Let your light so shine before men, that they may see your good works, and glorify your Father which is in heaven. (Matthew 5:16)

If we would face the future, no matter what it may be, with calmness of spirit, with an assurance that God governs in the affairs of men, let us as individuals and as a group live exemplary lives.

Let us see to it that the social evils now rampant in the world that bring such sorrow and degradation to mankind, that spread sorrow and misery throughout the world are reduced to a minimum in our own communities; for example, there is too much drunkenness, too much unchastity. The excessive consumption of intoxicating liquors in this state is a reflection upon all.

To curtail those evils, to spread love and peace, brotherly kindness throughout the world is our paramount duty. If we succeed to a commendable degree, we can say to the world—unbelievers, scoffers, and all others, "Come, our way of life is best because it works best. Our people are efficient, prosperous, and happy because we are a body who aid one another in the productive life. We waste none of our substance in vice, luxury, or ostentation. We do not dissipate our energy in brawling, gambling, or unwholesome habits. We conserve our resources of body and mind and devote them to the upbuilding of the kingdom of God, which is not a mystical but a real kingdom. It is a body of people dominated by ideals of productivity, which is mutual service. We do not strive for the things which satisfy but for the moment and then leave a bad taste. We strive for the things which build us up, and enable us and our children to be strong, to flourish, and to conquer. We strive to make ourselves worthy to receive the world by fitting ourselves to use the world more productively than others. We believe that obedience to God means obedience to the laws of nature, which are but the manifestations of his will; and we try by painstaking study to acquire the most complete and exact knowledge of that will, in order that we may conform ourselves to it."

The world faces a crisis—a terrible crisis. Opportunity is given for men to choose wisely and live, or disregard the Master's teachings and die. Down through the ages comes resounding the cry of Joshua—

. . . choose you this day whom ye will serve; . . . but as for me and my house, we will serve the Lord. (Joshua 24:15)

And the thrilling words of Peter when commanded not to speak at all, nor to teach in the name of Jesus:

. . . Whether it be right in the sight of God to hearken unto you more than unto God, judge ye.

For we cannot but speak the things which we have seen and heard. (Acts 4:19-20)

The choice today is between dictatorship with the atheistic teachings of communism, and the doctrine of the restored gospel of Jesus Christ, obedience to which alone can make us free.

God bless the Church, particularly our young people who are going to maintain its standards. God bless fathers and mothers who instil this faith in the hearts of children and proclaim it throughout the world, I pray.

Transforming Power of Faith in Jesus Christ

For I know that my redeemer liveth, and he shall stand at the latter day upon the earth:

And though after my skin worms destroy this body, yet in my flesh shall I see God:

Whom I shall see for myself, and mine eyes shall behold, and not another; though my reins be consumed within me. (Job 19:25, 26, 27)

Such was the heartfelt assurance of Job expressed in humiliation when everything else had been taken from him and even his body utterly wasted in affliction.

If a few more million men in the world could feel that testimony of the reality of our Redeemer selfishness would be less manifest, war among nations would be eradicated, and peace would reign among mankind.

"What think ye of Christ?" was the question Jesus put to a group of Pharisees when they, with scribes and Sadducees sought to entrap or confound the great Teacher by asking him entangling questions. He silenced the Sadducees in their attempt to ensnare him with regard to paying tribute to Caesar. He satisfied the scribes regarding the first and greatest commandment, and now he put to silence the Pharisees regarding their anticipated Christ.

To this congregation, to the Church, and to the world, I repeat this question as being the most vital, the most far-reaching query in this unsettled, distracted world.

Great minds in all ages who have contributed to the betterment of mankind have been inspired by noble ideals.

History is replete with men who, as Wordsworth puts it, "By vision splendid, were on their way attended." There is John Milton, for example, inspired with a desire as a boy of twelve to write a poem that would live for centuries. As a result, the world has "Paradise Lost," and, though blind, the poet as he approached the closing moments of his life, explained: "Still guides the heavenly vision." Sir Walter Scott wrote almost day and night to pay off a debt for which he was not really responsible. George Washington, guided by the desire to build a noble character and to be of service to his country, cried: "I hope I may ever have strength and virtue enough to maintain what I consider to be the most precious of all titles the character of an honest man." Abraham Lincoln's lofty soul, expressing himself:

With malice toward none; with charity for all; with firmness in the right as God gives us to see the right, let us strive on to finish the work we are in to bind up the broken wounds, to care for him who shall have borne the battle and for his widow and his orphans. To do all which may achieve and cherish a just and lasting peace among ourselves and with all nations.

These and others who live to their best, are the men "who realize in daily life their luminous hours and transmute their ideals into conduct and character. These are the soul architects who build their thoughts and deeds into a plan. Who travel forward, not aimlessly, but toward a destination. Who sail not anywhither but toward a port, who steer not by the clouds, but by the fixed stars. High in the scale of manhood these who ceaselessly aspire towards life's Great Exemplar."

But the highest of all ideals are the life and teachings

of Jesus of Nazareth, and that man is most truly great who is most Christlike.

What you sincerely in your heart think of Christ will determine what you are, will largely determine what your acts will be. No person can study this divine personality, can accept his teachings, without becoming conscious of an uplifting and refining influence within himself. In fact, every individual may experience the operation of the most potent force that can affect humanity. Electricity lightens labor in the home, imprisons alike on a disc the warbling tones of the mocking bird and the convincing appeal of the orator. By the turn of a switch, it turns night into day. The possibilities of the force resulting from the breaking up of the atom seem to be limitless, either for the destruction or the blessing of life. Other and greater forces are already glimpsed. None, however, is so vital, so contributive to peace and happiness of the human family as the surrendering of our selfish animal-like natures to the life and teachings of our Lord and Savior Jesus Christ. Writes George R. Wendling in "The Man of Galilee:"

Believe it! the most wonderful work in all the world is not to take iron, steel, and brass and make a locomotive; nor is it to take gold and diamonds and cog-wheels and make a watch; nor is it to take canvas and colors and brush, and paint an Angelus; nor yet is it to take pen and parchment and write an Iliad or Hamlet, but an infinitely greater work than all is to take an ignoble, cruel, impure, and dishonest being and transform him into an upright, gentle, noble, and pure man. Here we touch the creative power of the Galilean—and bow before the mystery.

Here we find the crowning glory of all the evidences, attested by millions of intelligent men and women, the fact, mysterious but not illusory, that his very presence is found, is realized, is verified, and that he is as helpful, as vital, and as inspiring now as when the matchless Beautitudes fell upon the ears of a listening multitude two thousand years ago.

Peter, the chief Apostle, is a striking example of this transforming power. He was a humble, reputably a rough, uncultured fisherman to whom Jesus of Nazareth became an inspiration. The vision that bade him say, "Thou art the Christ, the Son of the Living God," became the guiding light of his life. Conditions occasionally made him falter, but he regained the lightened pathway. Bigots scoffed at him, religious zealots, political charlatans arrested, imprisoned and shackled him as a dangerous enemy to society, but the heavenly vision lightened the darkened dungeon, burst open prison doors, struck off the fetters that bound his wrists, as well as his wavering soul, and gave him courage and strength to face his accusers with the sublime testimony: He "whom ye crucified, Jesus Christ, is the only name under heaven given among men, whereby we must be saved." (Acts 4:12.)

Only a comparatively well-to-do man, making a fairly good living by fishing, of whom the world would never have heard had he not been inspired by a testimony of the divine mission of the Man of Galilee—just a humble fisherman, who, by the light of that inspiration to him and a few others, "Many of the world's loveliest things have been created, many of the world's finest minds inspired."

Another good example is Paul, a contemporary of Peter, whose early life and teachings were entirely different from those of the fisherman, but who, when the vision of the risen Lord pierced his prejudiced mind, was inspired throughout the remainder of his days by one guiding thought expressed on the occasion of his great vision: "Lord what wouldst thou have me do?" Paul, as Peter, had his hours of discouragement. Pride sometimes perturbed him, and conformity to church authority was occasionally difficult. He, too, was mobbed, beaten, and imprisoned, put in stocks in a dungeon, but the heavenly vision of the risen Lord ever guided his footsteps.

Recall also the Prophet Joseph Smith who declared: "I had actually seen a light, and in the midst of that light I saw two Personages, and they did in reality speak to me; and though I was hated and persecuted for saying that I had seen a vision, yet it was true; and while they were persecuting me, reviling me, and speaking all manner of evil against me falsely for so saying, I was led to say in my heart: Why persecute me for telling the truth? I have actually seen a vision; and who am I that I can withstand God, or why does the world think to make me deny what I have actually seen? For I had seen a vision: I knew it, and I knew God knew it, and I could not deny it, neither dared I do it; at least I knew that by so doing I would offend God, and come under condemnation." (Joseph Smith 2:25.)

Through railings, scoffings, mobbings, arrests, imprisonments, persecutions that led to martyrdom, he, as Peter and Paul before him, ever strove to the utmost of his ability to follow the light that had made him a "partaker of the divine nature."

I quote these three outstanding leaders in the realm of religion to show how the assurance of the divine mission of our Lord and Savior not only transformed their personal lives to a greater or lesser degree, but influenced for good the entire world.

Since man's first advent on earth, God has been urging him to rise above the selfish groveling life of the purely animal existence into the higher, more spiritual realm. After several thousand years of struggling, mankind even now but dimly recognizes the fact that the greatest of the world's leaders are those who most nearly approach the teachings of the Man of Galilee. This is psychologically sound, because the thoughts a man harbors determine the realm in which he serves. "Be not deceived," writes Paul to the Galatians, "God is not mocked; for whatsoever a man soweth, that shall he also reap. For he that soweth to his flesh shall of the flesh reap corruption; but he that soweth to the Spirit shall of the Spirit reap life everlasting." (Galatians 6:7-8.)

A Great Drama

Today there is being enacted a great world drama, the final act of which we can only dimly surmise. In Korea, one of the bloodiest wars of modern times is raging. Engaged in it are soldiers from South Korea, United States, Great Britain, France, Turkey, Greece, Netherlands, Australia, Canada, New Zealand, Thailand, the Philippines, South Africa, and one or two other nations—all enlisted under the United Nations' banner. Political relationships leading up to their fighting as an international army need not concern us this morning, but there is one significant fact most worthy of attention: battling for the same cause are Buddhists, followers of Confucius, Moslems, and Christians. Opposed to them are communists, openly avowed to be anti-Christ. Two hundred twenty-nine thousand casualties are already reported in this conflict! It would almost seem to be the beginning of the great battle of Armageddon. More destructive to the spreading of Christian principles in the minds, particularly of the youth, than battleships, submarines, or even bombs, is the sowing of false ideals by the enemy. Particularly, during the last five years, Communist Russia has gained conquests over the satellites for the time being under her dominion, including China, and now threatening Japan by sowing seeds of mistrust in the body politic. Misrepresentation, false propaganda, innuendoes soon sprout into poisonous weeds, and before long the people find themselves victims of a pollution that has robbed them of their individual liberty and enslaved them to a group of political gangsters.

So it is with evil thoughts that may be permitted insidiously to enter and to find lodgment in the human mind. Thoughts harbored determine destiny.

"My spirit," says the Christ, "will not dwell in unclean tabernacles." The corruption that is in the world through lust, as mentioned in one of Peter's epistles, has its source in thoughts and schemes harbored in the individual mind. A man who takes advantage of his neighbor in a business deal when the opportunity offers, has prepared himself for the occasion by dishonest thinking. Young couples do not lose their chastity, named by the Book of Mormon as "precious above all things" without their having previously in thought justified the act. The husband who coolly turns from a loyal wife and family and seeks illicit relationship elsewhere, perhaps with a disloyal wife of a neighbor, has previously poisoned his soul with immoral ideas. Disgruntled members of society, fault-finders in wards and stakes, do not become such merely because of some offense real or imagined. What they say and do have been preceded by selfish desires or unattained ambition.

I mentioned communism in its war against individual liberty and free enterprise as surreptitiously sowing poisonous seeds within the body politic. It is also from within, morally speaking, that our cities become corrupt; not from outward, open assault on virtue, but from insidious, corrupt actions of trusted individuals. Our government has recently uncovered a gambling ring that covers a twenty billion dollar business in vice. Many large cities in the United States are connected with it and contaminated by it. Too many of these city officials license darkened rooms wherein men and women, and not infrequently teen-age boys and girls, may guzzle beer and whiskey and indulge in other vices sought by persons of low ideals. For the permission and perpetuation of such dens of iniquity in our cities, the public is not entirely free from blame. However, those who are elected to office—commissioners, peace officers, trusted servants of the people—are most directly responsible. Generally speaking, these men are honest in their intentions and actions to enforce the laws and if possible to eradicate, at least to reduce to a minimum, the evils upon which the underworld thrives. One or two, or a half a dozen unprincipled men, however, can frustrate the most earnest efforts of the upright officials. For example, officers informed that minors are permitted to enter a certain 'joint" will find when they get to the place that the proprietor has been "tipped off" and seemingly everything is within the law. If and when appreciation of such "tip-offs," and other favors, is expressed in secretive payments of money, those participating in the graft may meet in a room, a club, or in a private residence, ostensibly to play a social game of poker, and under this guise divide their ill-gotten gains. Thus do our cities, as well as individuals, become corrupt from within.

Such exploitation of the poor unfortunates whose thoughts and desires lead them only to gratify their appetites, indulge their passions to exist by deceit, cunning, and crime, are among the corruptions that Peter says "are in the world through lust."

Citizens should never lose sight of the fact, however, that—

> There is not vice so great but we can kill
> And conquer it if we but will.

Christ came to redeem the world from sin. He came with love in his heart for every individual, with redemption and possibility for regeneration for all. By choosing him as our ideal, we create within ourselves a desire to be like him, to have fellowship with him. We perceive life as it should be and as it may be.

The chief Apostle Peter, the indefatigable Paul, the Prophet Joseph Smith, and other true followers of the risen Lord recognized in him the Savior of the individual, for did he not say, "This is my work and my glory—to bring to pass the immortality and eternal life of man"—not the sacrificing of the individual for the perpetuation of the socialistic or communistic state.

Members of the Church of Christ are under obligation to make the sinless Son of Man their ideal—the one perfect being who ever walked on earth.

Sublimest Example of Nobility
God-like in nature
Perfect in his love
Our Redeemer
Our Savior
The immaculate Son of our Eternal Father
The Light, the Life, the Way
Head of the Church that bears his name
Restored in its fullness by the appearance
Of God the Father
And his Beloved Son
To the Prophet Joseph Smith.

O Thou great Friend to all sons of men,
Who once appeared in humble guise below,
Sin to rebuke, to break the captive's chain,
And call thy brethren forth from want and woe,

We look to thee! thy truth is still the Light
Which guides the nations, groping on their way
Stumbling and falling in disastrous night,
Yet hoping ever for the perfect day.
Yes: thou art still the Life, thou art the Way
The holiest know; Light, Life, the Way to heaven!

And they who dearest hope and deepest pray,
Toil by the Light, Life, Way, which thou hast given.
                                    (Theodore Parker)

The World Needs Appreciation of
the Principles Enunciated
by Jesus Christ

This morning just following the Tabernacle Choir broadcast, I expressed a few words of appreciation to the Tabernacle Choir members. Perhaps nowhere else in the world can you find several hundred singers who devote their time and their means, two or three times a week, to the service that that choral body is rendering. They will not take even their carfare. They have to pay, some of the mothers, for women and girls, to take care of the little babies and children while the mothers go out to render this service. They are radiating their influence throughout the world. To the members of the choir such effort seems somewhat insignificant, but to that little thing surprises the visitors who come to the block.

We should like the world to come and see today what you have done. I wish we could all see just how you have struggled to contribute your share of the money needed to complete this house. The bishop was not the only one to whose eyes tears sprang when he said, "I have seen members sell even their cow, and give all the money toward completion of this building."

I should like to see and know the details of some young girl who gave of her wages and denied herself a new dress or a new hat. A little thing? No, that is the big thing which the world needs. I should like to see the young man, the young deacon, who saved his meager wages and gave to the bishop to contribute to this. I should like to look into the homes of the parents whose boys or girls were on missions, or who are now on missions when this project began. You had to send out some $60 to $75, and besides that, give your contribution to the erection of this building. A little thing—it is an illustration of what the world needs.

Here's a quotation I wrote just before I left home from a book entitled, "Wake Up or Blow Up."

Under the heading he has this word, "America; lift the world, or lose it." This will give you an idea of his theme.

We could conquer the world's heart by serving it as Jesus said we should, but in this all-out attack of help, the church has a very basic responsibility. It must find the right kind of men. The technicians will fail unless they have the type of character that the church at its best produces.

These are the men—men of high honor; men with good habits, integrity, warm hearts, Christ-like, compassionate desires to help; democratic and congenial men who are loving and beloved. Unless the churches will send out such men as missionaries, America cannot fulfill her destiny as a leader in the nations.

The author of "Human Destiny," Pierre Lecomte du Nouy, expresses largely the same thought:

The time has come for nations as well as individuals, to know what they want. If civilized countries want peace, they must understand that the problem must be approached basically. The old scaffolding willed to us by past generations cracks on every side. It cannot be consolidated by makeshifts, by bits of string, by pots of glue and treaties gravely signed by highly dignified gentlemen.

In current life, in his relations with his fellow men, man must use his reason, but he will perpetrate fewer errors if he listens to his heart.

Then he says:

The state should be the servant of the man, protect him in his free, individual expansion and be worthy of him, of the individual. It should not dominate him. The value of a country is the sum of the values of its children. Any government which seeks to substitute its interest to the pursuit of individual development is regressive and threatens human dignity.

Some people may say that we are still far removed from the time when man will be sufficiently evolved to be fully conscious of himself and to be worthy of being treated in any way but as a child. This may be true, but all the more reason to help him to develop into organized society toward this goal, for as long as a state pursues an aim different from that which should be the aim of its members, no real progress is conceivable.

Now that gives the idea of what it is. "As long as there is no collective conscience rendering the nations," that is, the citizens, not the governments, "jointly liable for the engagements taken by their representatives, treaties will constitute a tragic comedy and it is surprising that anyone can still be their dupe. Yet the game continues and the abovementioned gentlemen who take themselves very seriously dictate and sign acts which are supposed to assure the peace of the world. For how long?"

Then he touches a principle already mentioned here today—that individual consciousness, that individual testimony, and with it a willingness to sacrifice, if necessary, for the establishment of the truths of the Gospel among the nations.

Examinations deal with a quantity of facts destined to be forgotten in three months or which are purely technical. Children are trained to behave decently in public, but nobody dreams of making them repeat daily as a prayer; "Every promise is sacred. No one is obliged to give a pledge, but he who breaks his given word is dishonored. He commits an unpardonable crime against his dignity. He betrays; he covers himself with shame; he excludes himself from human society."

If this is not in reality a prayer, it is a creed, a creed which by expressing faith in the dignity of man addresses itself beyond him to God from whom we have received it.

And then he makes an appeal for man, the individual man, to bring himself in harmony with the ideals enunciated by Christ.

Mankind has tried everything except Christianity. The world has tried hatred, impurity, graft, self-interest and has been brought to the brink of perdition. It is curious that we must stand up in the Twentieth Century and plead with people who bear his name that Jesus Christ was not a foolish ruler, a visionary leader, that his word is the illuminating word, that his way is the living way, that it is only safe to trust and follow him.

The Church must repent of her lukewarmness and rebuke with prophetic wrath the selfishness of men and break her cowardly silence and say to the world, "We've let you run affairs after selfish pagan methods until you have come to the brink of ruin. Unless you Christianize your industrial system, it cannot last. Unless you Christianize your institutions, they cannot endure.

Better foundations can no man lay than that which is laid by Jesus Christ. Too long have we imagined that the principles of Christ were for some other world. We have put the kingdom he came to establish beyond the stars, but this was not the purpose of his mission. This is not the meaning of his gospel. His laws are to be followed in the world in which we live, now and here, in street and market and factory. It will only be through obedience to moral law, the Sermon on the Mount and the Golden Rule, and whole-hearted response to the Fatherhood of God and the Brotherhood of Man and the suffering love of Jesus Christ that there can ever be frictionless society in our world.

"Blessed are the pure in heart for they shall see God," was one of the messages of the Savior. He had that in mind undoubtedly when he said to those two disciples, in answer to their question, "Master where abidest thou?" "Come and see."

You, brethren and sisters, did not think when you were making those contributions to this building, that you were illustrating, or making practical in your lives, the very principles, for which these men, worried about the future of this world, are pleading. When that first writer, the author of "Wake Up or Blow Up," makes his appeal for missionaries to go out, he did not have in mind missionaries who would go out and pay their own expenses, but you know that is what this Church is doing now.

Of course you know, sending them out to all parts of the world without compensation, wherever we are admitted, preaching the restoration of the Gospel to Joseph Smith in this day, each one contributing his time and each one carrying the responsibility to be honorable, to possess integrity, to radiate a sincerity which will go into the hearts of others, and lead the honest in heart to see the truth of his message.

"Come and see," we say to the world, and though we make mistakes and though we are frail and not accomplishing all that we have in mind, here in this little group of a million people you will find the application of the principles of the Gospel of Jesus Christ in daily routine and activity.

The success of that work depends upon you, upon me. The Lord always speaks to the individual, not to somebody else but to you. It is necessary for each individual to sense his relationship as a son or her relationship as a daughter of our Father in heaven. You are not just a cog in the wheel of the state. To be such I think is the greatest danger in the world today, and I find some in our Church who rather favor that.

They think the state is our protector. It isn't. The state as a servant, is here to protect you in your work, on your farm and in your business, and to see that justice is administered, and you have a right to that protection.

The state has not anything that you do not give it.

The government has no means but that which you give it, and we give it to the government so that it will protect each individual in his right. That is a fundamental principle of the gospel of Jesus Christ. Brother Lee emphasized the value of the individual when he referred to the strength of an individual testimony. You would not do what you are doing if you did not feel that this Church belongs to you. It is your Church. It does not belong to the president nor to his counselors nor to the Twelve.

That individual testimony is the strength of Zion, the priesthood and each man who holds that priesthood knowing of the dignity, knowing of the revelation and divine announcement that Jesus Christ has established this Church for the good of the individual.

You who have completed this Church edifice say in substance to each child, "Come and see. Come and learn the best way to live." And we should like all the world to know that in this house the fundamental principles of the Lord Jesus Christ will be taught.

Now I have in my mind not just faith, repentance and baptism. Our children have absorbed those principles, not only through teaching but more principally through the actual performance of these ordinances. But I do have in mind some of the following:

First, respect for parents. That is a fundamental principle of the Gospel. We should like boys and girls to understand from teachers who instruct them that one of the first duties of children is to honor their parents. It is a source of deep sorrow when a girl will challenge the advice of parents and marry contrary to their advice. It makes life tragically sorrowful when a father will cry and say, "What can I do?" as he realizes that his daughter is defiantly going to marry a rake. "Honor thy father and thy mother that thy days may be long upon the earth which the Lord thy God giveth thee." Respect for parents is a fundamental principle, and parents, it is your duty to sit down and talk with the children before they become rebellious. Win their confidence and they will not defy you.

Another principle which will be taught here in this building is reverence. That is a wonderful principle, too.

It is a source of refinement. One of the brethren referred to the necessity of restraint on the part of the children from marking the walls or breaking windows. This is the house of God. Any irreverent feeling that would prompt such desecration is contrary to the teachings of Jesus.

Why, when he saw those people in the temple, changing their money for the convenience of the Jews who came from other nations, when he heard the bleating of the sheep, the cooing of the doves that were brought there for the convenience of those who were going to offer sacrifices, he felt that his house, his Father's house, was desecrated. His whole being rebelled against it.

Yes, it was convenient for the foreigners who came to offer sacrifices, but the bleating of the sheep, lowing of the cattle, cooing of the doves should be out somewhere else and not in the house of God. The money changers were a convenience for those who came with foreign change, but their money should be changed not in the house of God but outside. And so our business dealings, ought not to be brought in here, nor our jealousies, nor our scheming. This is the house of God and should be revered as such.

George Washington fought for the liberties which we enjoy. He was a reverent man and was wounded to his heart when he heard that some of his soldiers were taking the name of God in vain. And he wrote a letter condemning such a practice. Soldiers should be above it. What an ideal: —to have an army praying to God and refraining from taking his name in vain! Come and learn that principle. Come and see, for Christ is here teaching just that principle through the Gospel which he has given to us.

We learn not only reverence, but also the principle of self-control. It is one of the sources of sorrow to find that so many couples wreck their married life on the shoals of divorce, and I find as I read the applications for cancellation of sealings and the reasons given, that very often one is because the husband cannot control himself. Sometimes it

is the wife, but very seldom. Principally it is the men who
try to dominate or who mistreat their wives who have promised to live in respect and serve throughout time and eternity. If the little principle of self-control could be practiced
in the home, there would be fewer heartbreaks, and dis-
rupted homes. The Word of Wisdom is given not only for
the benefit of the physical body but it is also given that men
may learn in little things to control their appetites. If they
can control their appetites, then they have strength to
control their tempers. If they control their tempers, they
can control their tongues which lash out and leave wounds
that sometimes take years and probably centuries to heal.
These are practical? Why, they are part of life itself. "Come
and see" and learn what the ideals are that will be taught
and promulgated in these classrooms, yes, and in the recre-
ation hall and particularly here in the chapel.

Not only self-control, but we shall learn here that the
value, the strength of each individual must come from within, not from what parents say, not from what the bishop
says, the president of the stake or the General Authorities.
Their words may awaken a thought in the mind, arouse a
determination, but that determination and that thought
must come from each individual's soul. You decide which
course you are going to take and the Lord will judge you
accordingly.

> Nae treasures, nor pleasures,
> Could make us happy lang;
> The heart aye's the part aye
> That makes us right or wrang.

So every penny, every dollar, every tens of dollars or
hundreds or thousands of dollars that you donate here pre-
sents to the world, an illustration of practical Christianity.
It is not just saying that you love the Lord but it is doing.
It was not easy, I know, to make the contribution that you
have, but you will be rewarded manyfold for having done

it because you lost yourself for the good of others, for the the cause of Christ.

"Not everyone that saith to me, 'Lord, Lord,' shall enter into the Kingdom of Heaven but he that doeth the will of my Father which is in heaven."

With all my heart I pray God to bless you for the good you have done for yourselves but more because of the good you have done to the world. Two thousand and more other wards and branches are demonstrating to the world just what practical Christianity is. The Church is growing. Its radiation is entering the hearts of thousands, millions perhaps from whom we never hear, but you are doing the work. You are missionaries.

Yes, the world is in a critical position and selfishness is at the bottom of it, and greed and hatred, but the leaven is working. Eyes are being turned to the Church of Jesus Christ, established by him and he is its head. God preserve the Church. God bless his servants who hold the priesthood. Protect our missionaries who are out in the field, teaching the fatherhood of God, the brotherhood of man, but more than that the restoration of the Gospel, and the reality of our Father and the reality of his Beloved Son.

God bless our soldier boys. They, too, are missionaries. A few of them slip, but the reports that come from them from different parts of the world show that most of them are true to their ideals. That is what counts. Christianity applied in the foxhole, on the battleground, among the generals and among those who are flying in the air.

We think of them tonight and we think of them when we kneel to pray.

May the day soon come when the influence of the Church will be felt even behind the iron curtain; for this gospel must be preached to all the world, to every nation, kindred, tongue and people.

Anniversary of Joseph Smith's Birth

Fellow members of the two Twenty-Seventh Wards, I esteem it a great privilege to meet with you in worship on this 146th anniversary of the birth of the Prophet, and the Sunday nearest to Christmas. This is an eventful occasion, and I pray that the spirit of the season will abide with us tonight while I try to give a message appropriate to these two great events.

I have chosen a text that will take our minds to a scene preceding the birth of the Savior. You will find it in the second chapter of Luke:

> And Joseph also went up from Galilee, out of the city of Nazareth, into Judaea, unto the city of David, which is called Bethlehem; (because he was of the house and lineage of David:)
> To be taxed with Mary his espoused wife . . .
> And so it was, that, while they were there, the days were accomplished that she should be delivered.
> And she brought forth her firstborn son, and wrapped him in swaddling clothes, and laid him in a manger; because there was no room for them in the inn.

Such is a brief account of a most significant event in the world's history. Those persons travelled with many, many others, bound to their native city to be taxed in accordance with the decree as mentioned in the paragraphs preceding what I have read.

Undoubtedly, they were weary. They had walked, Mary resting as best she could, and she could ride on the little donkey that carried their belongings. A few hours before that they had rested at the well, now known as Mary's Well. Then they had had several miles trudging still. Others had preceded them because they could travel with more speed.

And so it must have been early in the evening at least, and probably late in the evening. Darkness had set in when Joseph and Mary applied to the inn, and were told by the registrar, "There is no place."

You mothers can picture this more earnestly, and securely, more impressively, than anybody else. Undoubtedly, Mary had visions of an early birth. Seemingly she had not come prepared for the events that took place that night and the next day. That is why the babe was wrapped in swaddling clothes.

Imagine how she felt, and how Joseph, in sympathy with his wife, felt, when they were told, "There is no place in the inn," then stepping out in that darkness, and going to seek a place down in the stable, the humblest spot in the entire town. Others had preceded them there, and had already housed their animals. Some people were sleeping in the loft, undoubtedly, where travelers who could not afford to go to the inn found lodging.

My theme tonight can probably be best understood, or introduced, by a man by the name of Stetler, an educator, philosopher, who imagined that he was there that night, and this is what he says:

The city was crowded with strangers. I hurried to the little inn to find it jammed with folks trying to get lodging for the night. The answer came again and again from the innkeeper, "No room

in the inn." Being a friend of the innkeeper, I had no trouble in
getting lodging for the night.

Soon I observed a young man and his wife approach the desk
and ask for a room. "Sorry, sir, but there is no more room in the
inn," said the keeper sternly. "But I must have a place where my
wife can rest," pleaded the young man, and he leaned over and
whispered something to the innkeeper.

"The only thing I can suggest," replied the keeper curtly, "is
the stable. There you will find plenty of straw. Perhaps you can
keep warm," and with that he returned to his many wealthy and
distinguished guests.

Soon I retired for the night, but was awakened by the most
beautiful singing I had ever heard. It seemed to be coming from a
nearby hillside. The melody was not familiar to me, and while I
could not catch all the words, the message wafted over the air
seemed to be, "On earth, peace, good-will to men."

Shepherds coming in the next morning from the hillside related
a strange story. There had been an angel chorus, and an angel of
the Lord appeared, and spoke to them, saying, "For unto you is
born this day in the city of David, a Savior. Ye shall find the babe
wrapped in swaddling clothes, lying in a manger."

The shepherds had hastened to Bethlehem to see this miracle.
There was a great stir around the inn when it was learned that
during the night a child had been born to the young woman, who,
with her husband, had gone to the stable for shelter. I said to myself, "Why didn't I give up my room? No room for the Savior!
Great God, what an opportunity I have missed!" You say to me,
"Your imagination is running riot."

Well, I wonder how often there is no room for God in your
life and mine in this day and age. Somehow it seems the cry of the
innkeeper is still true. "There is no room in the inn."

A few years ago an incident happened in Edinburgh in
the winter of 1909, when no less a personage than the prime
minister of Great Britain delivered a lecture in the McCune
Hall of the University of Edinburgh on the subject, "The
moral values which unite the nations."

The gentleman presented in an interesting manner the
fundamental ties that unite the different nations of the
world—common knowledge, common commercial interests,
the intercourse of diplomatic relationship, and the bonds of
human friendship.

The audience greeted his masterful address with a great outburst of applause. As the presiding officer arose, and was about to express his appreciation, and that of the audience, a Japanese student who was doing graduate work at the University, stood up and leaning over the balcony, said, "But Mr. Balfour, what about Jesus Christ?"

Mr. Robin L. Sphere, to whom Professor Lang related this incident, writes that one could have heard a pin drop in the hall. Everyone felt at once the justice of the rebuke. The leading statesman of the greatest Christian empire in the world had been dealing with the different ties that are to unite mankind, and had omitted the one fundamental and essential bond, and every one felt, too, the dramatic element in the situation that the reminder of his forgetfulness had come from a Japanese student from a far-away non-Christian land .

A few years ago, and this you will remember, representatives from the leading nations of the world met in San Francisco to draw up a Constitution that would unite the nations of the world. The United Nations Charter was about finished when one of the small nations, I think from South America, suggested that they insert the name of God and appeal to him for guidance.

The suggestion was voted down. There was no room in the United Nations Charter for the Christ, for his name, or the name of his Father.

I am glad that the statesman who spoke about it did invoke the guidance of divinity, the divine guidance of the Son of Man, but I have always regretted that there was no room in the charter for his name.

Too often there is no room in our homes for the Savior, or for things that point to religion. We sometimes omit from those homes the prayer to Christ, and the prayer for divine guidance. Sometimes there is no room there because of intemperate parents, or profane parents. This will illustrate

what I mean. It is written by William H. Davis, and titled,
"The Little Ones."

> The little ones are put to bed
> And both are laughing, lying down,
> Their father and their mother, too
> Are gone on Christmas Eve to town.
> "O Santa Claus will bring a horse
> Gee up," cried Will with glee.
> "If I am good I'll have a doll
> From old Santa," laughed Emily.
> The little ones are gone to sleep;
> Their father and their mother now
> Are coming home with many more.
> They are drunk and make a merry row.
> The little ones on Christmas morn jump up
> Like skylarks from the grass,
> And then they stand as still as stone
> And just as cold as stones, alas.
> No horse, no doll beside their bed,
> No sadder little ones could be
> "We did some wrong," said little Will,
> "We must have sinned," sobbed Emily.

No room in that home for him who said, "Suffer little
children to come unto me, and forbid them not for of such is
the kingdom of heaven."

Campbell Morgan gives this short account of his experience when he and his bride first entered their new house.

My father came into my house soon after I was married, and
looked around. We showed him into every room, and then in his
rough way he said to me, "Yes, it is very nice, but nobody will
know, walking through here, whether you belong to God or to the
devil."

I went through and looked at the house again, and I thought,
"He is quite right."

No room in that house, so far as furniture or books are
concerned, for the Master. Often there is no room in our
hearts for the teachings of the Babe of Bethlehem. We lack

self-control. We fly in anger at a loved one who chances to make a mistake or who irritates us. We speak in anger, and probably strike, one of our little ones. We indulge in those things which Christ has advised us to avoid. It really means —all such things—that we have no room—there is no room in the inn. What else is it? You cannot explain it any other way, can you?

Recently, the United Nations Committee sensed the absence of something from that charter, and again the resolution was introduced that they offer prayer and appeal to God. I'm going to try to find out some day who gave that. I have never known.

So they compromised, sensing the need of divine help, but not wishing to offend atheistic nations, to rise and bow their heads in silence so that each one may pray as he wishes. I think that is a long way down the line of cowardice from the time when Benjamin Franklin and the other framers of the Constitution of the United States felt the same need of divine guidance. They too started out without prayer, but they seemed not to make any progress until finally that old gentleman, the oldest, I believe, in the committee, arose and said, "The longer I live the more convincing proofs I see that God governs in the affairs of men, and if a sparrow cannot fall to the ground without his aid, is it possible that an empire can rise without his aid?" and they asked a man each morning to offer prayer, and sincerely offered, with the result that we have the Constitution of the Unied States, giving to each individual liberty of conscience to worship God as he wished, the right to possess his own property, to speak his own mind, to publish what he would, do what he wishes so long as he does not trespass upon the rights of another, or deprive his neighbor of those same privileges.

As those two nations felt the need of God and his guidance, so do individuals. Sometimes, and many times, there comes into a man's heart or a woman's soul a sense of dependence upon some great power. Perhaps you felt it in school, you sincere students, when you realized that graduation meant so much to you, when you failed you could not stand the humiliation. I hope you sensed that keenly enough to go down on your knees, and if you did not, that you offered a silent prayer in your soul for God's guidance; that you did not say to him, "There is no room in my heart for you. I need you in my heart."

If you young people would sense that, you would find less sorrow because of yielding to temptation. There would be fewer parents with broken hearts because you yielded to that temptation. Strength comes from within, but that soul within is strengthened by a realization of dependence upon God.

Now is the time as never before for the so-called civilized nations, struggling for peace, to answer the question, "What of Christ?" If men ever reject the fact that Christ is our Lord and Savior, that his mission is to redeem man from sordid, animal life, of selfish indulgence in sin, and lift him into a realm shown only by him, of self-sacrifice, generosity, beauty and love; if the majority of nations fail to recognize Christ as the only name under heaven given among men whereby we must be saved; if doubting men reject the possibility of obtaining that spiritual assurance of Christ's divinity disclosed by Thomas when he reverently exclaimed, "My Lord and my God;" if men's acts be in accordance with rejections rather than in accordance with their acceptance of him as the one divine, then this world will continue to be torn by contention, made miserable by hideous warfare, and ignominiously wrecked on the shoals of materialism, selfish indulgence, and disbelief.

Without Jesus of Nazareth, the Crucified Christ, the Risen Lord, the world cannot survive.

Of all festivals throughout Christendom, Christmas comes most nearly being universally accepted and celebrated. There is something intrinsic about it that appeals to everyone from the stripling youth and the little toddling infant to the old philosopher walking in the sunset of life. It is the one season of the year when selfishness is subordinated, when the desire to give exceeds the desire to get— kindness, forgiveness, forbearance, love. These are among the simple virtues which make this holiday season so delightful.

The true spirit of Christmas is the spirit of the Christ, radiating through the centuries down the heavenly announcement of the birth of the Babe of Bethlehem comes the message, "Glory to God in the highest, peace on earth, good-will toward men."

The gift of a loving Father of his beloved Son who lived the one perfect life should ever be the central theme of Christmas celebrations. Let us cherish the hope that some day the friendly, unselfish, generous, mutually helpful spirit that characterizes the Christian tie will dominate human society.

When he came as a lowly babe, there was no room in the inn. Today every heart in every home should bid him welcome. If such were true, unselfishness, jealousy, enmity, and all things which bring unhappiness would be replaced by kindness, willing service and good-will.

As we do away with strife, suspicion, for a day, so let us do away with them continually. Christ came to give us peace, and life eternal. Let us accept his gift with gratitude, and show our thankfulness by following the pathway that leads to peace. The responsibility of establishing peace in the world rests not alone upon a union of nations. It rests upon every individual, upon every home, upon every hamlet and city. The source of happiness is within one's soul. So springs faith in Jesus Christ as our Lord and Savior.

First then, let each individual admit into his own heart the true spirit of Christmas. Then let it radiate throughout his home. A thousand such homes would make a truly

Christian city, and a thousand such cities, a truly Christian nation.

One hundred and forty-six years ago today another little babe was born—December 23, 1805. He grew to young manhood as other obscure little boys grew, but his soul became filled with the longing to know just which church is right, and that longing led him into prayer, and in answer to that prayer, the door was opened to admit the living Christ. It was through that prayer that the reality of Jesus Christ was revealed again to the world.

I say "the reality" because that vision gave to that young boy a picture of the personality of Deity, and between you and me there is no other way, there is no higher concept, that can come to the human mind in worship of those divine beings. You try it.

Men speak of the force that permeates all nature, and they call it God. They know it exists. There is not an intelligent person, I think, living, who does not recognie the existgent person, I think, living, who does not recognize the existence of a power or force beyond the comprehension of thing that man has. They call it God, but can you worship it? Can you invite that power into your homes, and say to your child, worship that power? I cannot. Perhaps my mind is not sufficiently great to comprehend it.

I recognize that force of electricity. I recognize the presence of a force, a ray, that came through a machine today, and I said to the doctor, "I know that thing exists, but you cannot see it."

"No, but we know it is there," he said.

"So it is," I replied, "with everything great in the world, with the greatest things in the world, including the Holy Spirit. You can feel it. You can sense it, but you cannot see it."

"Yes," he said, "and now we have the atomic bomb. No man has seen it."

All right, we have all these forces. We know they exist, but I cannot kneel down and pray to any one of them. Can you? When in your distress you ask God to come to you, give you power, are you thinking of a force? I will ask any man. But you personalize that, and see personality in Deity in God, no matter how you picture him, if you personalize Jesus Christ, who is in the image of God, you have that which ties your soul to his, and you feel a nearness which you cannot feel any other way.

That is the great message that Joseph Smith gave when he opened the door and let the Christ in. Are we going to shut him out of our lives, through the indulgence of the animal things that are practiced? You can find pleasure in so doing. There is pleasure in any animal indulgence which you wish to participate in, but it is groveling, it is unsatisfying. If we subdue those things and rise to the spirit life of Christ, we find true joy.

That life is expressed in a wonderful sentence, which he later said to the Pharisees and others, is the summary of all the commandments: "Love the Lord thy God with all thy might, mind and strength, and thy neighbor as thyself."

You say you cannot do it? Try it. We can approach it. We are approaching it this Christmas time. True, we are giving many times just because somebody else is going to give something to us, and we give sometimes for fear somebody will give it to us, and we will be embarrassed, but back of it all is the spirit of the Christmas, and if we can do that for a week during Christmas, we can do it two weeks after, and three weeks, and a month.

The Gospel is just a simple presentation of ideals by which we can rise one by one up to the spirituality of the Christ, and his life was devoid of everything which man usually possesses. He did not have a home which he called his own. The foxes had holes, the birds of the air had nests, but the Son of Man had nowhere to lay his head, and yet he rose to the heights and became after death, conqueror of death, creator of the world. No other being in the world has ever exerted such an influence, and of him one man said truly,

"A field without flowers, an alphabet without vowels, a continent without rivers, a night without stars, and a sky without a sun—these would not be half so sad as a world without a Bible, or a soul without Christ."

To apply his teachings in three words we should have in our hearts this Christmas Day and always three words, each commencing with "S". First, sincere faith in Christ the Lord.

Second, self-mastery. Do not under-estimate it. Do not brag about your temper. Do not justify an evil act, or a quick or an injurious act because you say you cannot control your anger. That is an admission of weakness. Do not say that you were tempted, and you could not resist it. That is worse than an admission of weakness. That says that you thought about that act before you committed it. Self-mastery, as Christ gave the lesson on the Mount of Temptation. He passed through every experience which you or I will pass through, temptation of the appetite, illustrative of the physical appetites and passions; temptation of pride—cast yourself down—a challenge; and the temptation of wealth, power. "All these will I give you if you will only fall down and worship," but he rose above them all and said, "Get thee hence, Satan, for it is written, 'Thou shalt worship the Lord thy God, and him only shalt thou serve.'" We too pass through those temptations in our own way. That is why I say the second great point is to hold to that self-mastery.

The third is service—service to our fellow men. Are you asked to do something in the Church? Do not refuse it. It is an opportunity in an organized way to render help to somebody in need. Are you asked to lead the choir? To sing in the choir? To go ward teaching? Do not refuse it. No matter how humble it seems to you. There is no position in the Church that is too humble for the greatest man to serve in.

"And inasmuch as ye do it unto the least of these, my servants, ye have done it unto me."

I like to call attention of the young people to the fact that Joseph Smith exemplified those high teachings in his life. People like to attack the Prophet. They like to say he was guilty of this and guilty of that. Men arrested him time after time, and finally thrust him into prison because of what they thought were ignominious things. But they don't know him, and they do not read his life.

Take the last day of his life, if you wish to see exemplified the spirit of the Christ—the last few weeks of his life. He felt impressed to lead the people out here in the west, and he started. He crossed the Mississippi River with Hyrum, his devoted brother, and with other great men, but there were enemies within the flock at Nauvoo—jealous men, men with hate in their hearts, and some of them influenced Emma, and she sent word with Porter Rockwell that "they are saying around here that you are a false shepherd fleeing from the flock."

Joseph turned again to Nauvoo, saying to Hyrum, "I'll stay. You go on."

Hyrum said, "No, I'll go back with you."

And Joseph returned with this great feeling in his heart: "If my life is of no value to my friends, it is of no value to me."

There is the Spirit of the Christ. A man 35 or 36 years of age has risen to high rounds on the ladder of spirituality when he can say that just out of the goodness of his heart, a natural spontaneous feeling which animates his life. And that was exemplified in the prison, and I would like to conclude with this thought, for it brings in both the greatness of the Prophet, and the reward of a righteous life by the Savior.

Joseph Smith, John Taylor, Hyrum, and Willard Richards were incarcerated. Dan Jones had left with a prophecy on his head which was afterwards fulfilled. Willard Richards had said, in answer to a question of the prophet, "Would you like to go away?"

He said, "Joseph, you did not ask me to go with you, or to come to Nauvoo. You did not ask me to cross the Mississippi River with you. You did not ask me to come here to Carthage, and I am not going away. But I will tell you what I will do. If they arrest you to take your life, I will die for you instead." And Willard Richards was a great man. You would not find a man like that devoted to another who was not just as noble as he himself, and nobler.

In that environment, Joseph asked that they sing "A Poor, Wayfaring Man of Grief," by Montgomery. Have you ever studied that carefully? It is not sung very often, but you remember, it is—

A poor wayfaring man of grief
Hath often passed me on the way
Who sued so humbly for relief
That I could never answer "Nay."
I had not power to ask his name,
Whereto he went or whence he came
Yet there was something in his eye
That won my love, I knew not why.

Then I shared with him my crust
And enjoyed manna. I dipped
And gave him the cup to quench his thirst
I drank, but he returned to me
And never thirsted more.
I found him in prison
The tide of lying tongues I stemmed
And honored him mid shame and scorn
Found him by the wayside, stripped, wounded
Nigh to death

I revived his spirits, and supplied
Wine, oil, refreshment—he was healed;
I had my self a wound concealed,
But from that hour forgot the smart,
And peace bound up my broken heart.
Then he asked if I for him would die
My flesh was weak, my blood ran chill
But the free spirit cried, "I will."

Then in a moment to my view
The stranger started from disguise
The tokens in his hands I knew
The Savior stood before mine eyes.
He spoke, and my poor name he named.
"Of me thou hast not been ashamed.
These deeds shall thy memorial be
Fear not, thou didst them unto me."

It is through those deeds that we let the Christ enter the inn. May our doors and our hearts always be open to him.

Dedicatory Services for the Monument

Monuments are links that unite one generation with another. We assemble here today to unveil and dedicate one of the great monuments of the world. In some respects it is most singular and outstanding. It is a monument designated by a sentence. In our country we have the Washington Monument, the Lincoln Monument, the Thomas Jefferson Monument, the Brigham Young Monument and others, to individuals. This monument is designated as "This is the Place" Monument. Every sentence, every phrase fills two purposes. It denotes a certain thing. It also connotes, sometimes, many things. Abraham Lincoln, for example, denotes a long, tall, angular individual, but it connotes the preservation of the Union and other historical features that are sacred to every true citizen of the United States. I think it would be interesting for a few moments to try to contemplate what "This is the Place" connotes.

A hundred years ago yesterday the great leader, Brigham Young, looked over this Valley and used that famous phrase: "This is the right place. Drive on." What did he have in his mind when he said: "This is the place?" By reading the reports of his sermons we find, first, that he had in mind the prophetic utterance of the man whom he loved, the Prophet Joseph, who said the Saints would go to the West, build cities, and become a mighty people in the midst of the Rocky Mountains.

Secondly, when that great leader uttered the sentence, "This is the Place," he had in mind that here they would find a place of refuge and peace.

Third, he had in mind that from this center there would radiate to all the world a message of truth insofar as it would be possible for that little band and those who followed them to declare that truth to the world. Perhaps back of it was to establish brotherhood, peace, and above all, faith in God our Father.

And fourth, he had in mind in this place we shall establish industry, worship, education and mutual service.

On one occasion soon after they entered the Valley he said to that little group: "First build your fort and protect yourselves from degradations. As soon as you have built your log house," and I quote, "let a sufficient number of rooms be appropriated for schools, furnished by the best teachers, not furnished by the best furniture, upholstered— furnished by the best teachers, and give every child among you an opportunity of continuing his education anew and see that he attends to it. That individual who has an opportunity to educate his children and does not, is not worthy to have children. Teach your children the principles of the kingdom that they may grow in righteousness."

These are some of the thoughts connoted in the mind of Brigham Young when a century ago he said, "This is the Place."

The Centennial Commission, with all associated, have tried to commemorate these ideals in the celebration that has been carried on now since January 1, 1947. They commemorate first the building of cities and these commonwealths, and to that end the program has been carried forward to every hamlet and county in this state. They have tried to commemorate the schools in education, in music, art, drama, and tragedy, physical prowess as it is exhibited in the highest and best in sports. They commemorate too the ideals of the pioneers in courtesy, service to one another and to visitors and strangers.

In conclusion, as we look upon this place and monument, I will say in the words of one of our outside friends:

" 'This is the place in all the West'
Exclaims the traveled stranger guest,
'Where Brigham and his Mormon band
First built in Utah's wonderland.
" 'And so 'twill be year after year
They will criticize or praise or cheer
When we have long since quit the race
Will still be heard, "This is the place." ' "

Missions and Missionaries
of the Church

Said the Savior to his Apostles:

Go ye therefore, and teach all nations, baptizing them in the name of the Father, and of the Son, and of the Holy Ghost.

Teaching them to observe all things whatsoever I have commanded you: and lo, I am with you alway, even unto the end of the world. (Matthew 28:19-20.)

Nearly every member of the Church understands that there are two great ecclesiastical divisions in the Church of Jesus Christ: one made up of the organized stakes and wards; the other, of the missionary work.

It is of this second division I wish to speak this morning.

I think many of us fail to realize the value and potent possibilities of this great branch of Church activity.

1. As an example of voluntary service in the cause of the Master, it is unexcelled.

2. As an incentive to clean living among youth, as a contributing factor to character building, its influence is immeasurable.

3. Its educative force and uplifting influence upon our communities is clearly manifest.

4. In contributing to the better understanding among nations, and to the establishing of international friendship, it is no insignificant factor.

5. It is the purpose of the Almighty to save the individual, not to make him a mere cog in the machinery of the state. Said he,

> Remember the worth of souls is great in the sight of God;
> And if it so be that you should labor all your days in crying repentance unto this people, and bring, save it be one soul unto me, how great shall be your joy with him in the kingdom of my Father!
> And now, if your joy will be great with one soul that you have brought unto me into the kingdom of my Father, how great will be your joy if you should bring many souls unto me! (D & C 18:10, 15-16.)

The text I have just quoted, "go ye unto all the world" is really the missionary injunction given by the risen Christ to his apostles. In effect he says:

Consider this work unfinished until all nations shall have accepted the gospel and shall have enlisted themselves as my disciples.

Now, that command was not given to men indiscriminately; for even to the Twelve to whom he addressed that commission he gave later a formal assignment and blessing saying:

> . . . as my Father hath sent me, even so send I you.
> And when he had said this, he breathed on them, and saith unto them, Receive ye the Holy Ghost. (John 20:21, 22.)

With the same direct commission from the risen Lord who with the Father appeared in person in the beginning of the nineteenth century, the proclamation of the gospel is being made by The Church of Jesus Christ of Latter-day Saints, to "every nation, kindred, tongue and people" as fast as means and personnel can carry it forward.

The missionaries, generally, are young men and women, ranging in age from twenty to thirty years, with a sprinkling among them of more experienced men and women.

It is well to say here that the direct responsibility of preaching the gospel rests upon the priesthood of the Church—not upon the women, though the efficiency of the latter in cottage meetings, in Primaries, and Sunday Schools, and in other phases of missionary work is of the highest order, and their willingness, even eagerness, to labor is not excelled by that of the young men.

Who are these youths chosen to represent the Church? They, too, as their mission presidents, come from the rank and file. They are farmers, artisans, factory workers, bank clerks, secretaries in business firms, and other vocations. Some who are married leave their wives and their children who help to support them in their work. All of them look forward to the time after their return when they, with congenial loving companions, may build happy homes.

As already stated, each pays his or her own expenses, in most cases, of course, with the assistance of parents. True Christianity is love in action. There is no better way to manifest love for God than to show an unselfish love for your fellow men. This is the spirit of missionary work. Our hearts respond to the cry of the poet:

> O brother man! fold to thy heart thy brother.
> Where pity dwells, the peace of God is there;
> To worship rightly is to love each other,
> Each smile a hymn, each kindly deed a prayer.
> ("Worship"—John Greenleaf Whittier)

These men go out in the spirit of love, seeking nothing from any nation to which they are sent: no personal acclaim, no monetary acquisition. Two or three years ago, many of these missionaries were just out of the army. Not a few had saved their government allowance to pay their expenses in the mission field if and when they should be called.

In this fact we get a glimpse of the helpful influence of the missionary system upon the youth. Every deacon, teacher, and priest, every elder in the Church understands that to be worthy to be a representative of the Church of Christ, he must be temperate in his habits and morally clean. He is taught that there is no double standard of chastity, that every young man, as well as every young woman, is to keep himself free from sexual impurity.

I once read one of the most impressive letters of a mother to a son that I think has ever been written. It contained only three words, except the signature. Those words were: "Quinn, keep clean," and was signed, "Lovingly, Mother."

These young men are instructed that they go out as representatives of the Church, and that a representative of any organization—economic or religious—must possess at least one outstanding quality, and that is: trustworthiness. He was right who said, "To be trusted is a greater compliment than to be loved." And whom do these missionaries represent? First, they represent their parents, carrying out the responsibility of keeping their good name unsullied. Second, they represent the Church, specifically the ward in which they live. And third, they represent the Lord Jesus Christ, whose servants they are.

These ambassadors, for such they are, represent these three groups and carry in that representation one of the greatest responsibilities of their lives.

Now, what is the outstanding message that they have to give to Christian, as well as un-Christian countries? There must surely be something distinctive to justify their presence in all parts of the world.

First, their message is that Jesus Christ is the Son of God, the redeemer and Savior of mankind. To these missionaries—"Jesus is not a legendary figure in history," to paraphrase a question asked by Hall Caine to the Christian world,

. . . he is not merely a saint to be painted in the stained glass of church windows, a sort of sacred fairy not to be approached and hardly to be mentioned by name. But he is still what he was in the flesh, a reality, a man of like passions with ourselves, a guide, a counselor, a comforter, a great voice calling to us to live nobly, to die bravely, and to keep up our courage to the last.

These missionaries declare with Peter of old:

. . . there is none other name under heaven given among men, whereby we must be saved. (Acts 4:12.)

The second distinctive message is this: Every missionary should clearly understand, and so declare in unmistakable words, the relation of this Church to other Christian organizations—that it is neither an outgrowth nor a division of any of them. True, the Church is generally classed with the Protestants; but Protestantism began with the great dissenters—Martin Luther, Philip Melanchthon, Ulrich Zwingli, John Knox, and others. These great reformers denounced corrupt practices in the Roman Church, particularly the selling of indulgences wherein delinquents could make satisfaction by money contributions, a practice carried on under one pretext and another until it became a regular financial expedient for increasing papal revenue.

It was extended even to souls in purgatory.

The great men whom I have named rebelled against this evil and others, and organized churches in protest.

Accordingly, when the second Diet of Spires in 1529 passed a resolution

. . . disallowing further religious innovations in the Lutheran states, whilst prohibiting the profession of the Zwinglian and Anabaptist forms of the reformed faith, the Lutheran minoriy protested, and this protestation was signed by fourteen cities as well as by the elector of Saxony, the landgrave of Hesse and four other provinces. Hence the name Protestant as a designation of the evangelical party.

Protestantism, under many different names, spread over Europe and later among the American colonies, and freedom to worship as one sincerely wished became more and more the proscribed right of the individual, but in the hearts of many a true believer in Jesus of Nazareth, there remained an abiding belief, a feeling that the authority to represent him had been taken from the earth, and that there

. . . can be no recovery out of that apostacy till Christ shall send forth new apostles to plant churches anew.

This in effect is what the Lord told Joseph Smith when as a fourteen year-old lad he inquired which of all sects was right and which should he join. Joseph was told to join none of them for, as has been heretofore quoted,

"they draw near to me with their lips, but their hearts are far from me; they teach for doctrine the commandments of men, having a form of godliness, but they deny the power thereof." (Pearl of Great Price, Joseph Smith, 2:19.)

A few years later, specifically, April 6, 1830, Joseph Smith received by the spirit of prophecy and revelation instructions from the Savior "to organize his Church once more here upon the earth."

Thus was established by direct revelation and divine authority from the Eternal Father and Jesus Christ who founded the Church of the Meridian of Times, the Church of Latter-days, which is set up as a fore-runner, if you please, to the establishing of the kingdom of God upon the earth. And in the words of President John Taylor:

Unless the Father had a Church and a people who had submitted to his law and were willing to submit to it with an organization of such a people gathered from among the nations of the earth under the direction of a man inspired of God, the mouthpiece of Jehovah to his people, I say that with such an organization there is a chance for the Lord, God to be revealed. There is an opportunity for the law of life to be made manifest, a chance for God to introduce the principles of heaven upon the earth and for the will of God to be done upon earth as it is done in heaven. (J.D. 18:140, Oct. 10, 1875.)

With these two great fundamental truths as the heart of their message, namely, (1) the divinity of the mission of the Lord Jesus Christ, the Savior of the world, and (2) the restoration of his gospel in this age, the missionaries are to the best of their ability, fulfilling the injunction to preach the gospel to every creature, baptizing them in the name of the Father and of the Son and of the Holy Ghost, teaching them to observe all things whatsoever the Lord has commanded.

This, then, brethren, is a world-wide Church organized preparatory to the establishing of the kingdom of God on earth by means of which

. . . the Lord God may be revealed, and an opportunity for the laws of life to be made manifest.

These thousands of missionaries and men who hold the priesthood everywhere are ambassadors of good will, the ultimate purpose of whose service is to change the hearts of men everywhere from selfishness and greed to tolerance, compassion, and brotherhood. And, so, with all our hearts we can sing:

> Go, ye messengers of glory;
> Run, ye legates of the skies;
> Go and tell the pleasing story
> That a glorious angel flies,
> Great and mighty,
> With a message from the skies.
>
> Go to ev'ry tribe and nation;
> Visit ev'ry land and clime;
> Sound to all the proclamation.
> Tell to all the truth sublime:
> That the gospel
> Does in ancient glory shine.
>
> Go to all the gospel carry.
> Let the joyful news abound;
> Go til ev'ry nation hear you,

Jew and Gentile greet the sound.
Let the gospel,
Echo all the earth around.

Bearing seed of heav'nly virtue,
Scatter it o'er all the earth;
Go! Jehovah will support you;
Gather all the sheaves of worth;
Then, with Jesus,
Reign in glory on the earth.
—John Taylor

Marriage and Divorce

And the Pharisees came to him, and asked him, Is it lawful for a man to put away his wife? tempting him.

And he answered and said unto them, What did Moses command you?

And they said, Moses suffered to write a bill of divorcement, and to put her away.

And Jesus answered and said unto them, For the hardness of your heart he wrote you this precept. (Mark 10:2-5.)

In all the problems and perplexities of human existence, Jesus Christ is the one safe guide to whom we can go for guidance and comfort. Mark's account of Jesus' answer to the Pharisees on divorce sets forth the Savior's attitude toward this vital question.

A careful study of this text, and other references that he made to marriage and divorce, leave little doubt that Jesus set forth the lofty ideal that marriage is of divine origin and that the marriage bond should be held sacred.

This lofty ideal of marriage is confirmed by modern revelation, and is recorded in the Doctrine and Covenants as follows:

And again, verily I say unto you, that whoso forbiddeth to marry is not ordained of God, for marriage is ordained of God unto man.

Wherefore, it is lawful that he should have one wife, and

they twain shall be one flesh, and all this that the earth might
answer the end of its creation;
   And that it might be filled with the measure of man, according to his creation before the world was made. (D & C 49:15-17)

When the Pharisees, seeking to justify the granting of
divorce, cited the fact that "Moses suffered to write a bill
of divorcement and to put a wife away" on the ground of
"some uncleanness," Jesus answered:

   . . . For the hardness of your heart he wrote you this precept.
But from the beginning of the creation God made them male and
female. For this cause shall a man leave his father and mother, and
cleave to his wife; And they twain shall be one flesh. What therefore God hath joined together, let not man put asunder. (Mark
10:5-9.)

In the light of scripture, ancient and modern, we are
justified in concluding that Christ's ideal pertaining to
marriage is the unbroken home, and conditions that cause
divorce are violations of his divine teachings. Some of
these are:
   Unfaithfulness on the part of either or both, habitual
drunkenness, physical violence, long imprisonment that dis-
graces the wife and family, the union of an innocent girl to
a reprobate—in these and perhaps other cases there may be
circumstances which make the continuance of the marriage
state a greater evil than divorce. But these are extreme
cases—they are the mistakes, the calamities in the realm
of marriage.
   On the other hand, to look upon marriage as a mere
contract that may be entered into at pleasure in response
to a romantic whim, or for selfish purposes, and severed at
the first difficulty or misunderstanding that may arise, is
an evil meriting severe condemnation, especially in cases
wherein children are made to suffer because of such separation.
   Modern living conditions contribute to these frustrations. Formerly a married woman had a home to care for,

often several children. Today, in many parts of our country, a married woman continues either to follow her vocation or to spend her time seeking new stimulations—no children to care for—no house to clean—no meals to cook. Under such a condition her leisure time activities become her all-absorbing interests—interests which often lead her away from her husband rather than to him.

When the steamship Marama dropped anchor outside the coral reef that surrounds the island Rarotonga, a passenger desiring to go ashore asked the captain why he did not sail nearer to the wharf. In answer the experienced seaman mentioned treacherous waters and pointed to an engine of one ship, the Maitai, and to the bow of another, still protruding out of the water—both carrying mute evidence of the danger of anchoring too close to the shore of this coral-bound island. "We anchor here," said the captain, "because it is safer to avoid being dashed to pieces, as those two vessels, on those dangerous reefs."

A flippant attitude toward marriage, the ill-advised suggestion of "companionate marriage," the base, diabolical theory of "free sex experiment," and the ready-made divorce courts are dangerous reefs upon which many a family bark is wrecked.

An ever-decreasing birth rate and an increasing divorce rate are ominous signs threatening the stability of the American home, and the perpetuity of our present form of constitutional government.

In some states of the union, it is almost as easy to get a divorce as it is to get married. As a result of this laxity, one out of every five marriages ends either in divorce or annulment.

The real source of security of our nation rests in the well ordered, properly conducted homes. The character of a child is formed largely during the first twelve years of his life. It is estimated that in that period the child spends approximately 3,240 hours in school, 416 hours in Sunday School and church, but 52,560 hours in the home, not counting twelve hours a day for sleep. In other words, he spends sixteen times as many waking hours in the home as in school, and one hundred twenty-six times as many hours in the home as in the Church.

In the homes of America are born the children of America, and from them go out into American life American men and women. They go out with the stamp of these homes upon them, and only as these homes are what they should be, will children be what they should be.

Luther Burbank, the great plant wizard, most impressively emphasizes the need for constant attention in the training of a child. He says:

Teach the child self-respect. Train it in self-respect just as you train a plant in better ways. No self-respecting man was ever a grafter. Above all, bear in mind repetition—the use of an influence over and over again, keeping everlastingly at it. This is what fixes traits in plants, the constant repetition of an influence until at last it is irrevocably fixed and will not change. You cannot afford to get discouraged. You are dealing with something far more precious than any plant—the precious soul of a child!

There are three fundamental things to which every child is entitled: (1) a respected name, (2) a sense of security, (3) opportunities for development.

The family gives the child his name and standing in the community. A child wants his family to be as good as those of his friends. He wants to be able to point with pride to his father, and to feel an inspiration always as he thinks of his mother. It is a mother's duty so to live that her children will associate with her everything that is beautiful, sweet, and pure. And the father should so live that the child, emulating his example, will be a good citizen, and, in the Church, a true Latter-day Saint.

Security

A child has the right to feel that in his home he has a place of refuge, a place of protection from the dangers and evils of the outside world. Family unity and integrity are necessary to supply this need.

"He needs parents who are happy in their adjustment to each other, who are working hopefully toward the fulfillment of an ideal of living, who love their children with a sincere and unselfish love; in short, who are well-balanced individuals, gifted with a certain amount of insight, who are able to provide the child with a wholesome emotional background which will contribute more to his development than material advantages."

Divorce almost invariably deprives children of these advantages.

How to Lessen the Breaking Up of Homes

1. Substitute the present tendency toward a low view of marriage by the lofty view which Jesus the Christ gives it. Let us look upon marriage as a sacred obligation and a covenant that is eternal or that may be made eternal.

2. Teach the young, both sexes, in the responsibilities and ideals of marriage so that they may realize that marriage involves obligation, and is not an arrangement to be terminated at pleasure. Teach them that pure love between the sexes is one of the noblest things on earth, and the bearing and rearing of children the highest of all human duties. In this regard it is the duty of parents to set an example in the home that children may see and absorb, as it were, the sacredness of family life and the responsibility associated therewith.

3. The number of broken marriages can be reduced if couples realize even before they approach the altar that marriage is a state of mutual service, a state of giving as well as of receiving, and that each must give of himself or herself to the utmost. Harriet Beecher Stowe wisely writes:

No man or woman can create a true home who is not willing in the outset to embrace life heroically, to encounter labor and sacrifice. Only to such can this divinest power be given to create on earth that which is the nearest image of heaven.

4. Another condition that contributes to the permanence of the marriage covenant is marriage in the temple. Before such a marriage is consummated, it is necessary for the young man and young woman first to obtain a recommend from the bishop. They should go to him in person, and the bishop who does his duty will instruct the couple regarding the sacredness of the obligation that they are as young people going to assume, emphasizing all the safeguards that have been named before. There in the presence of the priesthood the young people receive, before they take upon themselves the obligation, instruction upon the sacredness of the duty which is before them; and, furthermore, whether or not they are prepared to go in holiness and purity to the altar of God and there seal their vows and love.

5. Finally, there is one principle which seems to me to strike right at the base of the happiness of the marriage relation, and that is the standard of purity taught and practiced among the Latter-day Saints. It is a common saying throughout the world that young men may sow their wild oats, but that young women should be chaperoned and guarded. In the Church of Christ there is but one standard of morality. No young man has any more right to sow his wild oats than has a young girl. She is taught that second only to the crime of taking human life is that of losing her virtue. And that is the ideal among young men. That young man who comes to the bishop and asks for a recommend to take a pure girl to the altar is expected to give just the same purity that he expects to receive.

Conclusion

For the proper solution of this great problem we may turn with safety to Jesus as our guide. He declared that the marriage relation is of divine origin, that "marriage is ordained of God," that only under the most exceptional conditions should it be set aside. In the teaching of the Church of Christ, the family assumes supreme importance in the development of the individual and of society. "Happy and thrice happy are they who enjoy an uninterrupted union, and whose love, unbroken by any complaint, shall not dissolve until the last day."

The marriage ceremony when sealed by the authority of the holy priesthood endures, as do family relationships, throughout time and all eternity.

"What therefore God hath joined together, let not man put asunder."

God bless us all to look more earnestly and prayerfully and sincerely upon the sacredness of home and the marriage covenant.

Old Battles Yet to Be Fought— New Victories to Win

And they shall beat their swords into plowshares, and their spears into pruning hooks; nation shall not lift up a sword against nation, neither shall they learn war any more.

But they shall sit every man under his vine and under his fig tree; and none shall make them afraid; for the mouth of the Lord of hosts hath spoken it.

For all people will walk every one in the name of his god, and we will walk in the name of the Lord our God for ever and ever. (Micah 4:3-5)

So wrote the Prophet Micah, probably quoting Isaiah, 750 years before Christ. Over 2600 years ago, the eye of prophecy saw a time when "nation shall not lift up a sword against nation, neither shall they learn war any more." During the intervening centuries since that prophecy was uttered, many nations have lifted up sword against nations; in fact, war has been one of mankind's greatest evils.

Well may we wonder how many more years will pass before "they shall sit every man under his vine and under his fig tree; and none shall make them afraid"; when, in Lord Tennyson's words:

The war-drums throb no longer, and the battle-flags be furled,
In the parliament of man, the Federation of the world.

Restrictions incident to the great conflict have largely been abrogated; and once again we meet in a general Conference of the Church without fear of molestation from a murderous enemy. We join the Allied Nations in giving thanks that gangsters who, through evil manipulations and clever strategies seized control of Nations, have been defeated; that their attempt to set up dictatorial government has been frustrated; that freedom has been preserved, and liberty kept within the grasp of those who cherish the right of self-government.

In this great conflict God's overruling power has been manifest. Let the nations not forget him in the hour of victory.

Out of the war has come the harnessing of atomic energy. In discussing this new and terrible force, scientists and military experts are now writing articles saying that all present means of defense are inadequate, already antiquated, and must be changed if the world is to be protected from future devastation.

I would that these men of reputed wisdom and foresight would lay equal emphasis on the fact that *the future safety of the world depends not so much upon the changing of defense as upon the changing of men's way of thinking, and acting*. Men and nations must have a change of heart. Hate and envy, suspicion and greed must be supplanted by sympathy, forbearance, tolerance and justice before the hoped-for time comes that "nation shall not lift up sword against nation, neither shall they learn war any more."

Now that another terrible war is ended, the great question is—Are human minds equal to the problems that are theirs; are human hearts sufficiently filled with virtues needed in the present crisis? With this thought in mind, I echo the cry of one who pleads—

"O human hearts, beating through fear, through jealousy, through pride, through avarice, through bitterness, through agony, through death; beating shame and forgiveness, bewilderment and love.

"O my own country, my new world, prepare, prepare—not to avenge wrong, but to exalt right. Not to display honor, but to prove humility. Not to bring wrath, but vision; not to win war, but a people. And not people only, but all peoples. Not to exact justice from your enemies only, and not from your friends only, but from yourselves!"
Truly,

> The world is in the valley of Decision,
>   And out of it there is but one sure road;
> Eyes unsealed can still foresee the mighty vision
>   Of a world in travail turning unto God.

Yes, World War II is ended, but old battles are yet to be fought; new victories yet to be won before the peace for which we pray can be realized.

1. Man's Suspicion and Lack of Trust

Man's suspicion and lack of trust is one of the greatest enemies of peace. Nations are distrustful of one another. Thus, the seeds of envy and enmity are sown.

This lack of confidence in one's fellowman is even more of an individual than a national vice. We are prone to magnify weaknesses and to imagine vices in others that do not exist. We chew the cud of slander with satisfaction. Slander, "whose whisper over the world's diameter, as level as the cannon to its blank, transports his poisoned shot." Talk about battles yet to be fought! Back-biting and evil speaking head the list!

"If any man among you thinketh himself to be religious, and bridleth not his tongue, this man's religion is vain."

2. Battle Against Godlessness

The battle against godlessness must still be fought. Nietzche even before the first World War denounced Christianity as a cunningly devised system that has "debauched and undermined and sapped the vigor of the modern European world, and is the most powerful instrument of racial degeneration ever devised by common herd."

Nietzche is dead, but the poisonous seeds he sowed in his blindness and bitterness still produce fruit of skepticism and unbelief. In charity we can say that the Christianity he condemns is not the Gospel of Jesus Christ as taught by the Redeemer of Man. But egotists and misled people who cannot discriminate between truth and error still find themselves wavering with respect to the divine mission of Jesus Christ. Every true Christian, and especially every faithful member of the Church of Christ should be militant in defending the principles of the Gospel as given by our Lord and Savior, for, in the words of Mark Hopkins, "true Christianity promotes industry, honesty, truth, purity, kindness. It humbles the proud, exalts the lowly, upholds law, favors liberty, is essential to it, and would unite men in one great brotherhood. It is the breath of life to social and civil well-being here, and spreads the azure of that heaven into whose unfathomed depth the eye of faith loves to look."

There has been but one perfect character in this world —the peerless personality of Jesus of Nazareth, the Son of God, the Redeemer of the world. No man can do better than to accept Christ as the great exemplar and the safest guide.

It is not an easy thing in this old world to make God the center of our being. To do so we must determine to keep his commandments. Spiritual attainment, not physical possessions, not the indulgence and the gratification of the body, must become the chief goal. God should not be viewed from the standpoint of what we may *get* from him, but from what we may *give* to him. Only in the complete surrender of our inner life may we rise above the selfish, sordid pull of nature. We should seek first the kingdom of God and his righteousness. What the spirit is to the body, God is to the spirit. As the body dies when the spirit leaves it, so the spirit dies when we exclude God from it. I cannot imagine peace in a world from which God and religion are banished.

3. Selfishness

Another old battle still raging, and one we must win before permanent peace is established on earth is the battle against selfishness.

Selfishness is the root from which spring most human ills and suffering. It promises satisfaction, but its fruit is disappointing, and produces only ill-will and unhappiness. Selfishness and enmity caused the first recorded murder, and the first implied rejection of the great truth that man is his brother's keeper.

It was selfishness that caused the violation of the Munich Pact that led in, September 1939, to the murderous invasion of Poland, and the subsequent destruction of European nations with all its attendant horrors and human suffering. It was selfishness and inordinate ambition that caused the destruction of Pearl Harbor.

Unless the battle against selfishness is won at the peace table, our hopes for permanent peace may be shattered, and the world again stricken in warfare.

Nature's law demands us to do everything with self in view. Self-preservation is the first law of mortal life. But Jesus says: "He that findeth his life shall lose it: and he that loseth his life for my sake shall find it." Jesus on the Mount of Temptation triumphed over all appeals to selfishness, and thereby set an example to all men who would strive for spiritual attainment. There is no development of character without resistance; there is no growth of spirituality without overcoming. "He that overcometh and keepeth my works unto the end, to him will I give power over the nations."

4. Intemperance

A fourth old battle that is still raging, and in which the opposition seems to be gaining ground, is the battle against intemperance. The attitude of the Church of Jesus Christ towards temperance is unmistakable. February 27, 1833, the Prophet Joseph Smith received what is known as the Word of Wisdom for the benefit of the Council of the High Priests assembled in Kirkland, and the Church, and also the saints in Zion, given by revelation which sets forth the order and will of God in the temporal salvation of all saints in the last days. Wine and "strong drinks" are condemned as beverages, and the use of them condemned in all cases except in the use of wine for sacramental purposes, and even this should be "pure wine of the grape of the vine of your own make."

Tobacco is condemned also as being "not good for man."

At the time the Church took this decided stand against whiskey and tobacco, no state in the Union had passed any law against the liquor traffic. It is true that many temperance societies had been organized, and the cause of temperance was gaining impetus, but it was not until 1851—18 years after the revelation on the Word of Wisdom—that the first permanent prohibition law was passed in Maine. Later, religious denominations began to organize temperance societies. It appears, therefore, that the "Mormon" Church was among the very first organizations, if not the first organization or Church in the United States to legislate as an organized body against the use of alcoholic drinks and tobacco.

In 1912 President Joseph F. Smith in his opening address at the 78th Annual Conference said: "There is a general movement throughout the land looking toward local option of temperance among the people of our state and adjoining states. I sincerely hope that every Latter-day Saint will cooperate with this movement in order that we may curtail the monstrous evils that exist especially in our cities. I wish to say that I am in sympathy with this movement, and I know my brethren are united with me, and in harmony with the efforts that are being made to establish temperance throughout the land."

Many of you will remember how President Grant pleaded with the people in Utah to retain the 18th Amendment. To the day of his death he regretted that Utah was in the column of states that repealed the prohibition law.

Conclusion

I know of no force so potent in eradicating these enemies of peace from the human heart as the Gospel of Jesus Christ. True religion is today the world's greatest need—a sense by the individual of a relationship with God— that indefinable something which enters into the soul of man and which unites him with his Creator. "The wind bloweth where it listeth, and thou hearest the sound thereof, but canst not tell whence it cometh, and whither it goeth; so is every one that is born of the Spirit."

A celebrated British statesman, Edmund Burke, in the latter half of the century wrote: "True religion is the foundation of society. When that is once shaken by contempt the whole fabric cannot be stable nor lasting."

"I have now disposed of all my property to my children," said Patrick Henry; "there is one thing more I wish I could give them and that is the Christian religion. If they had that and I had not given them one cent, they would be rich. If they have not that, and I had given them all the world, they would be poor."

Only through the application of righteous principles by individuals and nations can a permanent peace be established, and nations learn war no more.

> O Brother Man! fold to thy heart thy brother;
>   Where pity dwells, the peace of God is there;
> To worship rightly is to love each other,
>   Each smile a hymn, each kindly deed a prayer.
> Follow with reverent steps the great example
>   Of Him whose holy work was 'doing good;'

So shall the wide earth seem our Father's temple,
Each loving life a psalm of gratitude.
Then shall all shackles fall; the stormy clangor
Of wild war music o'er the earth shall cease;
Love shall tread out the baleful fire of anger,
And in its ashes plant the tree of peace!
(John Greenleaf Whittier)

Our Individual Responsibility

It is important that we all be impressed with our individual responsibility and that we appreciate that this Church depends upon all the people, not upon just a few, and that those who fail to carry their share of responsibility are not wholly true to their trust.

Fortunately, there are many members and officers in the Church who are determined to carry out their individual responsibility—not because it has been urged upon them by someone else but because they know that it is their individual responsibility.

I believe we should be influenced in this as, reputedly, a group of sailors were many decades ago. It was during the anti-slavery agitation, that a meeting was called in Fanueil Hall, Boston. It seems that these sailors had been hired to break up the meeting. They went there in a body, danced around on the floor, sang, shouted, and in every way possible tried to prevent the speakers from addressing the meeting. In vain were they appealed to: Their love of liberty, the memory of their old home, the honor of Massachusetts were all invoked; but still they continued their disturbance and refused to be quiet.

Suddenly a man, evidently one of their own number, arose. Quieted for a moment by his appearance, and thinking they had found a champion, the mob ceased its noise.

The man said, "Boys, I would not be quiet unless I had a mind to." Encouraged by this remark, the mob burst into loud applause, which lasted some minutes. When it ceased because of the men's desire to hear more, the man continued: "No, I would not be quiet if I didn't have a mind to, but if I were you, I would have a mind to, not because of the memory of this hall, not for the honor of Massachusetts, not for loyalty to her government only, but because you are men; and honorable men always stand up for the liberty of right, justice, and free speech." They were quieted; their manhood had been touched.

I believe that we all should carry out the responsibility that is upon us, not merely because others have urged us to do so, but because we have it in our souls to do it.

And what is this responsibility that rests upon every member of the Church? In the 107th section of the Doctrine and Covenants we find the following in the 99th verse:

"Wherefore, now let every man learn his duty, and to act in the office in which he is appointed, in all diligence."

Two principles in that admonition stand out: first, the learning, the knowing what one's duty is; second, to act in all diligence in the performance of that duty.

To know one's duty, to learn the truth, is the duty of every Latter-day Saint, of every man and woman in the world, including those outside of this Church. There is a natural feeling which urges men and women towards truth; it is a responsibility placed upon mankind. But that responsibility rests upon the Latter-day Saints in greater degree than upon their fellowmen—because the Latter-day Saints have learned the truth that the everlasting gospel has been restored.

But knowing a thing, or merely feeling an assurance of the truth, is not sufficient. "To him that knoweth to do good, and doeth it not, to him it is sin." (James 4:17)

This thought brings us to consider the second duty mentioned in this revelation by the Prophet Joseph Smith. "Wherefore, now let every man learn his duty and to act in the office in which he is appointed, in all diligence." The man who knows what his duty is and fails to perform it is not true to himself; he is not true to his brethren; he is not living in the light which God and conscience provide. This comes right home to you and to me. When conscience tells me that it is right to go along in a specified line, I am not true to myself if I do not follow that. Oh, I know we are swayed by our weaknesses and by influences from without; but it is our duty to walk in the straight and narrow path in the performance of every duty!

And mark this: Every time we have opportunity and fail to live up to that truth which is within us, every time we fail to express a good thought, every time we fail to perform a good act, we weaken ourselves and make it more difficult to express that thought or perform that act in the future. Every time we perform a good act, every time we express a noble feeling, we make it easier to perform that act or express that feeling another time.

I am reminded of the story of the woman who "felt" sympathy; she knew how to sympathize with the poor heroine on the stage. This lady sat in her box, comfortable in her furs and fine silks, and as she looked at the performance, she wept in sympathy with the heroine who was suffering imaginary torments; and while that woman was sympathizing with the stage heroine, her own coachman froze to death on the carriage seat outside because of insufficient clothing.

It is not enough to "feel;" we must act so that it will benefit somebody.

Let us look around in our own ward next Sunday and try to estimate how many of the Latter-day Saints are absent from the sacrament meeting. It may be that a majority are absent. And those who are absent without a real excuse are neglecting one of the duties of a Latter-day Saint. Upon whom does the responsibility of bringing in these brethren and sisters rest? First, perhaps, upon the bishopric. As the bishop sits there, let him look around and notice if all the presidents of the various organizations in the ward are present. Let him note if the presidents of the priesthood quorums are absent.

But it is not the bishop's sole responsibility; this Church rests upon all and not upon a few. If one of the presidents of seventy's quorum in that ward is present, and he finds that some of the seventies are absent, the responsibility of bringing them to meeting rests upon him. If presidents of the various quorums of deacons are present, they should note what quorum members have absented themselves from that meeting and let them assume the responsibility of visiting those members. And so throughout the various organizations in that ward.

Where is the responsibility, then? It is divided as it should be, as God intends it to be, among the people composing The Church of Jesus Christ of Latter-day Saints; the responsibility does not rest upon the officers alone; it rests upon the members also. God has blessed us with a knowledge of the truth; and the knowledge of the truth is not enough unless it is expressed, unless it is bringing others to that knowledge. That is the spirit and responsibility of the Latter-day Saint, and it rests upon us all.

Every man, every woman, every boy and girl must bear a part of the responsibility of this Church.

"Wherefore, now let every man learn his duty," and act in all diligence in the performance of it.

"He that is slothful shall not be counted worthy to stand, and he that learns not his duty and shows himself not approved shall not be counted worthy to stand." (See D & C 107:99-100)

Reverence and Order in Conducting Worshipping Assemblies

You brethren have all heard about the value of the "Three R's" in education—"Readin' - 'Ritin' - and 'Rithmetic." I should like to speak about the "Three R's" in presiding and conducting our services. They are: *Reverence, Readiness, Respect.*

Carlisle says: "Reverence is the highest of human feelings." We need more reverence in our house of worship. In this regard, we have made much improvement in that last twenty years, I think. I have visited a number of the wards here in the city, and in other parts of the Church, and have felt the presence of the Lord in rich abundance, especially during the administration of the sacrament. There is a feeling of communion with the spirit. That is as it should be, not only during the administration of the sacrament but throughout the entire service. There should be a feeling of reverence as soon as we enter a house of worship. A bishop in this city said to me one day, after his chapel had been dedicated, that a workman went there following the dedication, and, as he came to the door, he hesitated about entering. He said, "I hesitate about going in. There is something here I haven't before felt." I don't know whether it was just imagination on the part of that workman, but I do know that that is how every man should feel who enters a chapel that has been dedicated as a place of worship.

"Reverence is the highest virtue," says Carlisle. I think love is the highest, but reverence includes love. Reverence is profound respect mingled with love. It is a complex emotion made up of mingled feelings of the soul. Reverence embraces regard, deference, honor and esteem. Without some degree of it, therefore, there would be no courtesy, no gentility, no consideration of others' feelings or of others' rights. On this subject, one writer says: "One finds lack of reverence even in the church. In every community there are those who treat the house of God as they treat a street-car, entering it and leaving it when they please. Even habitual church attendants often surprise and shock one by their irreverent behavior in the house of prayer. Those persons are not ignoramuses or barbarians; they are simply undeveloped in the virtue of reverence."

If there were more reverence in human hearts, there would be less room for sin and sorrow, and increased capacity for joy and gladness. To make more cherished, more adaptable, more attractive, this gem among brilliant virtues is a project worthy of the most united and prayerful efforts of every officer, every parent, and every member of the Church.

In no Latter-day Saint home should the name of God be taken in vain. That is where we should begin to teach reverence.

But I am particularly interested tonight in reverence in the House of God. One contributing factor to such reverence is adherence to the second "R"—Readiness. Preparation for Sunday services should begin in the bishop's council meeting held some day during the week. You bishops direct the most important meeting in this Church. It isn't the Sunday School, great as it is, and I am a lover of the Sunday School. It isn't the Mutual Improvement Association. Most important of all is the sacrament meeting. I know that Sunday School superintendents meet and prepare for Sunday School session in the morning, and as a result everything moves as clockwork. The presiding officer need not say a word. I have seen a Sunday School of five hundred persons conducted without the presiding officer moving from his seat, or even making an announcement.

Bishops, if you prepare for the sacrament meeting in your council meeting, you will have in hand all details before the service begins. Know who is going to pray, who is going to sing, and whether the singers are going to remain throughout the service. I may be too sensitive on this point, but it creates a discord in the harmony of the service when I see musicians invited (probably a double quartette) to sing one number, and then to have the bishop arise and say, "We shall have to excuse them from the meeting because they have another appointment." I should rather they would not come. We have met to worship. Let us have somebody come who will remain. I congratulate you boys tonight. (Referring to the boys' chorus.) This has not been your meeting. You have had to listen to matters that pertain to men, but you have remained throughout the entire service, and you have contributed to the reverence and to the impressiveness of this meeting.

By previous preparation, the bishopric know what boys are going to pass the sacrament. The deacons are going to be in their seats, and they realize that they are going to remain there during the meeting. Years ago it was not unusual to see the boys get up and some of them actually go out of the service. Another discord in reverence. If you have arranged and instructed these boys they will know that they are to retain their seats and assist in keeping order. You know who will speak and give a message appropriate to the occasion. It might be Christmas; Joseph Smith's birthday; perhaps the anniversary of the restoration of the Aaronic Priesthood. If you are prepared to give the people something worthwhile, a message instructive and inspiring, they will be pleased to attend meetings. "*Readiness,*" said an old philosopher, "is everything!"

And that brings us to the third "R"—*Respect.*

In presiding in our meetings there are two elements to keep in mind—conducting the exercise, and the presiding authority. The bishop is the presiding officer in the ward. Not infrequently, however, the stake president, for example, is in attendance, and when he is, proper respect should be shown him as a superior officer. The bishop has the right, of course, to go on and carry out his program, but respect would suggest that he say to the president of the stake, "What is your pleasure?" It may be that he has a special message. If not, he will answer, "Go on with your usual exercises or with the program that you have." It may be that one of the Twelve will be present. He then is recognized by the bishop and the stake president as a superior officer in the Church and shown respect accordingly.

In fast meeting, after your testimonies are given, proper respect would suggest that you say to the president of the stake, before the close of that fast meeting, "What is your pleasure?" The organization of the Church is so complete that there is never a question as to who presides.

These are the "Three R's"—*Reverence, Readiness, Respect.* God help us to use them for the increase of spirituality, for the salvation of the souls of the youth.

Counteracting Pernicious Ideas
and Subversive Teachings

Religious leaders, civic officers, and all lovers of law and order are today deeply concerned, and not without justification, about the recklessness and lawlessness of youth. Even young folks, themselves, are deprecating the disobedience of parental authority, manifested by some of their companions. It is a dangerous sign when home discipline breaks down, and the loving advice of a wise father and a loving mother is defied. We are told by an early American explorer that among the Iroquois Indians, "The crime which is regarded as most horrible, and which is without example, is that a son should be rebellious towards his mother"—an ideal that might well be cherished today among men who esteem themselves high in the scale of civilization.

Our Country's Most Precious Possession

Our country's most precious possession is not our vast acres of range land, supporting flocks and herds; not productive farms; not our forests, not our mines, nor oil wells producing fabulous wealth—our country's greatest resource is our children, our young men and women, whose characters will largely determine our nation's future.

If it were possible for me to speak directly to the young men and women of the Church, I would say that true joy of life is found not in physical indulgences and excesses, but in clean living and high thinking, in rendering to others not inconvenience, injury or pain, but encouragement, cheer, and helpfulness. This is simply saying to them that satisfaction in daily life is found in trying to keep the simple law —"Do unto others as you would have others do unto you." Right actions toward others bring joy; wrongful deeds result in pain and not infrequently remorse.

Conformity to the Lord's word or law will invariably contribute to man's happiness and salvation. Those who do not what the Lord commands will be subjected to justice and judgment. In other words, there is eternally operative in the moral world a law of compensation and retribution— compensation commensurate with conformity to law; *retribution* in actual degree to the extent of disobedience.

In this sense, the word "law" has a deeper significance than a rule or dictum prescribed by authority for human action. It means rather "a uniform order of sequence" as operative and unvarying as the law of the inclined plane, or of the law of falling bodies.

Confirmation of this may be found in the Lord's statement to Cain, the first disobedient son in recorded history: "If thou doest well, shalt thou not be accepted? and if thou doest not well, sin lieth at the door." (Genesis 4:7)

It is also stated by the Prophet Joseph Smith as follows: "There is a law irrevocably decreed in heaven before the foundations of this world, upon which all blessings are predicted:

"And when we obtain any blessing from God, it is by obedience to that law upon which it is predicted."

It is said that "the soul in the formative period of youth, while it is yet unspotted from the world, may be likened to a block of pure, uncut Parian marble, in which lie boundless possibilities of beauty or of deformity. From the crude marble one will chisel a form of exquisite grace and symmetry; another a misshapen monstrosity, each visualizing in the formless stone the conception of his brain. Thus we are molded by our ideals."

Thoughts are the seeds of acts, and precede them. Mere compliance with the word of the Lord without a corresponding inward desire will avail but little. Indeed, such outward actions and pretending phrases may disclose hypocracy, a sin that Jesus most vehemently condemned. "O generation of vipers," he cried out on one occasion, "how can ye, being evil, speak good things?" The Savior's constant desire and effort were to implant in the mind right thoughts, pure motives, noble ideals, knowing full well that right words and actions would inevitably follow. He taught, and modern physiology and psychology confirm, that hate and jealousy and other evil passions destroy a man's physical vigor and efficiency. "They pervert his mental perceptions and render him incapable of resisting the temptation to commit acts of violence. They undermine his moral health. By insidious stages they transform the man who cherishes them into a criminal."

Charles Dickens makes impressive use of this fact in his immortal story "Oliver Twist," wherein Monks is introduced first as an innocent beautiful child; but as "ending his life as a mass of solid bestiality, a mere chunk of fleshed iniquity. It was thinking upon vice and vulgarity that transformed the angel's face into the countenance of a demon."

It is almost impossible to believe that such a devilish nature as Bill Sikes', depicted in the same book, could be found in human form, but Dickens says himself: "I fear there are in the world some insensible and callous natures, that do become, at last, utterly and irredeemably bad. But whether this be so or not, of one thing I am certain: that there are such men as Sikes, who, being closely followed through the same space of time, and through the same current of circumstances, would not give by one look or action for a moment the faintest indication of a better nature. Whether every gentler human feeling is dead within such bosoms, or the proper chord to strike has rusted and is hard to find, I do not know, but that the fact is so, I am sure."

The operation of the same law in a positive way is illustrated by Nathaniel Hawthorne in "The Great Stone Face." Said Ernest to his mother one evening as they sat looking at an immense rock in which nature had chiseled a man's face with noble features and an expression "at once grand and sweet, as if it were the glow of a vast, warm heart that embraced all mankind in its affections and had room for more: 'Mother, if I were to see a man with such a face, I should love him dearly.'"

She answered: "If a prophecy come true, we may see him some time or other with exactly such a face as that."

That face was finally depicted in the countenance of Ernest himself. Having lived a life in which he had constantly kept before him the "vision splendid," there was chiseled in his own countenance the benign features of the great image. "When he spoke he expressed what was in his mind and heart. His words had power because they accorded with his thoughts; and his thoughts had reality and depth, because they harmonized with the life which he had always lived."

No man can disobey the word of God and not suffer for so doing. No sin, however secret, can escape retribution. True you may lie and not be detected, you may violate virtue without its being known by any who would scandalize you; yet you cannot escape the judgment that follows such transgression. The lie is lodged in the recesses of your mind, and impairment of your character will be reflected sometime, somehow in your countenance or bearing. Your moral turpitude, though only you, your accomplice, and God may ever know it, will canker your soul.

"The more I know intimately the lives of other men (to say nothing of my own)," said Huxley, in a letter to Charles Kingsley, "the more obvious is it to me that the wicked *does not* flourish, nor is the righteous punished. The ledger of the Almighty is strictly kept, and every one of us has the balance of his operations paid over to him at the end of every minute of his existence. . . . The absolute justice of the system of things is as clear to me as any scientific fact. The gravitation of sin to sorrow is as certain as that of the earth to the sun, and more so—for experimental proof of the fact is within the reach of us all—nay is before us all our lives, if we had but the eyes to see it."

Man is endowed with appetites and passions for the preservation of his life and the perpetuation of his kind. These, when held under proper subjection, contribute to his happiness and comfort; but when used for mere gratification, lead to misery and moral degradation.

Associated with these natural instincts is a sin that always seeks seclusion. It is the prostitution of love, the noblest attribute of the soul. God has instituted marriage and the family as the proper conditions of expressing in our lives this divine virtue. But sometimes men and women with low ideals and weakened wills permit their passions, like unbridled steeds, to dash aside judgment and self-restraint and to cause them to commit sin that may sear their conscience and leave in their hearts an everlasting regret.

In this day when modesty is thrust into the background, and chastity is considered an out-moded virtue, I appeal to youth to keep your souls unmarred and unsullied from this sin, the consequence of which will smite and haunt you intimately until your conscience is seared and your character sordid. A chaste, not a profligate life is the source of virile manhood, the crown of beautiful womanhood, a contributing factor of harmony and happiness in family life, and the source of strength and perpetuity of the race. The Savior has said that if any shall commit adultery even in his or her heart they shall not have the spirit, but shall deny the faith and shall fear.

Resist evil, and the Tempter will flee from you. If you keep your character above reproach, no matter what others may think, nor what charges they make, you can hold your head erect, keep your heart light, and face the world undauntingly, because you, yourself, and your God know that you have kept your soul untarnished.

The only thing which places man above the beast of the field is his possession of spiritual gifts. Man's earthly existence is but a test as to whether he will concentrate his efforts, his mind, his soul upon things which contribute to the comfort and gratification of his physical instincts and passions, or whether he will make as his life's end and purpose the acquisition of spiritual qualities.

Duty of Parents

Luther Burbank, the great plant wizard, most impressively emphasizes the need of constant attention in the training of a child.

Parents who do not know where their children are at nights are recreant to the sacred obligation of parenthood, and untrue to the high ideals of the Church regarding home life.

Free Agency

Free Agency is a divine gift, more precious than peace, more to be desired even than life. Any nation, any organized group of individuals that would deprive man of this heritage should be denounced by all liberty-loving persons. Associated with this fundamental principle is the right of individual initiative, and the right to worship how, where, or what one pleases, and the simple privilege, for example, to leave a country if one chooses without having to skulk out as a culprit at the risk of being shot and killed.

At heart communism is atheistic, and facism is equally antagonistic to freedom and to other Christian principles— even denying the divinity of Jesus Christ, and the existence of God.

Conclusion

Today there is great need in the world for men of integrity, men of honor, men whose word is as good as their bond, leaders of nations who will consider international agreements sacred. The philosopher Thoreau said: "It matters not half so much what kind of ballot you drop into the ballot box once a year, as what kind of man you drop out of bed into the street every morning."

Man's greatest need is real conversion to the eternal truths of the Gospel—to the truth that Jesus Christ came to give life and light to the human family.

Recently, a group of friends presented one of their number with a valuable and practical gift. In accepting it, the man said that wherever he might travel the possession of that gift would be a constant reminder of his friends' affectionate regard.

The Lord's Sacrament

The greatest comfort in this life is the assurance of having close relationship with God. I am speaking to men who know what that experience is. The sacrament period should be a factor in awakening this sense of relationship.

The Lord Jesus the same night in which he was betrayed took bread:

And when he had given thanks, he brake it, and said, Take, eat: this is my body, which is broken for you: this do in remembrance of me.

After the same manner also he took the cup, when he had supped, saying, This cup is the new testament in my blood: this do ye, as oft as ye drink it, in remembrance of me.

For as often as ye eat this bread, and drink this cup, ye do shew the Lord's death till he come.

Wherefore whosoever shall eat this bread, and drink this cup of the Lord, unworthily, shall be guilty of the body and blood of the Lord.

But let a man examine himself, and so let him eat of that bread, and drink of that cup.

No more sacred ordinance is administered in the Church of Christ than the administration of the sacrament. It was initiated just after Jesus and the Twelve had partaken of the last supper; and the saints in the early days followed that custom. That is, they ate before they administered the sacrament, but that custom was later discontinued by instructions from Paul to the saints to eat their meal at home so that when they met for worship they might meet as a body of brethren and sisters on the same level to partake of the sacrament in remembrance of the life and death, particularly the death of their Lord.

There are three things fundamentally important associated with the administration of the sacrament. The first is self-discernment. It is introspection. "This do in remembrance of me," but we should partake *worthily*, each one examining himself with respect to his worthiness.

Secondly, there is a covenant made; a *covenant* even more than a promise. You have held up your hand, some of you, or, if in England when signing a document, put your hand on the Bible, signifying the value of your promise or of the oath that you took. All this indicates the sacredness of a covenant. There is nothing more important in life than that. Until the nations realize the value of a covenant and promise and conduct themselves accordingly, there will be little trust among them. Instead there will be suspicion, doubt, and signed agreements, "scraps of paper," because they do not value their word. A covenant, a promise, should be as sacred as life. That principle is involved every Sunday when we partake of the sacrament.

Thirdly, there is another blessing, and that is a sense of close relationship with the Lord. There is an opportunity to commune with oneself and to commune with the Lord. We meet in the house that is dedicated to him; we have turned it over to him; we call it his house. Well, you may rest assured that he will be there to inspire us if we come in proper attune to meet him. We are not prepared to meet him if we bring into that room our thoughts regarding our business affairs, and especially if we bring into the house of worship feelings of hatred towards our neighbor, or enmity and jealousy towards the authorities of the Church. Most certainly no individual can hope to come in to communion with the Father if that individual entertain any such feelings. They are so foreign to worship, and so foreign, particularly, to the partaking of the sacrament.

I think we pay too little attention to the value of meditation, a principle of devotion. In our worship there are two elements: One is spiritual communion arising from our own meditation; the other, instruction from others, particularly from those who have authority to guide and instruct us. Of the two, the more profitable introspectively is the meditation. Meditation is the language of the soul. It is defined as "a form of private devotion, or spiritual exercise, consisting in deep, continued reflection on some religious theme." Meditation is a form of prayer. We can *say* prayers without having any spiritual response. We can say prayers as the unrighteous king in Hamlet who said: "My words fly up; my thoughts remain below. Words without thoughts never to heaven go."

The poet, contrasting the outward form of worship, and the prayer of the soul, said:

> The Power, incensed, the pageant will desert,
> The pompous strain, the sacerdotal stole;
> But haply, in some cottage far apart,
> May hear, well-pleased, the language of the soul,
> And in his Book of Life the inmates poor enroll."
> (Burns, "The Cotter's Saturday Night")

Meditation is one of the most secret, most sacred doors through which we pass into the presence of the Lord. Jesus set the example for us. As soon as he was baptized and received the Father's approval: "This is my Beloved Son in whom I am well pleased," Jesus repaired to what is now known as the Mount of Temptation. I like to think of it as the *Mount of Meditation* where, during the forty days of fasting, he communed with himself and his Father, and contemplated upon the responsibility of his great mission. One result of this spiritual communion was such strength as enabled him to say to the tempter: "Get thee hence, Satan: for it is written, Thou shalt worship the Lord thy God, and him only shalt thou serve."

Before he gave to the Twelve the beautiful sermon on the mount, he was in solitude in communion. He did the same thing after that busy Sabbath day, when he arose early in the morning, after having been the guest of Peter. Peter undoubtedly found the guest chamber empty, and when they sought him they found him alone. It was on that morning that Peter said: "All men seek thee."

Again, after Jesus had fed the five thousand he told the Twelve to dismiss the multitude, but Jesus went to the mountain for solitude. The historian says: "When the night came he was there alone." Meditation! Prayer!

I once read a book written by a very wise man, whose name I cannot now recall, which contained a significant chapter on prayer. The author was not a member of the Church, but evidently had a desire to keep in close communion with God, and he wanted to find the truth. Among other things he said in substance: "In secret prayer go into the room, close the door, pull down the shades, and kneel in the center of the room. For a period of five minutes or so, say nothing. Just think of what God has done for you, of what are your greatest spiritual and temporal needs. When you sense that, and sense his presence, then pour out your soul to him in thanksgiving."

I believe the short period of administering the sacrament is one of the best opportunities we have for such meditation, and there should be nothing during that sacred period to distract our attention from the purpose of that ordinance.

One of the most impressive services I have ever attended was in a group of over 800 people to whom the sacrament was administered, and during that administration not a sound could be heard excepting the ticking of the clock, eight hundred souls, each of whom at least had the opportunity of communion with the Lord. There was no distraction, no orchestra, no singing, no speaking. Each one had an opportunity to search himself introspectively and to consider his worthiness or unworthiness to partake of the sacrament. His was the privilege of getting closer to his Father in Heaven. That is ideal!

Brethren, we recommend that we surround this sacred ordinance with more reverence, with perfect order, that each one who comes to the house of God may meditate upon his goodness and silently and prayerfully express appreciation for God's goodness. Let the sacrament hour be one experience of the day in which the worshiper tries at least to realize within himself that it is possible for him to commune with his God.

Great events have happened in this Church because of such communion, because of the responsiveness of the soul to the inspiration of the Almighty. I know it is real. President Wilford Woodruff had that gift to a great extent. He could respond; he knew the "still small voice" to which some are still strangers. You will find that when those most inspirational moments come to you that you are alone with yourself and your God. They come to you probably when you are facing a great trial, when the wall is across your pathway, and it seems that you are facing an insurmountable obstacle, or when your heart is heavy because of some tragedy in your life. I repeat, the greatest comfort that can come to us in this life is to sense the realization of communion with God.

Great testimonies have come in those moments. It is just such an experience as that which came to my father in the north of Scotland when, as I have told some of you before, that he prayed to God to remove from him a spirit of gloom and despondency that overwhelmed him. After a night of worry and restlessness, he arose at daylight and repaired to a cave on the shore of the North Sea. He had been there before in prayer. There, just as the rays of the morning light began to come over the sea, he poured out his soul to God as a son would appeal to his father. The answer came: "Testify that Joseph Smith is a Prophet of God!" The cause of his discouragement flashing upon his mind, he said aloud: "Lord, it is enough!"

There are those in this audience who knew my father, and can testify to his integrity and his honesty. A testimony of that kind has one hundred percent value.

These secret prayers, these conscientious moments in meditation, these yearnings of the soul to reach out to feel the presence of God—such is the privilege of those who hold the Melchizedek Priesthood.

Now I know that some of you are saying to yourselves, "music helps to intensify that feeling of communion." When you stop to consider the matter, you realize that there is nothing during the administration of the sacrament of an extraneous nature so important as *remembering* our Lord and Savior, nothing so *worthy of attention* as *considering the value of the promise we are making. Why should anything distract us? Is there anything more sublime?* We are witnessing there, in the presence of one another, and before him, our Father, that we are willing to take upon ourselves the name of Christ, that we will always remember him, *always*, that we will keep his commandments that he has given us. Can you, can anybody living, who thinks for a moment, place before us anything which is more sacred or more far-reaching in our lives? If we partake of it mechanically, we are not honest, or, let us say, we are permitting our thoughts to be distracted from a very sacred ordinance.

I was speaking recently to one man about this. He said: "Oh, but the beautiful music of the choir helps us to concentrate." Concentrate on what? The more beautiful the music, the more your attention is attracted to it, to the player, or to the composer. If it is beautiful music poorly played, then the discord distracts your attention. Have that music in preparation up to the moment, yes, but when the prayer is said, and that young priest speaks for us, as he does, then remember that we are placing ourselves under covenant. It will be ideal if, during the fifteen minutes, every man, woman, and child will think as best he or she can of the significance of that sacred ordinance.

There is one other point which might be associated with the passing of the sacrament. It is a beautiful, impressive thing to have our boys administer it. They are the servants; they are waiting upon us and waiting upon the Lord; and have come there because they are worthy to officiate if the bishop has spoken to them properly. "Be ye clean that bear the vessels of the Lord." If every boy could sense this, quietly and with dignity he would pass the sacrament to us. Sometimes they pass it first to the organist, as if no moment should be lost before she starts to distract our attention. The music starts at once. No matter how good it may be, the tones of the organ, if we are respectful to the organist, divert our attention from the prayer that has just been offered.

Rather should that young man carry the sacrament to the presiding officer, not to honor him, but the office, as you honored our president tonight. That presiding officer may be the bishop of the ward; if so, let the young man carry the sacrament first to the bishop. After that, pass it to one after the other who sit either on the left or the right of the presiding officer, not going back to the first and second counselors and then to the superintendent. The lesson is taught when the sacrament is passed to the presiding officer. The next Sunday, the president of the stake may be there, who is then the highest ecclesiastical authority. Do you see what the responsibility of the deacons and the priests is? There is a lesson in government taught every day. It is their duty to know who is the presiding officer in that meeting that day. Next Sunday there may be one of the General Authorities. Those young men will have in mind the question, "Who is he today, and who is the presiding authority?"

But the lesson I wish to leave is: Let us make that sacrament hour one of the most impressive means of coming in contact with God's spirit. Let the Holy Ghost, to which we are entitled, lead us into his presence, and may we sense that nearness, and have a prayer offered in our hearts which he will hear.

My thought is partially expressed by Edwin Markham in the following lines:

> The builder who first bridged Niagara's gorge,
> Before he swung his cable, shore to shore,
> Sent out across the gulf his venturing kite
> Bearing a slender cord for unseen hands
> To grasp upon the further cliff and draw
> A greater cord, and then a greater yet;
> Till at last across the chasm swung
> The cable—then the mighty bridge in air!
>
> So we may send our little timid thought
> Across the void, out to God's reaching hands—
> Send out our love and faith to thread the deep—
> Thought after thought until the little cord
> Has greatened to a chain no chance can break,
> And we are anchored to the infinite!

God help us, brethren, so to live that we may sense the reality, as I bear you my testimony tonight it is real, that we can commune with our Father in heaven, and if we so live to be worthy of the companionship of the Holy Spirit, he will guide us into all truth, he will show us things to come, he will bring all things to our remembrance, he will testify of the divinity of the Lord Jesus Christ, as I do tonight, and of the restoration of the Gospel.

Sunday School Joys Ahead

With the consideration of the assigned topic "Sunday School Joys Ahead" I associate fond memories of Sunday School joys of the past.

"Remember the worth of souls is great in the sight of God. . . . And if it so be that you should labor all your days . . . and bring, save it be one soul unto me, how great shall be your joy with him in the kingdom of my Father!"

The source of all future joys in Sunday School work may be found in this text. First, in sensing the value of a human soul, and, secondly, in influencing him to live an upright life.

I commend the General Sunday School Union Board for emphasizing joy in the life of Sunday School officers, teachers, and children. Joy is sweeter than pleasure. Joy is an emotion excited with the acquisition or expectation of good. Pleasure is a state of gratification of the senses or mind and may be sensuous. It may be self-indulgence. It is nearly always transitory. Joy and happiness are permanent. Joy is pleasure not to be repented of.

Children are entitled to joy. When you are in the presence of youth you cannot help but exclaim with the poet:

How beautiful is youth! how bright it gleams
With its illusions, aspirations, dreams!
Book of Beginnings, Story without End,
Each maid a heroine, and each man a friend!

Every generation seems to worry about its young people. Then these young folks grow up and worry about their children.

As indicated already, I have confidence in youth, therefore hope for the ultimate betterment of the human family. I base my trust in young people because, abiding in every normal human being's soul is a hidden impulse or longing to be somebody worthwhile, to accomplish some good thing. Winston Churchill once said: "There is a treasure, if you can find it, in the heart of every man."

It is natural for children to play, to seek pleasure. They are by right inheritors of joy. They should obtain this inheritance in their homes. If not, then by all means let them experience it in the Church. To quote one writer: "Let gayety cease to be a commodity of export. . . . Let us multiply anniversaries, family parties, and excursions. Let us raise good humor in our homes to the height of an institution. Let the schools, too, do their part. Let masters and students, school boys, and college members meet together oftener for amusement. It will be so much the better for serious work. There is no such aid to understanding one's teacher as to have laughed in his company; and conversely, to be well understood, a pupil must be met elsewhere than in class or examination."

I wish to emphasize the fact that our homes should be more attractive, and that more of our amusements should be in the home instead of out on the streets.

Joy Found in Achievement

True joy for teacher and for student is found in five achievements:

1. In giving increased regard and reverence for the Sunday School organization. Sunday School is for everybody, particularly for the children and youth. No young man or young woman will feel that Sunday School is a "sissy" organization if opening exercises are reverently conducted; if they can sense the spirit of true worship; if they sense a control and not a laxity in discipline.

When all come to Sunday School they should feel that they are being invited into the presence of the Lord. They are guests at a spiritual banquet. They should not depart from the classroom hungry and disappointed. When you prepare a meal for your guests, you make thorough preparation. Remember that greater preparation is necessary for your guests in Sunday School, at the table of the Lord.

2. The joy of having in the class all who should be enrolled—The joy of finding the indifferent.

The second achievement is the joy of having in the class all who should be enrolled. And with this thought I wish to correlate the welcoming statements and the welcoming remarks made by Superintendent Bennion — the joy of finding the indifferent. Let me illustrate.

On Tuesday July 18, 1933, at about 3 o'clock in the afternoon, a little three-year-old lad was lost in the Bad Lands of North Dakota. He was bare-headed, bare-footed, and wore only a pair of coveralls. The Bad Lands are noted for their pitfalls, canyons, rattlesnake holes, and as a rendezvous for wild animals.

Upon discovering that the little boy was missing, his parents began an immediate search. Later in the evening neighbors and friends were notified, and an all-night search was made. Early Wednesday morning, a neighbor rode sixteen miles to give the alarm that a child was lost. Farmers, housewives, ranchers, sheepherders, cowboys, business and professional men, storekeepers, boy and girl scouts, law officers gathered on the town square of Shaffer to hear Sheriff Thompson's instructions as follows:

"Friends, we are all going out to the Bad Lands to find and bring back the little Cornell boy. The best way I know to do this is for all of us to form into one single line and march out there. Each man, woman, and child of us will be spaced a few feet from each other. Every gully and canyon in the way must be searched, every brush must be examined as we go along. This line, friends and neighbors, must not be broken; every waterhole, ravine, and cave must be searched thoroughly. Every square inch must be scanned by us as we go. It is the only way. I don't know how long our search will take, but Alfred Cornell is out in the Bad Lands somewhere, and when we turn back the little fellow will be with us. We can only hope that we shall not be too late. Now let us get going. I have appointed some of you deputies to ride on horseback so that there will be no slip up, and there will be none if I know anything about the people of this state."

The line was formed. At 6:30 Thursday evening, the boy was found kneeling in a water hole, his legs and feet were badly bruised and inflamed. His father and mother rushed to him and took him in their arms.

When that ten-mile line of human beings saw that the boy was found and really alive, a great cheer arose from two hundred and fifty voices!

Present-day statistics indicate that youth is a criminal age. On every hand there is evidence that boys and girls are wandering into the "Bad Lands" of society. Several years ago it was reported that in the United States there were twenty-seven million youth under twenty-one without religious instruction. One in fourteen boys age twelve to twenty is arrested and brought to court. According to reliable statistics, there are many boys and girls who have strayed off in the midst of dangers of immorality and crime. And parents are not walking all night crying for them and hunting them. No neighbor is riding sixteen miles to cry — "A child is lost!" Someone must give the alarm; someone must act as a leader and organize the forces.

Sunday School teachers, one of the greatest joys of future Sunday School work will be to reduce the number of the indifferent and wayward. "And if it so be that you should labor all your days in crying repentance unto this people, and bring, save it be one soul unto me, how great shall be your joy with him in the kingdom of my Father!"

3. Joy of winning confidence.

The third achievement is the joy of winning confidence—even greater than increasing the enrollment of your class, even of finding an indifferent youth, is the joy that comes from winning the confidence of those whom you teach. To have the confidence of a little child is one of the greatest responsibilities and blessings in the world.

After the 4 o'clock meeting last Friday on Temple grounds, I heard a man who, evidently, is a leader of boys, saying: "We are going to the Assembly Hall, boys." As they walked away, two of them had their arms around the shoulders of their teacher, and the others crowded as close to him as possible. A teacher who holds such confidence and respect has the greatest opportunity in the world to shape the young men's lives.

4. Joy of awakening a love for truth.

The fourth achievement is the joy of awakening a love for truth. Have you ever told a child a story and watched his or her eyes and the yearning for more? Well, the joy of Sunday School service comes from the realization of the great opportunity to train the mind, to encourage worthy habits, and to foster noble traits of character inculcated by wise parental teaching and example. Often the teacher faces the greater task of overcoming the false teachings of unwise, irresponsible parents. "All who have meditated on the art of governing mankind," says Aristotle, "have been convinced that the fate of empires depends upon the education of youth."

True education "is awakening a love of truth; giving a just sense of duty; opening the eyes of the soul to the great purpose and end of life. It is not so much giving words, as thoughts; or mere maxims, as living principles. It is not teaching to be honest, because 'honesty is the best policy;' but because it is right. It is teaching the individual to love the good for the sake of the good; to be virtuous in action because so in heart; to love and serve God supremely not from fear, but from delight in his perfect character." No one can successfully controvert the fact that upon the teacher rests much of the responsibility of lifting society to this high ideal.

5. The joy of character building.

The fifth achievement is the joy of character building. This leads us to the paramount duty, and to the real and supreme joy of Sunday School work. Wise parents and leading educators in the nation today realize that good citizenship can be obtained only through character development. The sincere teacher realizes that here is an opportunity to inculcate the virtues that contribute to the building of true womanhood and manhood. "Character is higher than intellect," said Emerson, "a great soul will be fit to live as well as to think."

But the Sunday School teacher's duty is not complete when he teaches only ethical principles. If he would have his children truly happy, he will lead them to have a testimony of the truth of the Restored Gospel of Jesus Christ. Happy is the man or woman who can say with Thomas in reverent assurance: "My Lord, and my God!"

Conclusion

All mankind seek happiness. Most people desire to make the most and best of themselves. Few, however, realize that a sure guide to such achievement is disclosed in the following declaration of Jesus of Nazareth: "Whosoever will save his life shall lose it: and whosoever will lose his life for my sake shall find it." This significant passage contains a secret more to be sought than worldly fame or dominion, something which excels in value all the wealth of the world. It is a principle, the application of which promises to supplant discouragement and gloom by hope and gladness, to fill life with contentment and peace everlasting. This being true, its acceptance would be a boon today to this distracted wartorn world! Why, then, is a thing so precious ignored by men and nations? Is the truth of the paradoxical statement, losing oneself to find oneself so elusive that mankind cannot grasp it? Or is it so in conflict with the struggle for existence that men consider it impractical? Even so, the fact remains that he who is "the way, the truth, and the life" has herein set forth an immutable law, obedience to which will ameliorate those social and economic conditions in which "man's inhumanity to man makes countless thousands mourn."

Specifically stated, this law is: We live our lives most completely when we strive to make the world better and happier. The law of pure nature, survival of the fittest, is self-preservation at the sacrifice of all else—the law of true spiritual life is to deny self for the good of others.

The Church of Jesus Christ of Latter-day Saints accepts as fundamental this law of life. Faithful members thereof believe that only in its application can true joy be found or a truly great character be developed.

Therefore, in the heart of every true Latter-day Saint the voice of the Lord is ever whispering this recorded revelation: "Remember the worth of souls is great in the sight of God;"

"And if it so be that you should labor all your days, and bring save it be one soul unto me, how great shall be your joy in the kingdom of my Father!"

With this end in view, thousands of men and women, serving willingly, offer every week to hundreds of thousands of children and youth instruction and guidance in character-building and spiritual growth. Thousands more are in the M.I.A. and Primary Associations. In addition to this army of officers and teachers, two hundred thousand men ordained to the priesthood have accepted the obligation to devote their time and talents as far as possible to the scattering of sunshine, joy, and peace among their fellowmen. In all such efforts, these men and women are but actuated by the high ideals of the Prophet Joseph Smith, who, exemplifying the teachings of Christ, said: "If my life is of no value to my friends, it is of no value to me."

Never was there a time in the history of the world when the application of this principle was more needed. Therefore let sincere men and women the world over unite in earnest effort to supplant feelings of selfishness, animosity, greed by the law of service to others and thereby promote the peace and joy of mankind.

God bless you, fellow workers, as you go forth to experience the joys ahead in Sunday School work, I pray.

The Teacher's Responsibility

I shot an arrow into the air
It fell to earth, I knew not where;
For, so swiftly it flew, the sight
Could not follow it in its flight.

I breathed a song into the air
It fell to earth I knew not where;
For who has sight so keen and strong
That it can follow the flight of a song?

Long, long afterward, in an oak
I found the arrow, still unbroke;
And the song, from beginning to end
I found again in the heart of a friend.
                              —Longfellow

These stanzas express beautifully the possible never-ending influence of a word or deed. Therein lies the compensation and joy of the teacher, whose name is not emblazoned before the public gaze; but whose instructions, like echoes, "roll from soul to soul, and go forever and forever."

On this Temple Block today, flowers, "sweet letters of the angel tongue," planted in picturesque designs, are blooming on every hand. Tens of thousands of tourists are passing through these grounds. Into the hearts of some of these more observant, thoughtful visitors, the flowers may send tender messages of nature's love of life and beauty. Even the most unresponsive of them would undoubtedly thrill with admiration as they glimpse what the poet felt so fully when he cried:

> Your voiceless lips, O flowers, are living preachers—
> each cup a pulpit, and each leaf a book.

This gorgeous display of thirty thousand blossoming plants are the result of daily labor and attention of ten or twelve men, to whose consistent effort, indeed to whose existence the ten thousand visitors give scarcely a passing thought.

Nor do these men, these gardeners, work for any such recognition. Their reward is in their weekly compensation and in the satisfaction of seeing expressions of pleasure and admiration on the countenances of visitors. They work quietly and constantly to make the world more beautiful and the result of their labor is a benefit to the multitude.

So in the garden of humanity there are millions of men and women whose lives contribute to the betterment of the world, from whose characters are radiating virtues that might still be lying dormant in their souls had it not been for the noble, unselfish influence of teachers of whom the world has never heard.

Of what infinite value to the community are these guides and trainers of youth who carve and shape the moral atmosphere in which the people live. Flowers shed beauty and fragrance for a brief time, then fade and die and are gone forever, but children, who through instruction from noble teachers become imbued with eternal principles of truth, radiate an influence for good, which, as their own souls, will live forever. "If we work upon marble, it will perish; if on brass, time will efface it; if we rear temples, they will crumble into dust; but if we work upon immortal minds, and imbue them with principles, with the just fear of God and love of our fellowmen, —we engrave on those tablets something that will brighten to all eternity."

Whenever I face a body of teachers, I feel that I am addressing a body of men and women who are representatives of a group who carry the second greatest responsibility in all the world. Parenthood is the greatest; teaching is the next. On the proper education of youth depend the permanency and purity of home, the safety and perpetuity of the nation. The parent gives the child an opportunity to live. The teacher enables the child to live well. The parent who gives life and teaches his child to live abundantly is a true parent-teacher. Today the customs and demands of society are such that the responsibility of training the child to live well is largely and in too many instances shifted from the parent to the teacher. In the ideal state, the teacher would be but the parent's ally, training the mind and encouraging worthy habits and fostering noble traits of character inculcated by wise parental teaching and example. But in reality, the teacher, instead of being merely an ally, must become the foster-parent in training the child in the art of living. If that were all, his responsibility would be great enough. It is not all. Often he faces even the greater task of overcoming the false teaching and the vicious training of unwise, irresponsible parents. In the light of self-evident facts, it is not apparent to every thinking mind that the noblest of all noble professions is that of teaching, that upon the effectiveness of that teaching hangs the destiny of nations. "All who have meditated on the art of governing mankind," says Aristotle, "have been convinced that the fate of empires depends upon the education of youth."

It is the teacher's responsibility to awaken in the child a love for truth, a desire to seek happiness in life through righteous living. Not to give a child happiness by proper guidance along the road of the Gospel of Jesus Christ is to deprive one's self and the world of a blessing. A child misdirected may be the loss to mankind of an eminent scientist, or of a discoverer of new truth, or of a man whose life and vision might have hastened that future day of

universal brotherhood and peace. Most truly is a child
"a fragile beginning of a mighty end." One of the greatest of life's tragedies is to see such a possible ending shattered in its early beginning. Such a misdirected soul
crossed my path recently. He is only seventeen years of
age; but thankless, disregardful, disgraceful in his attitude towards his mother and others who love him; tempes-
tuous in his temper, unrestrained in his appetites, dishonest in his dealings, defiant of all restraint, a violator of
civil law and of laws of morality. He has a brilliant mind
and in some respects is highly gifted, but he bids fair, even
before he sees his twentieth birthday, to join that wreck-
age of humanity which makes up the flotsam and jetsam
of human society.

In contrast consider the young Mormon soldier who
gave his life for his country in Italy. Instead of spending
the money he received from the government for cigarettes,
drinking intoxicants, indulging in riotous living, he con-
served his earnings to be used in the future for some useful
purpose. In case, however, that he should be called upon
to sacrifice his life for the cause for which he was fighting, he sent his money home, with a request that should
he never return, that his money should be used to support
some missionary who would be sent to preach the Gospel
of peace.

Why this conscientious, masterful, God-fearing man
in one case, and the despoiler of self and the despair of
his loved ones in the other instance. Perhaps we cannot
rightly say. So many elements enter into the forming and
the shaping of a life. However, in these two instances we
do know that the two characters differ largely because
of environment and early training. One got the ideal;
the other failed to see it. Teachers, until your boys and
girls get the true ideal as set forth in the Gospel of Jesus
Christ, your responsibility is not fully discharged. Your
duty, your life's work is "To train them to virtue; habi-
tuate them to industry, activity and spirit. Make them

consider every vice as shameful and unmanly. Fire them with ambition to be useful. Make them disdain to be destitute of any useful knowledge. Fix their ambition upon great and solid objects, and their contempt upon little, frivolous and useless ones." (John Adams)

To achieve this power and influence, it should be every teacher's ideal to appear before his or her class with:

1. A pleasing personality
2. Thorough preparation, and
3. A prayerful heart.

You teachers are familiar with the famous painting depicting Christ as a youth of twelve years standing before learned men in the temple. In that picture the artist had combined physical strength, intellectual fire, moral beauty and spiritual fervor. The artist pictures him as a perfect youth, an ideal for every boy in the land. I ask you, fellow-teachers, to take the artist's brush and canvas and try to reproduce that picture of perfect youth! You hesitate! You say you have neither the skill nor the training. Very well. Every person who enters the profession of teaching assumes the responsibility not of attempting to put on canvas an ideal picture of youth but of cooperating with every youth under his tuition to make out of a living, breathing soul a perfect character.

The responsibility of the teacher, however, does not end in his duty to teach positively. He enters the realm of what-not-to-do, as well as the realm of what-to-do. In the garden of the human soul, as well as in the fields of human endeavor, there are thorns and thistles as well as flowers and useful plants. Thrice worthy of condemnation is he who would crush in a boy's mind a flower of truth, and sow in its stead the seed of error! Touching this point, the greatest of all teachers has said: "Whoso shall offend one of these little ones who believe in me"—that is, cause one of these little ones to stumble—"it were better for him

that a millstone were hanged about his neck, and that he
were drowned in the depth of the sea."

> The sculptor might chip the marble block
> The artist a blot erase;
> But the teacher who wounds a little child
> Might never the scar efface.
>
> O, hesitate then, unskilled hands
> To strike the harp of the soul;
> The discordant tones and the broken strings
> Might meet you at judgment's roll.
> —David O. McKay

Wise parents and leading educators in the nation today realize that good citizenship can be obtained only
through character development. They recognize, with
Emerson, that "character is higher than intellect. A great
soul will be fit to live as well as to think." Leading youth
to know God, to have faith in his laws, to have confidence
in his Fatherhood, and to find solace and peace in his love,
—this is the greatest privilege, the most sublime opportunity offered the true educator.

I have mentioned the responsibility of the teacher
to appear before her class with a pleasing appearance, second, with thorough preparation, and third, with a prayerful heart. Now let me add one more paramount duty,
and that is to teach by proper example. If teachers are
true in their desire to make character a true aim in education, arouse faith in God and a desire to maintain the
standards of the Church, they will manifest that sincerity
in daily action. They will be what they expect their pupils
to become. Otherwise their teaching becomes hollow and
meaningless, their words and precepts but as a sounding
brass and a tinkling cymbal. To live an upright life, to
conform to high ethical standards is the responsibility and
duty of every teacher in the land. Greater even than this
is the responsibility of the Primary teacher. Her profession is higher than that of the teacher in the common

school, for in addition to her belief in the efficacy of ethical and moral precepts, the religious teacher assumes the responsibility of leading the youth into the realm of spirituality.

The responsibility and opportunity of the teacher are summarized thus in the 93rd section of the Doctrine and Covenants:

"I give unto you these sayings that ye may understand and know how to worship, and know what you worship, that you may come unto the Father in my name, and in due time receive of his fulness.

"For if you keep my commandments you shall receive of his fulness, and be glorified in me as I am in the Father."

Eternal Verities

Have you ever sat down and talked with men
In a serious sort of way of their views of life,
And pondered then on all that they had to say?
If not, you should, in some quiet hour,
It's a glorious thing to do
For back of the pomp and back of the power,
Most men have a goal in view.

That's what I should like to do with you graduates tonight—talk with you in a serious sort of way of your views
of life.

For what is a man profited, if he shall gain the whole world,
and lose (forfeit) his own soul (life)? or what shall a man give
in exchange for his soul (life)? (Matt. 16:26)

In quoting this passage, I have in mind to emphasize
the dual nature of man—physical and spiritual. The revised version, substituting as it does, the word "life" for
"soul" makes justifiable the conclusion that preserving
one's physical life is deemed more precious than the acquiring of an earthly emoluments, or the possession of the
wealth of the world.

However, that Jesus had in mind the soul as a spiritual entity is confirmed by Mark who, recording this incident, adds: "Whosoever therefore shall be ashamed of

me and of my words in this adulterous and sinful generation; of him also shall the Son of Man be ashamed, when
he cometh in the glory of his Father with the holy angels."
(Mark 8:38)

Luke confirms this thought as follows: "For what is
a man advantaged, if he gain the whole world, and lose
himself, or be cast away?

"For whosoever shall be ashamed of me and my
words, of him shall the Son of Man be ashamed, when he
shall come in his own glory, and in his Father's, and of the
holy angels." (Luke 9:26)

If we accept the spirit entity of man as real and eternal, how utterly foolish to ignore or to neglect its development by giving most, if not all, of our attention to physical
needs, pleasures, and passions.

If one makes the present world with its allurements,
riches, honors, pleasures, indulgences, etc., "the object of
supreme pursuit," and gain not only what one seeks, but
the whole world, yet along with it forfeits one's own soul,
one has gambled the only thing worthwhile, and lost. Isn't
that true?

Also, if we are in company where the teachings of
Jesus are unpopular, if, in order to stand well with others or to avoid criticism we yield to indulgences violative
of Christ's teachings, we demonstrate that we are ashamed
of him, and merit his being ashamed of us when he
"cometh in the glory of his Father with his angels." The
tendency to vary from true standards or modify ideals
is well illustrated in one of Oliver Wendell Holmes clever
bits of literature on "lie" and "truth."

I quote it having in mind a tendency we sometimes
have to modify, shape or change true ideals by which we
should guide our lives.

When we are as yet small children, long before the time when
those two grown ladies offer us the choice of Hercules, there comes
up to us a youthful angel, holding in his right hand cubes like dice,

and in his left spheres like marbles. The cubes are of stainless ivory, and on each is written in letters of gold—TRUTH. The spheres are veined and streaked and spotted beneath, with a dark crimson flush above, where the light falls on them, and in a certain aspect you can make out upon every one of them the three letters L, I, E. The child to whom they are offered very probably clutches at both. The spheres are the most convenient things in the world; they roll with the least possible impulse, just where the child would have them. The cubes will not roll at all; they have a great talent for standing still, and always keep right side up. But very soon the young philosopher finds that things which roll so easily are very apt to roll into the wrong corner, and to get out of his way when he most wants them, while he always knows where to find the others, which stay where they are left. Thus he learns—thus we learn —to drop the streaked and speckled globes of falsehood and to hold fast the white angular blocks of truth. But then comes Timidity, and after her Good-nature, and last of all Polite behavior, all insisting that truth must roll, or nobody can do anything with it; and so the first, Timidity, with her course rasp; and the second, Good-nature, with her broad file; and the third, Polite behavior, with her silken sleeve, do so round off and smooth and polish the snow-white cubes of truth that, when they have got a little dingy by use, it becomes hard to tell them from the rolling spheres of falsehood.

(Oliver Wendell Holmes,
"The Autocrat of the Breakfast Table")

When the schoolmistress protested that there are better reasons for truth than could be found in mere experience of its convenience and the inconvenience of lying, the author continues,

Yes, but education always begins through the senses, and works up to the idea of absolute right and wrong. The first thing the child has to learn about this matter is, that lying is unprofitable, afterwards, that it is against the peace and dignitiy of the universe.

(Ibid. page 123)

The power of choice is a God-given gift, and the purpose of life is happiness. Things which pertain to the physical nature are so easily obtained and the pleasure so immediate that many spend most of their time seeking them, and neglecting the permanent joys of the spirit.

We are living in what may well prove to be the most epoch-making period of all time. There is ample evidence on every hand that we are witnessing one of those tidal waves of human thought and emotion which periodically sweep over the world and change the direction of human endeavor. It is a time that demands clear thinking and sound judgment. Whether we are willing to admit it or not, this is a revolutionary period. There is social and political upheaval. Thoroughly tested, well-tried principles are being thrown into discard. Long accepted social theories," writes Charles Foster Kent, "have suddenly been rejected, and new ones are being adopted. Many of the moral standards of our fathers are being set aside in theory as well as practice . . . Religious dogmas long regarded as the cornerstones of religion and the church are being disproved or supplanted by the discoveries of modern science."

It is not strange, therefore, that the majority of the men and women in this war-shattered and war-threatening world are unhappy because they feel the foundations beneath them are tottering. As reported in the public press a year or so ago, an experienced United States Congressman, reputably one of the best lawyers in Congress said: "There isn't a person in this room now who can be certain that he can leave to his children the heritage of the privilege of being free."

Today, if ever, is a time for young people who are not satisfied with merely building "birds' nests" or with temporary desires and pleasures of the moment, to get in mind eternal verities, fundamental truths, and make them life's guiding stars.

If in this unsettled sea of human perplexities, yearnings, disappointments, and despair, we would pause and eliminate from our minds our immediate demands and schemes for livelihood, if we would set aside our desires for personal pleasure resulting from indulgence in gratification of appetites and passions, if we would for an hour or two withdraw ourselves completely from the physical, and sensual, the political, and even the social influence of this human world, and let our souls commune with self and with the Infinite—we should find that only in the recognition and adoption of eternal verities can the yearning of a sincere mind be satisfied and peace and happiness be realized.

The captain of the "Kon-Tiki," when midway in the Pacific Ocean, experienced in reality what I am now suggesting you try to experience in imagination. Floating on a raft with his five companions, a thousand fathoms of water beneath them, a myriad of glittering tropical stars in the firmament above, he writes: "Whether it was 1947 B.C. or A.D. suddenly became of no significance. We *lived*, and *that* we felt with alert intensity. We realized that life has been full for man before the technical age also —in fact fuller and richer in many ways than the life of modern man. Time and evolution somehow ceased to exist; *all that was real and that mattered were the same today as they had always been and would always be.*"

The captain seemed to feel what our poet said about truth:

> . . . Tis the last and the first,
> For the limits of time it steps o'er:
> Though the heavens depart, and the earth's fountains burst,
> Truth, the sum of existence, will weather the worst,
> Eternal, unchanged, evermore.

If as I say, we could divest ourselves of all immediate wants and perplexities, and talk with self in a serious sort of way we should find ourselves giving value to like realities. Out of such soul-communion would come a recognition that no matter what physical, material, political, industrial and other changes may occur, no matter how theories of governments may change; how fashions, customs, and ideals may be accepted and abandoned, there remain unchanging verities eternally operative in the universe, ever contributing to the spiritual progress, to the peace, to the happiness of the individual and of the race.

With this recognition would come certain fundamental questions, the answer to which can be found only by reference to eternal truth. A few of these vital problems might be as follows:

> *First* The ever-present reality and mystery of life and immortality of the human soul.
>
> *Second* The existence of God and our relation to him. Is it possible for man's spirit to be in harmony with that Divine Being?
>
> *Third* These eternal verities accepted, the question arises what is the noblest aim in life—pleasure, wealth, or character?
>
> *Fourth* Every human heart yearns for love even more than the body yearns for food. Every normal person seeks a soul mate, and recognizes the family as the true source, for love's expression.

Such questions enter either in a fleeting or contemplative degree the mind of every thinking or contemplating person.

Let us consider for a moment how the history and purpose of the Brigham Young University would answer these vital problems.

Reality and Mystery of Life

It advocates reverence for life in all its own manifestations. Now that means more than I have time to elaborate. Unjustifiably injuring a child or any other human being is a manifestation of an uncultured nature—sadism in any degree is beastly. Cruelty to animals reflects disharmony with nature.

> He prayeth best who loveth best
> All things both great and small
> For the dear God who loveth us,
> He made and loveth all.

How sweet association would be—what a peaceful community all persons would live in if we had a kindly attitude—a sincere reverence for life!

One of the most interestingly illuminating chapters on the origin of life is found in a recent work by Mr. A. Cressy Morrison, past president, New York Academy of Sciences, and the American Institute of the City of New York. Says he:

> Nature did not create life; fire-blistered rocks and a saltless sea did not meet the necessary requirements. Did Life brood over this earth and over "other earths," awaiting its opportunity to glorify Cosmos with understanding? Gravity is a property of matter; electricity we now believe to be matter itself; the rays of the sun and stars can be deflected by gravity and seem to be akin to it. Man is learning the dimensions of the atom and is measuring its locked-up power, but LIFE is illusive, like space. WHY? Life is the only source of consciousness and it alone makes possible knowledge of the works of God which we, still half blind, yet know to be good. Life is an instrumentality serving the purposes of the Supreme Intelligence. LIFE IS IMMORTAL.
>
> Life pushes forward, building, repairing, extending, and not found in inanimate things. Is this intelligence? Is it instinct? or does it just happen? You can answer this yourself. The writer does not know, but he believes it came as an expression of Divine power, and it is not material.
>
> (A. Cressy Morrison, "Man Does Not Stand Alone," page 44)

From its beginning, the Brigham Young University has had the revelation in the Doctrine and Covenants that "intelligence, or the light of truth, was not created or made, neither indeed can be.

"All truth is independent in that sphere in which God has placed it, to act for itself, as all intelligence also; otherwise there is no existence." (D&C 93:30)

What an impressive example of inspiration to the Prophet Joseph Smith. When answering your students' questions on "intelligence" or the origin of life, you teachers are not hampered or hesitant when you give these revelations as eternal verities.

Thus we have the glorious truth that that uncreated, ever-existent intelligence animated spiritual bodies, "for man is spirit. The elements are eternal, and spirit and element, inseparably connected, receive a fulness of joy;

"And when separated, man cannot receive a fulness of joy.

"The elements are the tabernacle of God; yea, man is the tabernacle of God; even temples; and whatsoever temple is defiled, God shall destroy that temple." (D&C 93:33-35)

Thus may be found in this Church university without wonderment or equivocation the source not only of life, but of intelligence, and the answer to the question of human immortality.

I heard your president say on an important occasion last week that this school is destined to be the greatest university in the world and if we maintain these ideals, nothing can prevent its becoming so.

Another thought in this connection: when President Brigham Young called Brother Karl G. Maeser into his office, and said: "We want you to go to Provo to organize and conduct an academy to be established in the name of the Church—a Church school," he at least implies that our Lord and Savior, Jesus Christ, would be kept in mind as the head, center and life of this institution. How could it be otherwise when the school was to be established in the name of the Church, which is the Church of Jesus Christ!

"The whole question of the very life or speedy death of Christianity," writes George R. Wendling in 'The Man of Galilee,' "lies nevertheless wrapped up today as it always has been in the question of Deity of Jesus Christ. Hence the paramount question today is, and always will be, the supernatural character of the great Galilean. The inspiration of the Bible, the doctrine of a future state and other problems which perplex the seeker after religious truth, are all subordinate to this question of the divinity of Jesus Christ. They fasten themselves to it and arrange themselves about it dependently as a spiritual stairway is attached to a massive column leading up to clouds of doubt and darkness or up into the sunlight."

Permeating this school from the day of its opening to the present is the ever abiding testimony given of old, but ever new—

> I know that my redeemer liveth, and that he shall stand
> at the latter day upon the earth;
> And though after my skin worms destroy this body, yet in
> my flesh shall I see God:
> Whom I shall see for myself, and mine eyes shall behold,
> and not another; though my reins be consumed within me.
> (Job 19:25-27)

We come to the second question—*The existence of God and our relation to him.* Can we get in harmony with him?

One of the fundamental conditions contributive to a person's right thinking and acting is a reverence for God. A growing disbelief in a supreme being among many misguided people is a principal source of crime. When God becomes the center of our thoughts, we become conscious of a new aim in life. To nourish and satisfy the body and its desires as all other animals do, is no longer a chief end of mortal existence. Spiritual attainment, not material possessions, becomes the chief goal. With a sincere belief in God, "Thou shalt-not's" are easily resisted; vulgarity, profanity, indulgence in appetites and passions, cheating, lying, etc. seem below human dignity.

Let us keep in mind, students, that "God and the unseen world are not merely objects of surmise. We know them in experience. In the process of building character we have genuine knowledge of the forces which enter vitally into those characters. We experience a divine power which makes for ideals of wealth and sustains us in our struggle to attain them.

Science deals with the world out there beyond us—it knows only symbols of reality which are interpreted to the consciousness through the senses. But when we deal with what takes place in our own inner consciousness we send the shaft down deeper into reality. There if anywhere we touch reality in completer sense. "By being religious," says Professor James, "we establish ourselves in possesion of ultimate reality at the only point at which reality is given us to equal!"

The question of the possibility of communion with the Infinite is answered in the founding of this great institution. When Dr. Maeser decided to accept the assignment given him to found a Church school, he went to President Young's office, and addressing the president, said: I am about to leave for Provo, Brother Young, to start my work in the Academy. Have you any instructions to give me?"

"Brother Maeser," answered the president thoughtfully, "I want you to remember that you ought not to teach even the alphabet or the multiplication tables without the Spirit of God. That is all. God bless you. Good-bye."

In those few instructions we hear the echo of the Savior to the Twelve:

"Howbeit when he, the Spirit of truth is come, he will guide you into all truth: for he shall not speak of himself; but whatsoever he shall hear, that shall he speak: and he will shew you things to come.

He shall glorify me: for he shall receive of mine, and shall shew it unto you. (John 16:13-14)

The man who first stood at the head of this institution had been given a practical demonstration of the influence of the spirit upon the mind of man, when through the operation of that spirit, he and Brother Budge understood one another though each spoke in a different language.

May I give you what I call a "heart petal" as we sit in sacred communion. When I sat in school a student as

you, I wondered about the reality of the gift of tongues
and the interpretation of tongues. I did not doubt it because it was part of the Church, but I wondered. Tonight
I want to bear you witness that the interpretation of
tongues is a reality. I witnessed it in New Zealand at the
Hui Tau at Huntly in 1921; again in Aintab when President J. Wilford Booth was interpreting in the Turkish language what I was speaking in English; and a third experience in Holland—when President Zappey was interpreter.
And so from experience I knew that such a miracle as related by Brother Maeser and Brother Budge may be actual. This Church school stands for the ideal that we may
so live as to be "partakers of the divine nature."

What about the third? *What ideal permeates the
school regarding the noblest aim of life?*

None of the twenty-nine students who were present
at the opening of the school on April 24, 1876 is now alive,
but fortunately we have on record a statement of one of
those older students regarding the early purpose and aim
of this institution. He was one of the chief justices of the
Supreme Court of the United States when he wrote:

> I had heard such enthusiastic praise of the Academy that the
> reaction to my first view of this building was one of doubt and
> disappointment. Fortunately the building was not the school, but
> only the house in which the school lived, and the discovery of the
> school itself was as though I had opened a rough shell and found
> a pearl. The soul of this school was Karl G. Maeser. When I came,
> as I soon did, to realize the tremendous import of that fact, the ugly
> structure ceased to trouble my eyes, my doubts vanished, and were
> replaced by the comfort of certainty and a feeling of deep content.

Dr. Maeser's ability to teach covered the entire field
of learning, including that of teaching others to teach.
Far more important than anything else, he was a teacher
of goodness and a builder of character. He believed that
scholastic attainments were better than riches, but that
better than either were faith, love, charity, clean living,
clean thinking, loyalty, tolerance, and all the other attri-

butes that combine to constitute that most precious of all possessions—good character! Good character does not consist in the mere ability to store away in the memory a collection of moral aphorisms that run loosely off the tongue. Seneca gave the world a book of beautiful, fully written moral maxims, but he stood in the Roman senate and shamelessly justified Nero's murder of his own mother. Character to be good must be stable, must have taken root. It is an acquisition of thought and conduct which have become habitual. And acquisition of real substance so firmly fixed in the conscience, and, indeed, in the body itself as to insure unhesitating rejection of an impulse to do wrong.

Twenty-nine students were imbued with that high idea. Today over seven hundred graduates leave the university with faith in the eternal verities of *reverence for God and for sacred things;* with a knowledge that *honesty and fair-dealing are eternal verities essential to man's happiness;* that *without faith in God and confidence in one's fellowmen* "civilization will become bankrupt, order will become disorder, restraint and control will be lost, and evil will prevail."

Fourth, *the yearning of the soul for love.*

There is another ideal which has permeated this school and which it will always uphold as one of the eternal verities ever operated for the happiness and good of mankind. That is, modesty and chastity among youth are to be cherished and guarded as life itself. This is an ideal associated with love and strikes right at the base of happiness in the marriage relation. It is a common saying throughout the world that young men may sow their wild oats, but young women should be chaperoned and guarded; and be it said to their credit, that generally speaking the young women are protected. The young men, however, are given too free license, if statistics tell the truth. In the Church of Christ there is but one standard of morality. No young man has any more right to sow his wild oats in youth than has a young girl; and she is taught that second only to the crime of taking human life is that of losing her virtue; and that is the ideal among honorable young men. The young man who comes to his bishop to ask for a recommend to take a pure girl to the marriage altar in the temple, is expected to give just the same purity that he hopes to receive.

Reverence for life in all created things—faith in God, in his Beloved Son—an assurance that spiritual communion with them may be actual—the joyous experience of living uprightly—practicing honor, truth, integrity, fair dealing, being true to future wife or husband—these are eternal verities which give happiness and spiritual expansion.

The world needs fundamental truths that never change —the eternal truths of the Gospel of Jesus Christ.

"For what is a man profited, if he shall gain the whole world, and lose his own soul? or what shall a man give in exchange for his soul?"

May God help you graduates and all of us to cherish worthy ideals and noble aspirations. Whatever our work, our joys, or our sorrows, let us ever remember that back of the work, back of the joys, and the sorrows, ever glows our ideal. How constantly and consistently we cherish it in our minds and follow it will determine whether we shamble as failures along life's highway or fulfill the divine purpose of our being.

The Ideals of Womanhood

How aptly are the words written thousands of years ago in tribute to another woman, women in general, but I now apply them to Sister Ruth May Fox:

"Who can find a virtuous woman? for her price is far above rubies. The heart of her husband doth safely trust in her, so that he shall have no need of spoil . . ." or, in the modern translation, so he shall have gain.

"She will do him good and not evil all the days of her life . . . Strength and honour are her clothing; and she shall rejoice in time to come. She openeth her mouth with wisdom: and in her tongue is the law of kindness. She looketh well to the ways of her household, and eateth not the bread of idleness. Her children arise up, and call her blessed; her husband also, and he praiseth her." (Proverbs 31: 10-12, 25-28)

I join with all Israel in saying to Sister Fox, "God bless you for what you have done, for what you are and what your influence will continue to be throughout all Israel."

Perhaps some of you think that the impressive drama presented [Lamps of Glory] is not based on facts. It is. I do not know the instance, but as I understand it, I said in my heart that Esther might have been a young girl in England ninety years ago, and Ronald, her sweetheart to whom she was engaged. Ronald was down in Australia seeking to make his fortune before he would return to England to take his sweetheart as bride, and while he was away she heard the message of Mormonism and with her adopted parents accepted the gospel. While, let us call him Ronald, was in Australia he heard the terrible stories about the Mountain Meadow Massacre and the Danites and polygamy with which he associated these other terrible things. He returned, however, to England and in high anticipation hastened to his sweetheart's home to have her name the wedding day. But she said: "I have something to tell you first. I have joined the Church."

"Well, that is all right. I will join it with you."

"No, you do not understand. I have joined The Church of Jesus Christ of Latter-day Saints."

"Well, that is all right. One church is just as good as another. Name the day."

"You do not understand. I have joined the Mormon Church."

"What?" he said, "I cannot understand how you have been so deceived."

Well, I need not tell you the story. He finally said: "You choose between the Mormons and me."

But the light shone also in her soul, and she said: "If that is your decision, I choose the Church."

When that light gets into the soul it is as a guide, the most precious thing in all one's life. Ronald left England. Back to Australia he went, but stopped on his way in Salt Lake City to see for himself, then continued on and returned a year or so later and investigated for himself. He observed as best he could the great leader, Brigham Young. He sat in the old tabernacle that was built before the present edifice, and he found out that he had been deceived, that it was he who was in error and not Esther. So he returned to England, asked her forgiveness, and they were married.

The adopted parents endowed them richly, comparatively speaking, for those times. And so they prepared to come to Utah. When they got to Liverpool, they learned of an Emigration Fund, which meant that if they would travel in handcarts and not in luxury as they could, seven other families could come for the same price that the voyage would cost them. He turned to Esther and said: "What shall we do?"

She said: "We will deposit our funds and take other families with us."

Unfortunately they were delayed in the east and came with that unfortunate handcart company that was caught in the storms on the plains of Nebraska and Wyoming, and they saw some of those who had been helped by their means placed in temporarily marked graves in the morning before the journey was continued. And out on the plains, sometime in September, a little baby girl was born to Esther, and members of the company held a blanket over mother and babe when the little one was washed and dressed.

I think it was about 1907 that I sat at the table as a guest of that little baby girl born on the plains, and around her, crowning her with glory, were nine children, and it was from her lips that I received in detail the story of her mother and her father as I have briefly sketched it to you. She was Mrs. Leigh of Cedar City.

These two are but typical of many others, illustrating the heroism and faith of the Mormon women.

Looking among my treasures recently, I picked up a piece of old homespun cloth. It was woven by my grandmother. My grandfather clipped the wool from the sheep out of which the cloth was made. There were no factories in Utah then. The nearest factory was over a thousand miles from this city. It was carded and spun into thread by my grandmother who had walked across the plains. It was old and threadbare, but genuine, not a shoddy thread in it.

Recently I saw my daughter and her husband examining a sample of a modern piece of cloth which they wished to use for a special purpose. As she picked the threads apart and examined them closely, she suddenly exclaimed, "Why, this is nothing but paper." Outwardly it outshone in newness and attractiveness the old piece of homespun, but in reality it was shoddy.

What that piece of homespun is to a modern substitute for genuineness, fundamental, unchanging virtues that have stood the test of ages are to promises of pleasure, indulgence, and false ideals of modern society. Those old fundamental ideals are genuine. Some of them which appeal to you today are attractive but false. Outwardly the latter seem glamorous and glorious, but when tested and tried in the scrutiny of experience, there is nothing which remains but the dust of disappointment.

This week I presented the following question to each of ten daughters, "Will you please name for me the outstanding virtues that you admire in your mother?" I did that because I can think of no higher ideal that a daughter should have than her mother, no one whom she should love more. In the words of Tennyson:

"Happy he with such a mother! faith in womankind
Beats with his blood, and trust in all things high
Comes easy to him; and though he trip and fall,
He shall not bind his soul with clay."

When each daughter says in her heart:

"The holiest words my tongue can frame
The noblest thoughts my soul can claim,
Unworthy are to praise the name
More precious than all other.
An infant, when her love first came,
A girl, I find it still the same,
Reverently I breathe her name,
The blessed name of mother.
                    —George Griffith Fether

The ideals mentioned by these girls are genuine, everlasting, in an ever-changing world. Summarized they are as follows: "Some of the qualities I appreciate in my mother," writes one, "first, her willingness to inconvenience herself for others." Note the second: "Her faith and trust in me. Third, her faith in the gospel of Jesus Christ. Fourth, Cheerfulness; her cheerful attitude in face of difficulties. Fifth, sympathy with what I do, and understanding of my problem." And, sixth, "ability to make a lovely home."

Just one other sample:

"Mother has always had complete faith in me. She has a strong testimony, great faith, and has always been active in Church organizations. She has always been kind, gentle, thoughtful, understanding, one to whom I can always turn, and one whom I can always trust, willing to sacrifice all for her children. She has set me the perfect example of clean living, never having touched alcohol, tobacco, or stimulating drinks. She taught me a love, appreciation, and understanding of the gospel while very young. She has always given me encouragement, inspiration, and a desire to live life in its fulness through love and service to my fellow-men."

Note the summary: Unselfishness, honesty, patience, congeniality, neatness and cleanliness, faith, love of the beautiful, trust and faith in her children, a perfect lady.

To each daughter, then, her mother seems:

"As pure as some serene
Creation minted in the golden moods
Of sovereign artist; not a thought, a touch,
But pure as lines of green that streak the white
Of the first snowdrop's inner leaves—
—Tennyson

Not one of them even imagined, not one visualized her mother with teeth and breath stained with nicotine, nor her clothes impregnated with the vile fumes of tobacco smoke. It is beyond the imagination of any one of these girls, as I hope it is beyond yours, even to associate with mother, indulgence in views held by modern society regarding sexual promiscuity. "Strength and honor are her clothing, and she shall rejoice in time to come." Mother is worthy of the confidence, love, and admiration of her daughter because in her youth she ever wore the crown of virtue.

Home is the center from which woman rules the world. It is there she teaches her child self-restraint, develops in him the confidence and strength that spring from self-control. It is there the child learns respect for the rights of others. It is in a well-directed home that men and women first develop a consciousness that true happiness lies in conforming one's life to the laws of nature and to the rules of social conduct.

A married woman who refuses to have children, or who having them neglects them for pleasure or social prestige, is recreant to the highest calling and privilege of womankind. The home is the best place in the world to teach the highest ideals in the social and political life of man; namely, perfect liberty of action so long as you do not trespass upon the rights and privileges of another.

Home is the best place to inculcate true religious ideals. The great need in the American home today is more religion. Parents should make it obvious, both by their actions and their conversation, that they are seriously interested, if not in outward forms, in the fruits of religion. The example of parents should emphasize the need of honesty in our dealings with our family, our neighbors, and all with whom we come in contact—kindness to our employees, fair play to our employers, a good measure to our customers. Talk about these intangibles should become common practice in our homes and offices if we want to succeed in solving family difficulties.

The ideals of true womanhood may sometimes seem as old-fashioned as that old piece of homespun cloth, but they are as unchanging and everlasting as the soul itself. Modern indulgences and pleasures that lead girlhood away from these fundamental principles of happiness are shallow and shoddy, deceiving in their promises and ultimately disappointing.

The highest ideal of our young girls today, as for our mothers who crossed the plains, is love as it may be expressed in marriage and home-building, and this virtue in which love finds true expression is based upon the structural and not the physical side of our being. If marriage and home-building be based upon physical attraction alone, girls, your love will sooner or later become famished and life a heavy, disheartening existence.

This truth is emphasized by the following quotations taken from "Our Home":

"Spiritual love lives by its own right, but the physical lives only by the lease of the spiritual. They can live together only on one changeless and eternal condition and that condition is the supremacy of the spiritual over the physical . . . Let woman remember that this doctrine appeals to her with doubled force. It is through you, O woman, that the world must heed it. Whatever other wrongs you may submit to, whatever rights may be denied you in the social world, remember that in this matter you should proclaim yourself the sovereign ruler. Your voice may be silenced in the roaring mart, you may be pushed aside by the mad crowd, but behind the silken folds that hide the sanctity of wedded joy you are the sovereign divinely ordained. By the necessities and consistencies of your being, by every argument from the exhaustless realm of natural history, by every law of nature and of God, you bear the badge of rightful sovereignty."

"The cords of love must be strong as death
　　Which hold and keep a heart,
No daisy chains, that snap in the breeze,
　　Or break with their weight apart;
For the pretty colors of youth's fair morn
　　Fade out from the noonday sky,
And blushing love in the roses born
　　Alas! with the roses die!

But the love, that when youth's morn is past,
  Still sweet and true survives,
Is the faith we need to lean upon
  In crises of our lives;
The love that shines in the eyes grown dim,
  In the voice that trembles, speaks;
And sees the roses that years ago
  Withered and dried in our cheeks;

That sheds a halo around us still,
  Of soft immortal light,
When we change youth's golden coronal
  For a crown of silver white;
A love for sickness and for health,
  For rapture and for tears;
That will live for us, and bear with us
  Through all our mortal years.

And such there is, there are lovers here,
  On the brink of the grave that stand,
Who shall cross to the hills beyond, and walk
  Forever hand in hand!
Pray, youth and maid, that your end be theirs
  Who are joined no more to part;
For death comes not to the living soul,
  Nor to the loving heart!"

Mothers and daughters, where can be found a group made up of more precious persons, the epitome of all that is beautiful, the personification of all that is good. With all my heart I say, God bless you, and I pray that he may do so, in the name of Jesus Christ. Amen.

Woman's Influence

I realize as I stand before you that I am probably filled with partiality and am highly susceptible to the presence of a group of such noble women. I admit I am partial. Just to meet with seven thousand or more sisters in the Church, actuated by one high ideal, is in itself an inspiration; and as I stand before you I am indeed very thankful that my training and experience through life have made me sympathetic with womankind. I owe that to my sainted mother and the experience in an ideal home with lovely sisters who contributed to the beauty of that home; and later, to the inspiration of a noble wife who has devoted her whole life to her home and her children. I acknowledge, too, the inspiration of the influence of circumspect, pure-minded women with whom I have associated in the Church. I have heard of women who have contributed in their lives to unpleasantness and discord, and who have chosen to revel in that which is low and vulgar, but I know nothing about that side of life and so when I say that this gathering is glorious I mean it. Here we have assembled the purest and best. Someone said, "God could not be everywhere, and so he gave us mothers." Well, that is partially true. God can be and is everywhere present with his Spirit, but I agree that there is no one in life who can make us feel nearer heaven than can mother, a true mother.

It is these thoughts I think, and this training, which have prompted the theme that I should like to present to you at the closing of this great conference, and I should like to preface that theme by reading a paragraph or two from the instructions given to the Relief Society by the Prophet Joseph Smith. Said he on April 28, 1842, when he faced the first group of members of the Relief Society:

I now turn the key in your behalf in the name of the Lord, and this Society shall rejoice, and knowledge and intelligence shall flow down from this time henceforth; this is the beginning of better days to the poor and needy, who shall be made to rejoice and pour forth blessings on your heads.

When you go home, never give a cross or unkind word to your husbands, but let kindness, charity, and love crown your works henceforward.

If the men had been there, I am sure the Prophet would have said, Don't go home and say cross, unkind words to your wife. That is what we say to you men who are here today.

Don't envy the finery and fleeting show of sinners, for they are in a miserable situation; but as far as you can, have mercy on them, for in a short time God will destroy them, if they will not repent and turn unto him.

Let your labors be mostly confined to those around you, in the circle of your own acquaintance, as far as knowledge is concerned it may extend to all the world; but your administering should be confined to the circle of your immediate acquaintance, and more especially to the members of the Relief Society. Those ordained to preside over and lead you are authorized to appoint the different officers, as the circumstances shall require. (History of the Church, Vol. IV, p. 607.)

I commend to you the reading of that entire address as given on that occasion. That blessing and promise of the influence of the Relief Society indicates how highly the Church of Jesus Christ esteems womankind. The placing of women on that lofty pedestal is a far cry from the time when she was bargained for as cattle and other chattels by her so-called superior companion, man. With the turning of that key came the promise that knowledge and intelligence shall flow down from this time henceforth, indicating the mighty influence to be wielded by this organization.

Another point: In emphasizing or referring to the duty and right of women to render aid to the sick, the Prophet said truthfully that none are "better qualified to give such service than our faithful and zealous sisters, whose hearts are full of faith, tenderness, sympathy, and compassion." Truly, "When pain and anguish wring the brow, A ministering angel thou."

One other point: The Prophet said as far as knowledge is concerned it may expand to all the world, and that is being rapidly realized. That thought is indicated graphically on your programs of this conference. There are stars, have you noticed, indicating where organizations of the Relief Society may be found in North and South America, Europe, South Africa, Australia, New Zealand, and on the isles of the sea, indicating how widespread is this organization in the comparatively short space of one century,—a well-organized channel through which knowledge and intelligence may flow continually. How wide-spread this influence for good is, only a comparatively few realize.

> They say that man is mighty,
> He governs land and sea;
> He wields a mighty scepter
> O'er lesser powers that be;
>
> But a mightier power and stronger
> Man from his throne has hurled;
> And the hand that rocks the cradle
> Is the hand that rules the world.
> (Wm. Ross Wallace)

What I am trying to point out and to emphasize on this glorious occasion is that the influence of the Relief Society is rapidly becoming world-wide; consequently, that influence carries with it great responsibilities. Do you remember reading what William George Jordan says about the influence of one individual.

> Into the hands of every individual is given a marvelous power for good or for evil,— the silent, unconscious, unseen influence of his life. This is simply the constant radiation of what a man really *is*, not what he *pretends* to be . . . Man cannot escape for one moment from this radiation of his character, this constantly weakening or strengthening of others. He cannot evade the responsibility by saying it is an unconscious influence. He can *select* the qualities that he will permit to be radiated. He can cultivate sweetness, calmness, trust, generosity, truth, justice, loyalty, nobility,—make them vitally active in his character,—and by these qualities he will constantly affect the world.

Nor can the Relief Society escape, even if it would, the responsibility of its ever-increasing influence.

In the quotation that I have just read from the Prophet appears this excellent admonition: "Let your labors be mostly confined to those around you in the circle of your own acquaintance." As far as knowledge is concerned, that will go to the whole world, but your "administering should be confined to the circle of your immediate acquaintance, and more especially to the members of the Relief Society." Too many overlook the immediate needs of those right around us and neglect our duties in our own homes.

In an excellent work entitled "The Simple Life," by Charles Wagner, we find this thought emphasized in the following lines:

> First, then, be of your own country, your own city, your own home, your own church, your own work-shop; then, if you can, set out from this to go beyond it. That is the plain and natural order, and a man must fortify himself with very bad reasons to arrive at reversing it.

Then he continues:

> Strange infirmity, that keeps us from seeing our fellows at our very doors! People widely read and far-travelled are often not acquainted with their fellow-citizens, great or small. Their lives de-

pend upon the cooperation of a multitude of beings whose lot remains to them quite indifferent. Not those to whom they owe their
knowledge and culture, not their rulers, nor those who serve them
and supply their needs, have ever attracted their attention . . . To
certain wives, their husbands are strangers, and conversely. There are
parents who do not know their children: their development, their
thoughts, the dangers they run, the hopes they cherish, are to them a
closed book. Many children do not know their parents, have no
suspicion of their difficulties and struggles, no conception of their
aims. And I am not speaking of those piteously disordered homes
where all the relations are false, but of honorable families. Only, all
these people are greatly preoccupied: each has his outside interest
that fills all his time. The distant duty—very attractive, I don't deny
—claims them entirely, and they are not conscious of the duty near
at hand. I fear they will have their trouble for their pains.

I emphasize this increasing power and influence of the
Relief Society and of womankind in general, having one
purpose in mind: *That increased attention be given and
more intensified efforts put forth to maintain and preserve
the dignity of motherhood.* With all my heart I commend
the message of Sister Spafford to perpetuate the truth that
home is the true foundation upon which is built the structure of true civilized Christian society.

Now how may this be done? I said my theme was suggested by the training and experience I have had throughout my life with noble women. First then, sisters, continue
to counteract by every means possible the false idea growing more and more prevalent that sexual relations before
marriage may be indulged in with impunity. Our girls are
the future mothers, and they should understand how far
from the truth is the claim made now quite generally that
there is no more sin in such indulgence than in kissing. I tell
you there is. Such teachings emanate from the enemy of true
happiness and are the teachings of Satan himself. Every
virtuous young woman, who anticipates the true glory and
responsibility of motherhood, senses the evil of such teachings and indulgence. So does every young man who honors
fatherhood and has in his heart even a spark of chivalry for

future mothers of men. In this principle of chastity in youth lies the basic foundation of happiness in the marriage relation.

Second, continue to apply your influence to give greater emphasis to the fundamental teaching that marriage is for the purpose of building a home and of rearing children. That is the best channel through which love may be truly expressed. In this connection, I refer to a letter that appeared in the Deseret News. In the Deseret News the other night appeared an article written by an unwise, misguided young wife, which indicates a view of life that should never be entertained by a Latter-day Saint girl. She tells how happy she is. She has been married five years. She and her husband are "crazy" about each other. They ski and skate and dance and drive nice places to dinner and go to the symphony and good movies and lectures, and they are having a good time, buying a little home that is beautifully decorated and furnished. She has a good job that pays her well, and he has a job. This girl writes: "Actually, we don't want a family and that is that. We both feel that children would be a kind of foreign element in this little world that is so perfect and so all our own."

I apologize even for reading it to you sisters, but I do commend the writer in the News who told her this, among other things:

> You may go against nature for a while when you are young and think you are getting away with it, but all the while she is exacting her fees. The wives who live for themselves and their husbands alone nearly always lose out. They lose their beauty, their alertness, their interest in life. Their faces are so often empty and vacuous, even if pretty. Believe it or not, they very often lose their husbands, who unconsciously grow to miss the things that Nature knows a woman should be giving to her husband.
>
> On the other hand, those who sacrifice and suffer a bit develop the beauty that expression gives to faces, the beauty of responsiveness, of a deep, inner joy that makes even a plain woman attractive—the amazing beauty of fulfillment. And that love you are so anxious to preserve—you haven't the least idea what an enormous quantity

of it there is. It grows bigger and stronger and more everlasting with every baby a happily married wife gives to her husband.

Wifehood is glorious, but motherhood is sublime. There are those who can't be blessed with motherhood, but those who can and who take the attitude of this girl are not a credit to their sex.

Third, sisters, apply your influence to have more religion in your homes. Every Latter-day Saint home should have evidence therein of their membership. Children growing up should come in contact with things religious. I ask you now, have you in your home the Church works, ready at hand so that the children going to Sunday School, Primary, Mutual Improvement, and so on, can turn to them when they need help? Have you a religious verse in the bedroom of the boys, or a saying of the Savior? I wonder if you have a good painting of the Savior hanging up over the bed of your boy. Little things like these give to home a religious atmosphere.

Our children hunger for true religion and there is no better place to instill it into their hearts than the home.

Sisters, my heart is full of gratitude to you and blessing that you may continue to exercise the great world-wide influence that the Prophet has blessed you to exercise, and may the exercise of that influence be felt in your own neighborhood. May your daughters so live that their children may say of them, as you and I can say of our mothers, that

> The noblest thought my soul can claim,
> The noblest words my tongue can frame,
> Unworthy are to praise the name,
> More precious than all others.
> An infant, when her love first came,
> A man I find it still the same,
> Reverently I breathe her name,
> The precious name of Mother.

Section Two —

Youth, the Home and the Family

Youth and a Better Future

"Whether it be right in the sight of God to hearken unto you more than unto God, judge ye.

"For we cannot but speak the things which we have seen and heard."

❖   ❖   ❖   ❖   ❖

"For there is none other name under heaven given among men, whereby we must be saved."

Forty-eight years ago I sat as a graduate in the U of U Class of 1897!

I remember with what compassionate feelings—feelings almost akin to pity—I regarded the poor, old, gray-haired men of seventy and seventy-five! As I looked forward to attaining their maturity, what a long distance it seemed between our joyous twenties, and the decrepit seventies!

Now, having reached that milestone, I wonder at the immaturity of youth to think that a man only three score and ten is old! Surely, age must have been older then than now!

Of one thing, however, we may be sure: That

"Years rush by us like the wind,
We see not whence the eddy comes,
Nor whitherward it is tending
And we seem, ourselves, to witness their flight

Without a sense that we are changed.
Yet time is beguiling man of his strength
As the winds rob the trees of their foliage."

It is your life ahead of you, and of the responsibilities it entails that I have in mind as I speak of youth and a better future.

The scriptural passage that I have quoted illustrates three human qualities or virtues characteristic of true leadership. These are (1) a consciousness of a righteous cause, (2) an invincible resolution to uphold it, and, (3) the assurance of the one safe guide.

Notwithstanding the frequent declarations of many who see only calamities ahead of us, it is our intent to consider the making of a better world. It is surprising how many thoughtful people are speaking and writing ominously of the future. Hayden, for example, warningly writes:

"Today, as never before, mankind is seeking social betterment. Today, as seldom if ever before, human society is threatened with disintegration, if not complete chaos. All the ancient evils of human relationships, injustice, selfishness, abuse of strength, become sinister and terrible when reinforced by the vast increase of material power.

"The soul of man cowers, starved and fearful, in the midst of a civilization grown too complex for any mind to visualize or to control."

And Mr. John C. Mirriam, president of the Carnegie Institute, writes, "Changes that have taken place over the whole world in the past two centuries, make it evident that we are approaching a crisis in which either civilization will collapse or we must discover the formulae necessary for establishing such an understanding among nations as will permit continuity in peace and in constructive effort."

I am hopeful that the younger generation will eventually recognize such "formulae." It is at least justifiable to express such a hope in the presence of youth. The future is yours to make or to mar as you choose. The world is sick of strife; it yearns for peace. Only the perverseness of human nature can darken the oncoming years.

Youth—conviction—courage—a combination potentially capable of determining the kind of world we shall live in. Though not the wisest, youth is the best, the most radiant time of life.

> "All possibilities are in its hands
> No danger daunts it, and no foe withstands,
> In its sublime audacity of faith,
> 'Be thou removed,' it to the mountain saith,
> And with sublime feet, secure and proud,
> Ascends the ladder leaning on the cloud."

The Future

Occasionally, even during the tender years, the reality of the present is slightly disturbed by fancy flights of thought into the uncertain future—and by the time graduation comes the fact that you must take a part therein becomes as sure as the course of the sun toward the western sky. Facing that future, as you do today, you might well exclaim with King Henry IV: "O heavens! that one might read the book of fate, and see the revolution of the times!"

Even while the glories of youthful prime gladden your hearts and brighten your hopes with anticipated success, there rests unfelt upon your shoulders the weight of a coming responsibility. Yours the challenge to shape the future. Into your hands and in the hands of a million other youths will be placed the banner of civilization.

Courage

To carry it successfully forward will demand courage, or what Luke calls "the boldness of Peter and John"—that quality of mind which enables one to encounter danger and to overcome difficulties. It is a virtue admired by everybody. Our souls have been stirred, and our eyes filled with tears as we have heard of the military courage of our boys in uniform. We thrill even at spontaneous courage as it leaps forth in time of crisis. But the courage I would have youth possess, as they take their part in the better future, is neither physical nor military—it is the fearlessness to act in accordance with their convictions. Courage to do right whether alone or in public—courage to be true to a trust.

Youth Responsibility

There are approximately a million full-time and part-time college students enrolled in the United States. Nearly forty-five thousand will graduate this May and June. If it were possible to obtain the dominantly motivating idea of that group, we could pretty definitely determine the future of our government. "The destiny of any nation," says Goethe, "at any given time, may be determined by the thoughts of the young men under twenty-five."

In the "Lady of the Lake," when Roderick Dhu would summon his clansmen to battle, he placed the fiery cross in the hands of a valiant henchman. No mountain crest, no trembling bog or false morass could halt this trusted courier in the speedy performance of his assignment. His duty performed, he passed the fiery torch to the second courier, the heir of Duncan's line, who, leaving the funeral rites of his deceased sire, accepted the trust, and even in the face of death paused not an instant until he had placed the symbol in the hands of his successor. Though Norman's bridal vows had just been spoken, Clan Alpine's cause, his chieftain's trust, took precedence.

As to these young men was successively given the charge to summon Clan Alpine's warriors, so there has come successively to youth through the ages, a transferred trust to carry forward the cause of humanity. The passing of this responsibility from one generation to another, unlike Scott's story, has been imperceptible, and lingered along sometimes for years, but the responsibility has been as definite as that which passed from Clan Alpine's courier to courier.

Nor can youth evade that responsibility if they would. When it comes they may as recreants refuse to go forward, or even turn in an opposite direction as traitors to their trust, but onward or backward, each generation marks success or failure in man's struggle upward.

Early Training Determines Progression or Retrogression

Whether youth's contributive acts will be progressive or retrogressive, cultural or beastly, will depend largely upon the kind of training given by those who place the banner in their hands.

A striking example of this has been enacted as if in drama within the last quarter of a century. Blinded by false ideals and fired by vain ambition, a paranoiac, with the power of a once mighty nation behind him, said: "The plow will be the sword, and the bread of posterity will be watered by the tears of war." And again, . . . "What I am after is a violently active, dominating, intrepid, brutal youth. There must be no weakness or tenderness in it. I want to see once more in its eyes the gleam of pride and independence of the beast of prey."

It seems incredible that leaders of a reputably cultured people could, in less than a generation, step back to barbarism and revel in bestiality. And that, too, in an age when advancement in material sciences exceeds all other ages in the world's history.

Civilization Imperiled

As a consequence of that return to barbarism nations grapple at one another's throats in a death struggle. Millions have been killed, wounded, and unaccounted for. Homes have been blown to splinters, and their occupants left to wander helplessly and aimlessly, facing starvation and death. Men defeated have been compelled to labor for their conquerers. Nations once free have lost their independence. Millions of people have been forced to surrender all guarantees of personal liberty. Art galleries, monuments, historic buildings, and cities containing treasures of untold value to humanity have been ruthlessly destroyed. The holocaust of war continues and innocent men, women and children are being maimed, mangled, and murdered. Man has subdued the earth, harnessed the waves, conquered the air. His slightest whisper encircles the globe in a second. He controls the mightiest forces of nature and commands them to contribute to his comforts and whims. But all this material advancement has brought man neither safety, security, nor peace. These marvelous inventions which make New York and London eight-hour neighbors; which enable us to sit in comfortable chairs, and see the struggle of nations and the crumbling of empires—all these are not yet making secure the progress and happiness of man. Something is lacking. What is it?

Unifying Ideal Lacking

They lack the unfailing guide—a divine ideal. "The world has many good people in it today, more, we are ready to believe, than ever before," writes Dr. Batten, the author of "The Social Task of Christianity." "But these people possess no unifying ideal, no organic principle, no coherent view of life, no synthetic program of action. Society is coming to self-consciousness, and is beginning to take note of its troubles and needs. But it has no clear sense of direction, no organizing impulse, no all-inclusive ideal, no mighty impulsion . . .

"The great need of today is some social ideal which shall put meaning into man's life, and courage into his heart, some synthesis which shall unite mankind into one body and marshal them as one army to confront the ills of the world, and to seek the perfection of society."

And Dr. Charles A. Ellwood in "Man's Social Destiny" confirms this view as follows:

"Our civilization is imperiled today simply because it is ill-balanced. Our spiritual culture lags so far behind our material culture in its development that we have no adequate control over the latter. Our science, our education, and our government can do much to help correct this lag in our spiritual development. But in the main this must be done, if done at all, by religion and by the Church. For religion is the creator and the conservator of our social ideals; and the Church is their chief propagator."

Conquest or Chaos

A million young Americans, and millions of others have given their lives that the world may have another chance to live decently. Theirs is the conquest, ours the responsibility. Man makes war—man can end war if he will.

From the hands of those million dead come to the youth now living the banner and charge to carry forward to yet greater conquests.

The dominant motive in man and in nations is still self-preservation, self-advancement, self-comfort without consideration for the welfare of others, material achievements, accumulation of money, accentuation of power at the subjugation, even the enslavement of the individual. From the root of selfishness spring all the pestilential vices that disrupt the harmony of human relationships. Envy, hatred, greed, bigotry, the exercising of unrighteous dominion in governing men and crushing them, unrestrained passion, ungoverned appetites, drunkenness and debauchery—these are enemies to be conquered in the better future.

You may call it a Utopian dream, if you will, but selfishness must be subdued before mankind can experience peace. No peace or freedom can come to this world so long as men live only for themselves. Self-preservation is the first law of nature, but it is not a law of spiritual growth. He who lets selfishness and his passions rule him binds his soul in slavery, but he who, in the majesty of spiritual strength, uses his physical tendencies and yearnings, and his possessions to serve purposes higher than personal indulgence and comfort, takes the first step toward the happy and useful life.

This truth was taught not only "in the beginning" when the gospel was first revealed to man, but also when Jesus began his earthly ministry. On the Mount of Temptation was enacted the first scene in Christ's earthly drama of the abundant life. There he resisted the challenge to gratify his appetite; he turned aside the appeal to his vanity and pride; he scorned the bribe of worldly wealth and power as in spiritual victory he said to the Tempter: "Get thee hence." Only thus by the brilliant triumph of the spirit over the flesh can we hope for a better world.

Human Nature Must Be Changed

Your fellow alumni of four years ago accepted the challenge, and have met in deadly conflict dictatorship and inhuman aggression. Thus far they have won a glorious victory, but many will fight no more. Others are too maimed to continue longer the struggle.

Yours now the task to carry on!

Down through the ages men have retreated before the formidable enemies you now face; and thinkers, and some philosophers declare hopelessly that these enemies cannot be conquered, except only by changing human nature, and that, they insist, cannot be done.

I believe with the English writer, Beverly Nichols, that it can be done, and that "human nature can be changed, here and now."

"Human nature *has* been changed in the past.

"Human nature *must* be changed on an enormous scale, in the future, unless the world is to be drowned in its own blood.

"And only Christ can change it . . ."

Need of A Guiding Light

In the incident depicted by our text, Peter courageously declares what we shall think, what we shall declare: That "there is none other name under heaven given among men, whereby we must be saved." Molders of a better future need the assurance that Christ is the unfailing guide.

The Nazi creed advanced the conception that a self-centered, "super-race" might dominate the world by the application of material achievements divorced from religious or even ethical considerations. "It accented power, authority, and obedience, but denied human equality and the worth of the individual." Nazi youth fought for these false ideals with fanatical zeal.

Courage alone is not sufficient; a firm conviction is not sufficient. There must be the assurance that the conviction is in harmony with justice, with truth and righteousness.

Dominant Principles in the Better Future

At San Francisco there were representatives from 50 nations earnestly and conscientiously sought to formulate plans that would end war and establish a lasting peace. There assembled were men of different political views, and of varying opinions as to the best form of government. But no matter what their political differences, if they but applied fundamental Christian principles, for example, the age-old formula "do unto others as you would have others do unto you," the objective of the conference would have been attained.

Likewise others of Christ's teachings, containing unchanging principles eternally operative in this changing world, should be applied by all who would work sincerely for a better future. For example, consider how contributive to the ending of war would be the application of individuals and nations of just two of the divine injunctions relating to arbitration and mutual happiness:

"Moreover if thy brother shall trespass against thee go and tell him his fault between thee and him alone; if he shall hear thee, thou hast gained thy brother.

"But if he will not hear thee, then take with thee one or two more, that in the mouth of two or three witnesses every word may be established." (Matthew 18:15, 16.)

Though man may not overcome selfishness entirely, if, as conflicts arise, he would but subdue it sufficiently to submit to Christ's principle of arbitration, brute force, as manifested in this military conflict would cease.

Again, Jesus taught that men and women fail to live truly, and really amount to nothing unless they have spirituality. The spiritual force underlies everything, and without it nothing worthwhile can be accomplished. "Spiritual needs can be met only by spiritual means. All government, laws, methods, and organizations are of no value unless men and women are filled with truth, righteousness, and mercy. Material things have no power to raise the sunken spirit. Gravitation, electricity, and steam are great forces, but they are all powerless to change the motives of men and women. The wealth of a Rockefeller cannot heal a broken heart, and the wisdom of all our universities cannot turn into the paths of righteousness a wayward soul. Men can be born again only through religion."

Young men and women, the future awaits you! It is yours! If you would end war and give peace to the world, you have campaigns to organize, and conquests to achieve. These are campaigns planned for the establishments of justice—these are conquests of the soul. Whether it is better to walk along the easy road of selfishness and indulgence than to strive through self-mastery and service for the realm of spirituality you must decide. "Whether it is better to serve God than man, judge ye."

In the words of John Oxenham:

"God grant us wisdom in these coming days,
To pledge our souls with nobler, loftier life,
    To win the world to his fair sanctities,
To bind the nations in a pact of peace,
    And free the soul of life for finer loyalties.

Not since Christ died upon his lonely cross,
    Has time such prospect held of life's new birth;
Not since the world of chaos first was born
    Has man so clearly visaged hope of a new earth.

Not of our own might can we hope to rise
    Above the ruts and soilures of the past,
But, with his help who did the first earth build,
    With hearts courageous we may fairer build this last.

Thoughts for a Summer Day

Earnestly I urge parents to gather their families around them and to instruct them in truth and righteousness and in family love and loyalty. The home is the basis of a righteous life, and no other instrumentality can take its place nor fulfill its essential functions. The problems of these difficult times cannot better be solved in any other place, by any other agency, by any other means, than by love and righteousness, precept and example, and devotion to duty in the home.

May you be blessed in teaching and caring for and drawing near to you those whom God has entrusted to you and in watching over your own. As you do so, love at home and obedience to parents will increase; faith will develop in the hearts of the youth of Israel; and they will gain power to combat evil influences and temptations and to choose righteousness and peace and thus be assured an eternal place in the family circle of our Father.

Advice to Youth

We hear a good deal of talk about our young people these days. Some say that they are indifferent, that they are losing their interest in the Church. I do not agree with this accusation. I realize that temptations were never stronger than they are today, but the young people who resist these temptations deserve all the greater credit.

O youth of the Church, think of the responsibility of keeping your name unsullied! Think of bringing comfort and happiness to the parents who gave you mortality! There is the fundamental thought that will lead you toward God and worship in true religion. He is a recreant indeed who, to gratify his appetite or his passions, will bring a stain upon the honored name he bears or sorrow to the hearts of his parents. If a youth comes from such a home, with such right thoughts as respecting the rights of other persons and of society, he will not go far wrong in his acts toward his fellowmen.

These Are the Tender Years

Who are these children that come to gladden the hearts of man and wife and make them father and mother? More than once I have used this definition: The child is as a sweet new blossom of humanity, fresh fallen from God's home, to flower here on earth.

That many agencies are affecting the child you well know. But in The Church of Jesus Christ of Latter-day Saints, first comes the home. Upon fathers and mothers the Lord placed one of the greatest responsibilities that can come to human beings. Hear again what he says:

". . . inasmuch as parents have children in Zion, or in any of her stakes which are organized, that teach them not to understand the doctrine of repentance, faith in Christ the Son of the living God, and of baptism and the gift of the Holy Ghost by the laying on of the hands, when eight years old, the sin be upon the heads of the parents." (D&C 68:25.)

I believe that parents generally are doing this, yet I am convinced that there is still much opportunity for improvement in this regard. The outlines of your family evening programs will enable you to do more.

Teach by Example

Make every hour, every moment that you spend together as a family precious indeed. Your example will teach your children more effectively than what you say. Out of our homes come the future leaders of the Church and of the government.

There are little cords of influence that are binding and shaping the little babe's life, the little boy's life, until youth begins to be bound by the cable and later in life by the chain—the chain of habit.

Forces that are throwing out these little cords into the children's lives are the home, the playground, the school, the gang, and society. Unnumbered thousands of people are working today, trying to direct the influences of the school, the playground, society, and business so that these cords will lead youth in the right direction. All these forces are outside the home.

But the first and most important agency in child development and education is the family. "The virtuous home is the basis of all national prosperity."

"The strength of the nation, especially of a republican nation," says one writer, "is in the intelligent, well-ordered homes of the people.

"To make men out of boys, and women out of girls, there is no place like home."

Influences of Home

What are these fundamental home influences in child life? I shall name first physical environment. The physical security of the child is dependent upon the protection largely of his home. A good home involves a fair knowledge on the part of the parents, and especially of the mother, of needed physical care, proper nutrition, hygienic living, preventing disease, adequate shelter, proper clothing, pure food, including water, fresh air, and protection from accident. A good home requires good health habits through parents' instruction and example in eating, and proper exercise. I need not dwell upon this phase of the fundamental conditions of a good home; if we can have properly ventilated homes, if we know what kind of food to give to the children, we are contributing to the health and happiness of the home.

I wish to offer as the second influence opportunities for education. Parents must lead in the cultural development and show a willingness to answer questions. A child who is asking questions is contributing happiness to your life. Fortunate is the child whose parents can leave their work occasionally to encourage him in constructive play or to spend a few hours with him in nature study. Who can tell the cultural value of such association of a child with his mother—a child who beholds the glorious sunset, the beauties of nature, and who sees the snow-capped peaks through his father's or his mother's eyes? In later life he will never look at either without thinking of his parents. These are the tender cords that lead youth into paths of tenderness and humanity.

Let us inculcate into the lives of our children a nobility of soul that leads them instinctively to love the beautiful, the genuine, the virtuous, and as instinctively to turn from the ugly, the spurious, and the vile.

Within the Family Group

These are important, the physical and cultural environment, but I have merely mentioned them to lead you up to what I consider the most important, even though it is the most abstract in a child's life. I refer to the personal influence of the home. The most important factor in child life is in the interaction of personalities within the family group.

Who can measure the influence of the home? Health is important, and physical environment and culture equally important, but most important of all is that combination of personal influence centered in sacredness in the mother. If we can only get the spirit of the gospel in our homes— just get our boys and girls to feel that love for parents and

for each other and love for the gospel through mother—
our problems are solved.

God help us to put into our homes, to a great degree,
the ideals of the gospel of Jesus Christ. To be practical
let us have these boys kneel with us more frequently in
prayer. That is one practical thing to do. Through family
prayer let parents and children come into the presence of
God.

Many years ago there was a story told in one of our
early school books about some young people who were
sailing down the river towards Niagara Falls. A man on
the shore cried out to them: "Young men, Ahoy, the
rapids are below you!"

But they heeded not his warning call until they
realized too late that they were in the midst of the rapids.
With all the power at their command they failed to turn
their boat upstream, "So," said the man who tried to warn
them, "shrieking and cursing, over they went!"

The lesson left an indelible impression upon me, but
today it seems incomplete. It is one thing to stand on the
shore and cry, "Young men, Ahoy—there is danger ahead,"
and it is another thing to row into the stream, and, if possible, get into the boat with the young men, and by companionship, by persuasion, by legitimate force, when necessary, turn the boat from the rapids. Too many of us are
satisfied to stand on the shore and cry, "There is danger
ahead."

This morning, I have in mind giving a warning to all
young people relating to three dangers threatening the success and happiness of Youth:

First, the pernicious habit of smoking cigarets.

Second, the increasing number of divorces.

Third, the tendency to hold less sacred the moral
standards.

The Habit of Smoking

In 1833 the Prophet Joseph Smith received a revelation "showing forth the order and will of God in the temporal salvation of all saints in the last days." (D&C 89:2.) It relates to the physical, the intellectual, the moral, and the spiritual nature of man. It deals particularly with the relation of man's appetite to health and vigor. A person's reaction to his appetites and impulses when they are aroused gives the measure of that person's character. In such reactions are revealed the man's power to govern, or his forced servility to yield. That phase of the Word of Wisdom, therefore, which refers to intoxicants, drugs, and stimulants, goes deeper than the ill effects upon the body, and strikes at the very root of character building itself.

Strong Drinks and Tobacco Not Good for Man

The revelation says that strong drinks and tobacco are not good for man. This is a clear, definite statement which has stood the test of well over a century. It was made by a man only twenty-seven years of age, who from the standpoint of human learning, knew but little about physiology, hygiene, or the relation of mind and body to character and spirituality. His knowledge came from inspiration. With a conviction unwavering, with an assurance that the statement would stand all tests and experiments, he declared that strong drinks and tobacco, excepting only when used externally, are not good for man.

During the last one hundred years, the marvelous advance of science has made it possible for man to determine by experiments the ill effect of intoxicants and drugs upon the nerves and tissues of the human body. Observation and experiment have demonstrated their effects upon character. All such experiments and observations have proved the truth of the young man's statement: "Strong drinks and tobacco are not good for man."

Respect for another's rights and property is fundamental in good government. It is a mark of refinement in any individual; it is a fundamental Christian virtue. Nicotine seems to dull, if not to kill completely this trait of true culture, and women unfortunately have become its pitiable victims, and the worst offenders in society. There are still a few public conveyances that carry non-smoking compartments; a few eating places with signs, "No Smoking." In violation of such placards, it is not infrequent, however, to see a woman with utter disregard for the feelings of her fellow-passengers, among the first in an airplane or on a train to light a cigaret.

Many public buildings are often littered with burnt-out matches and stubs of cigarets and cigars. Most costly fires in hotels, apartment houses and homes are started by burning cigarets carelessly dropped or thrown aside.

If men and women must smoke, and it seems that many are now slaves to that habit, then for the sake of cleanliness and neatness, as well as of consideration for others, let them refrain from marring furniture, carpets, etc., and from strewing ashes and cigaret stubs in buildings where people assemble either for pleasure or instruction.

I appeal to young men and women everywhere to refrain from this obnoxious habit, not only for the effect it has on their character, but also because of the alarming proofs from doctors and scientists that it is one of the chief causes of cancer.

Increasing Number of Divorces

Another threat to our society is the increasing number of divorces and the tendency to look upon marriage as a mere contract that may be severed at the first difficulty or misunderstanding that may arise.

One of our most precious possessions is our families. The domestic relations precede, and, in our present existence, are worth more than all other social ties. They give the first throb to the heart and unseal the deep fountains of its love. Home is the chief school of human virtues. Its responsibilities, joys, sorrows, smiles, tears, hopes, and solicitude form the chief interests of human life.

To make a happy fireside clime
To weans and wife,
That's the true pathos and sublime
O' human life.

                              Robert Burns

When one puts business or pleasure above his home, he that moment starts on the downgrade to soul-weakness. When the club becomes more attractive to any man than his home, it is time for him to confess in bitter shame that he has failed to measure up to the supreme opportunity of his life and flunked in the final test of true manhood. No other success can compensate for failure in the home. The poorest shack in which love prevails over a united family is of greater value to God and future humanity than any other riches. In such a home God can work miracles and will work miracles.

Pure hearts in a pure home are always in whispering distance of heaven.

In the light of scripture, ancient and modern, we are justified in concluding that Christ's ideal pertaining to marriage is the unbroken home, and conditions that cause divorce are violations of his divine teaching.

Marriage is a sacred relationship entered into for purposes that are well recognized—primarily for the rearing of a family.

I know of no other place where happiness abides more securely than in the home. It is possible to make home a bit of heaven. Indeed, I picture heaven as a continuation of the ideal home. Some man has said: "Home filled with contentment is one of the highest hopes of this life."

An ever-decreasing birthrate, and an increasing divorce rate are ominous signs threatening the stability of the home and the perpetuity of any nation. In order to lessen the breaking-up of homes, we should substitute the present tendency toward a low view of marriage by the lofty view which Jesus Christ gives it. Let us look upon marriage as a sacred obligation and a covenant that is eternal or that may be made eternal.

Young people of both sexes should be taught the responsibilities and ideals of marriage so that they may realize that marriage involves obligation and is not an arrangement to be terminated at pleasure. They should be taught that pure love between the sexes is one of the noblest things on earth and the bearing and rearing of children the highest of all human duties. In this regard, it is the duty of parents to set an example in the home that children may see and absorb the sacredness of family life and the responsibility associated therewith.

The number of broken marriages can be reduced if couples realize even before they approach the altar that marriage is a state of mutual service, a state of giving as well as of receiving, and that each must give of himself or herself to the utmost.

The most vicious enemy to home life is immorality.

Of this evil, Victor Hugo writes impressively:

"The holy law of Jesus Christ governs our civilization; but it does not yet permeate it; it is said that slavery has disappeared from European civilization. That is a mistake. It still exists; but it preys now only upon woman, and it is called prostitution."

This corroding evil is just as demoralizing to men as to women. In The Church of Jesus Christ of Latter-day Saints there is no double standard of morality. The young man should approach the marriage altar just as fit for fatherhood as his sweetheart is worthy of motherhood.

Chastity, not indulgence during the pre-marital years, is the source of harmony and happiness in the home, and the chief contributing factor to the health and perpetuity of the race. Loyalty, dependability, confidence, trust, love of God, and fidelity to man are associated with this diadem in the crown of virtuous womanhood and virile manhood. The word of the Lord to his Church is: "Keep yourself unspotted from the sins of the world." (See James 1:27; D&C 59:9.)

Foundation of a Noble Character

The foundation of a noble character is integrity. By this virtue the strength of a nation, as of an individual, may be judged. No nation will become great whose trusted officers will pass legislation for personal gain, who will take advantage of public office for personal preferment, or to gratify vain ambition, or who will, through forgery, chicanery, and fraud, rob the government, or be false in office to a public trust.

Honesty, sincerity of purpose, must be dominant traits of character in leaders of a nation that would be truly great.

"I hope," said George Washington, "that I may ever have virtue and firmness enough to maintain what I consider to be the most enviable of all titles—the character of an honest man."

It was Washington's character more than his brilliancy of intellect that made him the choice of all as their natural leader when the thirteen original colonies decided to sever their connection with the mother country As one in eulogy to the father of our country truly said: "When he appeared among the eloquent orators, the ingenious thinkers, the vehement patriots of the Revolution, his modesty and temperate profession could not conceal his superiority; he at once, by the very nature of his character, was felt to be their leader."

Let us in The Church of Jesus Christ of Latter-day Saints, as citizens of this beloved land, use our influence to see that men and women of upright character, of unimpeachable honor, are elected to office; that our homes are kept unpolluted and unbroken by infidelity; that children therein will be trained to keep the commandments of the Lord, to be honest, true, chaste, benevolent, and virtuous, and to do good to all men. (See Thirteenth Article of Faith.)

Cherishing such ideals, we can with all our hearts say with the poet Longfellow:

> Thou, too, sail on, O Ship of State Sail on,
>   O Union, strong and great!
> Humanity with all its fears,
> With all the hopes of future years,
> Is hanging breathless on thy fate!

Blueprint for Family Living

Many years ago, President Joseph F. Smith then of the First Presidency, later president of the Church, said in a commencement address at the old Latter-day Saints College: "Educate yourself not only for time but also for eternity. The latter of the two is the more important. Therefore when we shall have completed the studies of time, and enter upon the commencement ceremonies of the great hereafter, we will find our work is not finished, but just begun."

With all my heart I believe that the best place to prepare for that kind of eternal life is in the home. But home life pays earthly dividends as well. I know of no place other than home where true happiness can be found in this life.

Every home has both body and spirit. You may have a beautiful house with all the decorations that modern art can give or wealth bestow. You may have all the outward forms that will please the eye and yet not have a home. It is not home without love. It may be a hovel, a log hut, a tent, a wickiup, if you have the right spirit within, the true love of Christ, and love for one another—father and mother for the children, children for parents, husband and wife for each other—you have the true life of the home that Latter-day Saints build and which they are striving to establish.

In such a home God has placed upon parents the responsibility of instilling eternal principles into the minds of children. Church schools, Sunday Schools, Mutual Improvement Associations, Primary, and priesthood quorums are all helps in government, established here to assist in the upbuilding and guidance of the youth, but none of these—great and important factors as they are in the lives of our youth—can supplant the permanence and the influence of the parents in the home.

The home is truly the first unit of society, and parenthood is next to Godhood. The relationship of the children to the parents should be one which would enable those children to carry out ideal citizenship as they become related to the state and to the larger forms of society. The secret of good membership in the Church or good citizenship in the nation lies in the home. If and when the time ever comes that parents shift to the state the responsibility of rearing their children, the stability of the nation will be undermined, and its impairment and disintegration will have begun.

The character of the child is formed largely during the first twelve years of his life. It is estimated that in that period the child spends sixteen times as many waking hours in the home as in the school and more than a hundred times as many hours in the home as in the church. Each child is, to a great degree, what he is because of the ever-constant influence of home environment and the careful or neglectful training of parents.

A good home requires good health habits through parents' instruction and example in eating, sleeping, and proper exercise.

Home is the best place for the child to learn self-control, to learn that he must submerge himself for the good of another. Then when he gets out into society where he meets with his playmates, he will better realize that he must give them respect and consideration. The home is the best place in which to develop obedience which nature and society will later demand.

Homes are made permanent through love. Oh, then, let love abound. Though you fall short in some material matters, study and work and pray to hold your children's love.

A child has the right to feel that in his home he has a place of refuge, a place of protection from the dangers and evils of the outside world. Family unity and integrity are necessary to supply this need.

I wish to emphasize the fact that our homes should be more attractive and that more of our amusements should be centered in the home.

Establish and maintain your family hours always. Stay close to your children. Pray, play, work, and worship together. This is the counsel of the Church. Unhesitatingly, I affirm that my home life from babyhood to the present time has been the greatest factor in giving me moral and spiritual standards and in shaping the courses of my life. Sincerity, courtesy, consistency in word and in deed, unselfishness are dominant virtues exemplified in the lives of my parents and others in the two homes, my father's and my own, that have proved a safeguard and guidance.

Do you know how I spell Home?

Honor

Obedience

Mutual service

Eternity of the marriage relation

—these spell home, and they comprehend the spirit in which the principles of life and salvation should be taught to children.

The dearest possession a man has is his family. In the divine assurance that family ties transcend the boundaries of death and continue throughout endless ages of eternity, I find inspiration. When the union of loved ones bears the seal of the Holy Priesthood, it is as eternal as love, as everlasting as spirit. Such a union is based on the doctrine of immortality and eternal progress of man.

Ten Contributing Factors to
a Happy Home

I should like to name, this afternoon, a few conditions that contribute to a happy home, this not only to the young people, but to you, my fellow parents—husbands and wives.

FIRST: As a contributing factor to a happy home—and this to you young folks—ever keep in mind that you begin to lay the foundation of a happy home in your pre-marital life. Some young folks say, "We shall sow our wild oats now while we are young, and settle down later." You know, as I do, that if you sow wild oats you are going to reap wild oats. "Whatsoever a man soweth, that shall he also reap." (Gal. 6:7.)

There is spreading generally throughout the world, and too much so throughout the Church, an idea that girls may have the same freedom in promiscuous relations as the world has generally condoned with impunity to men. Do not be deceived! Young men and women should ever keep in mind that chastity during young manhood and womanhood is the highest ideal they can cherish, having happiness and home life in mind.

Resistance—self-mastery during youth—is a contributing factor to manhood. It is not a weakness in man. And I am sure you all agree with me it is the crowning glory of womanhood. It is the foundation of a happy home. It is one of the contributing factors to the perpetuation of our race. I care not what certain sociologists say in regard to the necessity of indulgence. I know the truth whereof I speak when I plead with young men and young women who look forward to the greatest source of happiness in life to keep themselves loyal and true to their future husband or wife.

SECOND: Choose your mate by judgment and inspiration, as well as by emotion. Farmers know the value of breeding. They are very careful to choose the right kind of stock. They know that profit lies in it. Inheritance —breeding in the human family—is just as important or more so. I shall not take time to elaborate upon that.

THIRD: Approach marriage with the lofty view it merits. Marriage is ordained of God. It is not something to be entered into lightly, terminated at pleasure, or ended at the first difficulty that might arise. In our Church we have the highest idea of marriage ever given to man. We admonish young men and young women so to live as to be worthy to enter the House of God.

That means that they have, during their teens and courtship, been true to the ideals of their future wife and future husband. And as they stand and plight each other's troth, they do so with the assurance on the part of the young husband that she who now gives her life to him is as worthy of motherhood as the purest of virgins; and that he to whom she gives her life in marriage is just as worthy of fatherhood; that the source, the spring of life, is pure and unpolluted; and that if children bless that union, those children have a kingly birth, unshackled by disease.

FOURTH: The noblest purpose of marriage is procreation. Home is children's natural nursery. "I love these little people," said Charles Dickens, "and it is not a slight thing when they who are so fresh from God love us."

The Savior himself rebuked his disciples when mothers and children crowded to caress him or touch his garment. "Suffer the little children," he said, "and forbid them not to come unto me, for of such is the kingdom of heaven."

You know what a growing tendency there is in the Church now to limit families. Happiness in the home is enhanced by the children around the fireside, climbing on father's knee, receiving the caresses from mother. I think this expresses that better than I. I think it is Frances H. Lee who said:

> What's the happiest time of a woman's life?
> Is it her school-girl days
> When thoughts and hopes half-formed are rife
> Amid her glad wild ways?
> Ah! No, not then.
> The happiest time is yet to come—but when?
>
> What's the happiest time of a woman's life?
> Is it her virgin prime,
> When love awakes, ere she's a wife,
> Is it that golden time?
> Ah! No, not then.
> A happier time is coming yet—but when?
>
> What's the happiest time of a woman's life?
> Is it her wedding day,
> When vows are pledged, and as a wife
> She's bound to him to aye?
> Say, is it then?
> Ah! No, not yet; the time is coming. When?
>
> The happiest time of a woman's life?
> Ah! It has come at last;
> For hark! I hear a little voice,
> And footsteps toddling fast;
> And the happiest hours, I know, are these,
> When children are playing about her knees.

The FIFTH factor contributing to happiness is this: Let the spirit of reverence pervade the home, so that if the Savior happened to call unexpectedly, he could be invited to stay and not be made to feel out of his element.

I am reminded of a young son who had just married, who invited his father to see the new home. He showed him the kitchen, modern equipment, the living room, dining room, the bedrooms, spacious closets and all. As they finished the tour of the house, the father said, "Very good, very good, but I see no signs of God in your home." The young man went back and went through his house and said:

"Father was right. I have no sign of true religion." There was no picture of the Savior; there was no model of religion. He changed some of his decorations. Reverence at the home, right in the beginning, is a fundamental, contributing factor to happiness in that home.

"Prayer in the home will make a man cease from sin, or sin will make a man cease from prayer."

SIXTH: Let husband or wife never speak in loud tones to each other, "Unless the house is on fire."

In naming this fundamental factor, I mention swearing, a vice which should be so foreign from a Latter-day Saint home that even the thought of it should not come into mind.

SEVENTH: Learn the value of self-control. I do not know who wrote the words, but there is a sentence in a poem:

> Boys flying kites haul in their white-winged birds,
> You can't do that when you're flying words.
> Thoughts unexpressed may sometimes fall back dead,
> But God himself can't kill them when they're said.

I believe lack of self-control is one of the most common contributing factors of unhappiness and discord. We see something in the order which we dislike. It is easy to condemn it. And that condemnatory word arouses ill-feeling. If we see it, and we refrain from speaking, in a few moments all is concord and peace instead of animosity and ill-will. Self-control—controlling the unruly member, the tongue, is one of the greatest contributing factors to concord in the home, and one which too many of us fail to develop.

Self-control on the part of governing children: I think the children should be properly directed and controlled, not permitted to run around without any limitation to their actions as they affect other members of the household. I think a child should be taught self-control and obedience from the age of three, particularly between the ages of three and five. Modern psychologists and psychiatrists teach differently, but I know medical men of experience who agree that a little child can learn to obey during that early period, and if you parents fail in this, you will have difficulty in later years. Do I mean that you should be cruel to that child? No! It is unnecessary. But it means that when you say "No," you mean what you say.

EIGHTH: Foster home-ties by continued companionship. I do not believe in the saying that "absence makes the heart grow fonder." It is companionship that fosters love, and when you have vowed your troth and made a covenant to be true to each other, do everything to foster that love, to cement it for eternity. There is nothing sweeter in the world than the companionship of husband and wife, and the confidence and love of children in a Latter-day Saint home. Whenever you can, take those children with you on a picnic or a trip; even though once a summer, do so, and let them have the memory of it. Fathers, take your boys with you on a trip if you can. They will remember that, too, through life; and husband and wife, go together whenever possible, rather than seek the companionship of your associates in business—which is perfectly right, and you should do so, but never at the sacrifice of companionship with wife and children.

NINTH: Make accessible to children proper literature, music, and appropriate moving pictures.

TENTH: Finally, by example and precept, encourage participation in Church activity, thus establishing life's two paramount ideals: First, to build character; and second, to render service. Let those children feel that if they would make home happy; if they would just in a small degree, repay the kindness of parenthood and the sacrifices that mother and father have made, they will develop in themselves a noble character—that is all the father asks, that is all the mother asks, and you owe that, young man, to your father and mother. Young woman, you are recreant if you fail to give your parents the satisfaction of seeing you become a pure and worthy girl who will some day contribute to a home as happy as yours is today.

I am reminded of one of the finest things that Edgar A. Guest ever wrote, and I shall take the time to read it:

We've never seen the Father here, but we have known the Son,
The finest type of manhood since the world was first begun,
And summing up the words of God, I write with reverent pen,
The greatest is the Son he sent to cheer the lives of men.

Through him we learned the ways of God, and found the Father's
    love;
The Son it was who won us back to him who reigns above.
The Lord did not come down himself to prove to men his worth,
He sought our worship through the child he placed upon the earth.
How can I best express my life? Wherein does greatness lie?
How can I long remembrance win, since I am born to die?
Both fame and gold are selfish things; their charms may quickly
    flee,
But I'm the father of a boy who came to speak for me.

In him lies all I hope to be; his splendor shall be mine;
I shall have done man's greatest work if only he is fine.
If someday he shall help the world long after I am dead,
In all that men shall say of him my praises shall be said.

It matters not what I may win of fleeting gold or fame,
My hope of joy depends alone on what my boy shall claim.
My story must be told thru him; for him I work and plan;
Man's greatest duty is to be the father of a man.

Your greatest duty, son or daughter, is to see to it that your life, your character, reflect credit upon your father and your mother. The responsibility of sonship, the responsibility to be a worthy daughter of noble parents are among the greatest in all the world. In the home let the element, the atmosphere breathe forth character which is one of the highest aims in life, and that is developed through Church service, as well as through courtesy and consideration in the home.

Besides service, as I have indicated, you do have your character, but next to that you take home the service you have rendered.

Paraphrasing the words of the Savior:

"There deeds shall thy memorial be.
Fear not, thou didst them unto me."
(From "A Poor Wayfaring Man of Grief")

Some Paragraphs on Home

I look upon the home as the basis from which radiate all good influences. If, in every home in the land, there were a competent father and a helpful mother, our officers of the law would have much less to do in protecting society from the lawless.

✿　✿　✿

Homes are made permanent through love. Though you neglect some of your business, though you neglect some of your cattle, though you fail to produce full crops, study to hold your children's love.

✿　✿　✿

In every well-ordered home in the Church, the glad free spirit of childhood is led to honor its country and to worship its God; and every man sees in the home the nucleus of eternal companionship and everlasting life.

✿　✿　✿

Aaronic Priesthood work, seminary classes, Sunday Schools, the activities of the Mutual Improvement Associations, and the Primary are all helps established to assist in the upbuilding and guidance of youth, but none of these —great and important factors as they are in the lives of our youth—can supplant the permanence of the influence of the parents in the home.

✿　✿　✿

The relationship of the children to the parents should be one which would enable those children to carry out ideal citizenship as they become related to the neighborhood, the Church, and to the larger forms of society. Be extremely careful of those activities which require you to be away from your small children. The secret of good citizenship lies in the home. The secret of instilling faith in God, faith in his Son, the Redeemer of the world, faith in the organizations of the Church, lies in the home. There it is centered.

✤　✤　✤

The home is truly the basic unit of society, and parenthood is next to Godhead. Let us see that our home is such that if an angel called, he would be pleased to remain.

✤　✤　✤

In no better way can high achievement in life be better realized than in excelling in the art of home building. In that kind of home we may experience on earth a taste of heaven.

✤　✤　✤

Would you have a strong and virile nation?—then keep your homes pure. Would you reduce delinquency and crime?—lessen the number of broken homes. It is time that civilized peoples realize that the home largely determines whether children shall be of high or low character. Home-building, therefore, should be the paramount purpose of parents and of the nation. The secret of good citizenship lies in the home.

✤　✤　✤

I praise God for the instructions he has given his people regarding the sacredness, the sanctity, and permanence of the family relationship and the home. We are living in a most momentous age. We see on every hand manifestations of commotion. The world seemingly is stirred as it has never been stirred before. In the midst of this world confusion, the home, the fundamental institution of society, is also threatened. One of the highest ideals of life is to keep secure and free from sorrow the homes of the Church and of the nation.

❀   ❀   ❀

You members of The Church of Jesus Christ of Latter-day Saints know that your family ties are eternal. There is nothing temporary in the home of the Latter-day Saint. There is no element of transitoriness in the family relationship of the Latter-day Saint home.

The Greatest Trust—
The Greatest Joy

We believe that the home is the center, the bulwark of true civilization. We do not believe in the ideology that teaches that there is no God, that the state is supreme, or that it has control of the individual. The home is the center of civilization, and the responsibilities of the home rest upon the parents of the home.

The Church is an aid to the training of children; so also is the state, but neither is supreme. The Lord himself has said,

"For this shall be a law unto the inhabitants of Zion, or in any of her stakes which are organized.

"And they shall also teach their children to pray, and to walk uprightly before the Lord." (D&C 68:26, 28.)

That is a law.

The greatest trust that can come to a man and woman is the placing in their keeping the life of a little child. If a man who is entrusted with other people's funds defaults whether a bank, municipal, or state official, he is apprehended and probably sent to prison. If a person entrusted with a government secret discloses that secret and betrays his country, he is called a traitor. What must the Lord think, then, of parents who, through their own negligence or wilful desire to indulge their selfishness, fail properly to rear their children, and thereby prove untrue to the greatest trust that has been given to human beings? He has said: ". . . the sin be upon the heads of the parents." (Ibid., 68:25.)

The Home and the Church

Out of the homes of America go the future citizens of America, and what those American homes are will largely determine what our citizenry will be in the future. Indeed, Victor Hugo said: "The future of any country may be largely determined by the attitude of its young men between the ages of 18 and 21." Well, before those boys reach that age, their characters are pretty well established. One of our leading statesmen, Herbert Hoover, writing on this very subject a number of years ago, said:

After we have determined every scientific fact, after we have erected every public safeguard, after we have constructed every edifice for education or training or hospitalization, or play, yet all these things are but a tithe of the physical, moral, and spiritual gifts which motherhood gives and home confers.

None of these things carry that affection, that devotion of soul, which is the great endowment from mothers.

The home is the best place in the world to teach the child his responsibilities, to give him happiness in self-control and respect for the rights of others. Unhappiness in the child's life, as in the adult's life, springs largely from nonconformity to natural and social laws. The home is the best place in which to develop obedience, which nature and society will later demand. Some mothers foolishly overlook that and let children do as they please. That is all right within certain limits.

Let the child do certain things just as he pleases, so long as he does not interfere with the rights of a little brother or sister; and then the parent has the right to curtail him. A person's individuality is best safeguarded and developed through conformity with social conventions. If he has learned the rules of the game, he may hope to modify them; and until he has learned them, his attempts at modification will be amateurish. If these rules are never learned, then personal individuality is cramped and happiness constricted.

Home Contributes to Happiness

It is easy to understand, then, how the home contributes to the happiness of the child. First, by teaching obedience; second, by teaching him to be considerate of the rights of others; third, by being a place where confidence and consolations are exchanged; and, fourth, by being a place which serves as a haven of seclusion and rest from the worries and perplexities of life. Such a home is possible. There are thousands of such homes in the Church. From those homes go the future citizens of America. Upon every Latter-day Saint rests the responsibility of developing just such a home.

It is the duty of the Church to teach religion. The home should also do it; but the Bible has been taken not only out of the schools, largely it has been taken out of our homes as well. There is quite a laxity in teaching religion in the homes. Family prayers are being neglected.

Parents, if you do not do anything else, kneel down in the morning with your children. I know your mornings are usually busy, getting the children off to school and father off to work; but have some time when you can kneel and invite God into your home. Prayer is a potent force. You will hear some men reason that prayer is only what you think. Well, if it were just what you think, even that would benefit you. Prayer is a potent force, and into the homes of America we need to invite God, for this is a Christian nation.

Sunday Schools Foster Religion

The function of the Sunday School is to foster religion—to give religious education. To inculcate moral and religious ideals in the lives of children was the dominant motive in the mind of Robert Raikes of Gloucester, England, when he first established the Sunday School, and also in the mind of Richard Ballantyne when he organized that school in the little, log house on First West and Third South in Salt Lake City.

Today we have thousands of officers and teachers— every one of whom gives his or her services gratuitously— devoting 52 Sundays every year, and hours of study during each week for the betterment of children and youth: training them to have virtue; habituating them to industry, activity, and spirituality; making them consider every vice as shameful and unmanly; firing them with ambition to be useful; making them disdain to be destitute of any useful knowledge; and leading them into the joy of the Christ-life, into the friendship of God and the guidance of his Holy Spirit.

There is not a home in the Church, not an individual, that may not and should not come within the radiance of one or more of these teachers. The worth of each Sunday School upon the boys and girls, and upon the community, depends first upon the character, preparation, and devotion of the officers and teachers. No teacher who smokes a cigaret can conscientiously and effectively teach children to refrain from the use of tobacco. A teacher has no right to set an unworthy example to those children who trust him. "What you are," says Emerson, "thunders so loud in my ears, I cannot hear what you say."

Choose Spiritual Life

In both the home and in the Church, with all its auxiliaries and priesthood quorums, there is but one ideal, and that is to inculcate high ideals. The mission of the whole Church is to lift our young people, and the older ones, above the animal plane into the realm of spirituality. I think that is the whole mission of life. The Savior has given us the example. He rose above all things physical and temporal and lived in the spirit, and it is our duty to approach that ideal.

Let us choose the spiritual life. Let us conquer the animal in us. The Christ-life beckons. Christ is our Lord, our Savior, our Guide, our Light. He has restored his Church with all its opportunities for spiritual development. Let us be more determined to make beautiful homes, to be kinder husbands, more thoughtful wives, more exemplary parents to our children; determined that in our homes we are going to have just a little taste of heaven here on this earth. And may there come into our homes the true spirit of Christ, our Redeemer, whose reality, inspiring guidance I know to be real!

Responsibility of a
Latter-day Saint Home

A few months ago, the Supreme Court of the United States declared unconstitutional the repeating of a prayer in school. It might sound presumptuous for us to judge the Supreme Court on this, but just the thought that this has occurred is a lesson to every member of the Church all over the world. There is greater responsibility upon the home than ever before.

The Supreme Court urged—the one man who dissented, at any rate, urged—that the home should be the place where religion is taught, and I should just like to say a few words on the responsibility of keeping that home a Latter-day Saint home. President Curtis gave me a good text when he related the story of the two boys who went out to get the tenth load of hay. My brother and I were those two boys. Father stopped down by the creek to get a cool drink of water before he joined us with pitching— we pitched the hay in those days with pitchforks. We did not have the modern way of putting up hay by baling it.

We had hauled nine loads into the barn. We were just loading the tenth, which, of course, would go to tithing, tithing in kind. We boys drove just where we left the last shocks of hay, and father walked halfway towards us, then said, "No, boys, drive over on the knoll where the timothy grows." There was wild grass where we left the hay.

I said, "No, sir, take it as it comes," and I meant it, too. I thought that was fair. "Wire grass" was poor hay to pitch when we were feeding cows and horses.

By that time father was up by the rack, and he said, "Drive over on the knoll there where we have better hay, timothy and red top." And I repeated what I had said to him at some distance. I said, "Take it as it comes."

"No, David, this is the tenth load," he repeated. "The best is not too good for the Lord."

Four-Point Guide

That is the best sermon on tithing that I have ever received. But it is more than that. It is a lesson making your home a school of training, making your home a place where the principles of the Gospel are practiced as well as taught; and I name four things which I am going to leave with you, not as a sermon, but just as a guide.

Keep in mind the fact that the best is none too good for the Lord. What does the Lord want? What does he need to make his glory complete? I shall repeat it for you: "This is my work and my glory to bring to pass the immortality and eternal life of man."

What would the Lord be if there were no men, if there were no children? The earth would be created just the same. Creation is going on now, all around us. Sister McKay and I stood down in Mexico one day, a few days after the volcano had erupted in a man's field. We went down there a year later and there was the volcano in a mountain. That is part of creation. You see volcanos all over the world in all places. You can hear of an earthquake even today. It changes the life and existence of men just as happened last week. Creation is going on. But what would mountains be if there were no human beings, if there were only salted seas thrusting themselves against the shore every minute?

Everything in existence is confined to certain laws, physical laws, and they must obey those laws. To only one creature did God give part of himself, and that was the power of choice. That is a wonderful thing—free agency. To every human being he has given the power of choice, not to any other animal in the world. You are free to choose to be a saint, or free to choose to be a sinner, and you are responsible for it. The Lord will not keep you from being a saint; he will do all he can to make you a saint. He will not keep you from being a sinner; he will do all he can to influence you not to be a sinner, but yours is the choice. In making your life, always keep in mind "The best is not too good for the Lord."

Responsibility in Home

Now, what is the responsibility in the home? Children will follow your example. If you are inconsistent, you are teaching them to be inconsistent. If you are untrue, you are teaching them to be untrue. If you are profane, you are teaching your children to be profane. Yours is the choice. Father, making us get the best hay, proved to us boys that he was consistent in his belief in tithes, that he was consistent in his faith in God. He believed with all his heart that God is real, that God is our Father. When he prayed night and morning as he did, he taught his children faith in God, and he set the example. He asked the children in his home to take their turns and pray. Sometimes when he was off in the fields watering his potatoes or his alfalfa he would take time to tell of an experience he had had in Scotland. He told it so naturally that these boys knew that he was telling the truth.

His life was consistent with his teachings, and that I put down as the first example of a happy, successful home, sincerity in your belief in God the Father and his Son and in the Gospel of Jesus Christ and live it in the home.

The unfortunate thing about the statement regarding prayer in school being unconstitutional is that children going to school will be in an atmosphere where divine influence is a thing apart from life. Not to have a prayer in school is not the harm that will result from that unconstitutional act, but the young children will grow up in school feeling that teaching of God, of religion, is a thing apart from life itself.

A child should grow up feeling that he or she could go to the Father and pray for help in studies, in passing examinations, get help in preparing a talk or an essay, to feel that he or she is in the presence of a divine creator, an intelligent being, to whom the young boy or the young girl, the teenager or a young married couple may go and receive divine assistance. So if you have happiness in your home, put down sincerity as one of the fundamentals.

Second, consistency. What you say in the home to your wife, say it as courteously as you would to a stranger outside. If you are tempted to take an oath, do not take it. You would not take it in the presence of your Father in heaven. Why take it in the presence of your children?

Lesson in Boyhood

That lesson, too, came to me as a young boy just as impressively as when pitching the tenth load of hay. I was riding a horse, carrying a bucket with some nails—I will not take time to tell you all about it—but the horse jumped aside, and I fell off, and swore at him. I did not know father was around. But when I got back to the yard, he said, "David, are you in the habit of swearing?"

"No sir." That was true. I was not in the habit of it.

"I heard you say a very profane word. I think you had better unbridle your horse, go up to the house and wash your mouth," making me feel that I had defiled my mouth. It was consistent to his teachings. "You have fouled your language, your mouth, by cursing that mare." Consistency next to sincerity.

And the third I name, self-control.

Fourth, service. Help each other in the house, in preparation of plays, games. Help your ward, take an active part in your ward, serving somebody else, helping to make the world better.

Sincerity, consistency, self-control, service. Do you know, that was taught by the pioneers when they crossed the plains? Every morning the pioneers in the first company, and most companies that followed, knelt down and asked for guidance and protection for that day. If they were in the wagon, they knelt in the wagon. Those who were driving teams knelt there by the side. There was an hour for prayer. That is faith, sincerity.

Prepared for Eventualities

Second, they had to be prepared for eventualities. Every man who carried a musket was to be sure that it was properly loaded, ready to fire in case of an attack of Indians or buffalo. If he was riding in a wagon, he carried it so it would be ready for use. First, prayer, faith, sincerity; second, preparation—preparation for today comes under consistency. Be just as polite in the house as you are in society. Why should you not be? Children, seeing your politeness, your consideration, consistency, will themselves partake of that same consideration.

And the third thing in crossing the plains, President Young said, every man must be just as considerate of his neighbor's cattle as he is of his own. Take just as much care of those oxen that belong to your neighbor as those that belong to you. Make your homes places of harmony, peace and love. Home may become heaven on earth, a taste of heaven on earth, if Latter-day Saints make them ideal.

Let those elements be manifest whenever you are around, especially in the chapel. The whole building is dedicated to God, is his building. Let us take care of it, coming here just as reverently as we are at home when we kneel down to pray. Be consistent. Let that reverence show that we have faith in God. Be considerate of each other, just as the father is considerate of mother, and mother of father, and as children should be of parents.

Our most precious possession is the youth of the land, and to instruct them to walk uprightly and to become worthy citizens in the kingdom of God is our greatest obligation.

Religious freedom and the separation of church and state are clearly set forth in the first amendment to the Constitution of the United States, and no governmental agency can have any supervision, control, or jurisdiction over religion. Though our public schools may emphasize moral, ethical, and spiritual values as essential elements in the public school program, they cannot favor any particular religion or religious system. The teaching of religion is therefore definitely a responsibility of the home and the Church.

In discharging this responsibility, I say again, members of the Church should ever keep in mind two paramount obligations: (1) to put and to keep your home in order; and (2) to proclaim the divinity of Jesus Christ and the essentiality of his teachings to the salvation of the human family.

If, upon examination, you were to find that termites are undermining the foundation of your house, you would lose no time to have experts make thorough examination and have the destructive insects exterminated. You would have the weakened materials removed and the foundation strengthened and, if necessary, rebuilt.

Well, more important than the building of your home is the rebuilding and purifying of your home.

"Our home joys," says Pestalozzi, "are the most delightful earth affords, and the joy of parents in their children is the most holy joy of humanity. It makes their hearts pure and good; it lifts them up to their Father in heaven."

Well, you know, and I know, that such joys are within the reach of most men and women if high ideals of marriage and home be properly fostered and cherished.

But there are destructive termites of homes, as well as of houses, and some of these are backbiting, evil-speaking, faultfinding on the part either of parents or of children. Slander is poison to the soul. "Slanderers are like flies that pass all over a man's good parts to light only on his sores." In the ideal home, there is no slanderous gossip about day schoolteachers, about public officials or Church officials. I am more grateful now, as years have come and gone, to my father, who with hands lifted said, "Now, no faultfinding about your teacher or anybody else."

Quarreling and swearing also are evils that lower the standards of the ideal home. I cannot imagine a father or mother swearing in the presence of children or even letting it pass their lips.

Another deterrent to happiness in the home is the refusal to bear the full responsibility of motherhood and fatherhood. Members of the Church who are healthy and normal should not be guilty of restricting the number of children in the home, especially when such action is prompted by a desire for a good time, or for personal gain, or to keep up with the neighbors, or by a false impression that one or two children in a family can be better educated. These are excuses which members of the Church should not harbor, for they are unjustified.

The question of size of families, I know, brings up many problems: the question of woman's career, the false cry of "quality, not quantity," which one writer rightly says should read "extinction, not preservation," or the matter-of-fact question of daily living and getting on in the world.

With the high ideal of marriage as revealed to the Prophet Joseph Smith, members of the Church should have but one goal, and that is to keep in mind the fact that marriage, the foundation of society, is "ordained of God" for the building of permanent homes in which children may be properly reared and taught the principles of the gospel.

The following, I am sure, will strike a responsive chord in the hearts of the majority of parents in the Church. I quote:

> Every period of human life is wonderful; the irresponsible age of childhood, the thrilling years of adolescence and courtship, the productive, fighting, burden-bearing era of parenthood; but the most wonderful time of life comes when the father and mother become chums of their grown-up, successful sons and daughters, and can begin to enjoy their children's children. . . .
>
> Youth is confined with restrictions, limitations, schedules, and dominations; adolescence is full of mysteries, longings, and defeats; early fatherhood is absorbed in struggles and in the solution of problems; extreme old age is shadowed by eternal mysteries; but middle age and normal old age, if life has been rightly and fully lived, are filled with the thrills, not merely of success, but of companionship with children and grandchildren.
>
> Every normal individual should complete the full cycle of human life with all its joys and satisfactions in natural order; childhood, adolescence, youth, parenthood, middle age, and the age of grandchildren. Each age has satisfactions which can be known only by experience. You must be born again and again in order to know the full course of human happiness. When the first baby is born a mother is born, a father is born, and grandparents are born; only by birth can any of these come into being. Only by the natural cycle of life can the great progressive joys of mankind be reached.
>
> Any social system which prevents the individual from pursuing the normal cycle of life, from marrying young, from rearing a family before the age of fifty or so, and from obtaining the deep, peculiar joys of middle life and grandparenthood defeats the divine order of the universe and lays the basis of all sorts of social problems.
>
> When a young man and woman of the right biological type marry in the early twenties and are prepared to earn a living and support and rear a family, they have started in the normal cycle of life. They are likely to give society far fewer problems of crime, immorality, divorce, or poverty than are their unmarried companions. They will have children and rear them while they are strong, enjoy them when they are grown up and successful, depend upon them in weakness, and profit by the finest type of old-age insurance ever invented by man or God, an insurance which pays its annuities in

material goods when necessary, but which mainly pays in the rich joys of love and fellowship . . . The crowning joys of human experience will come in middle age and onward, through the companionship, love, and honor of children and grandchildren. (R. J. Sprague.)

We appeal to all members of the Church to set their homes in order and to enjoy the true happiness of harmonious family life.

Home and Family— Source of True Happiness

I have confidence in the membership of the Church. That confidence does not waver. I have confidence in the young people. True, some of them tarry, some of them seem to be indifferent; but at heart they are generally pretty well anchored. I have confidence in our parents, generally speaking, they are doing their best to establish homes; and that is the topic about which I should like to speak this morning.

Marriage and Courting

I believe in being happy. It is man's privilege to be happy if he chooses the path that leads to it. I am going to point out, this morning, one of the best sources of happiness in life—the greatest source of happiness. The Prophet Joseph Smith said, on one occasion, that "happiness is the object and design of our existence and will be the end thereof if we pursue the path that leads to it; and this path is virtue, uprightness, faithfulness, holiness, and keeping all the commandments without first knowing them. We cannot expect to know all or more than we now know unless we comply with or keep those we have already received."

That is a fundamental prophetic statement from a prophet of the Lord! Do you note that he does not mention pleasure? That is a wise discrimination. Young folks, note that especially; he does not say that pleasure is the end of existence, the object of life. No, he says happiness; and there is a difference between happiness or joy, and pleasure. Any living thing, particularly in the higher scale of life, may experience pleasure; but happiness comes only to the human soul. I do not know of any better definition of pleasure than that given by Robert Burns. In his "Tam O'Shanter," he describes pleasure and associates it with a scene in which pleasure is frequently experienced. Note his definition:

> But pleasures are like poppies spread,
> You seize the flower, its bloom is shed;
> Or like the snowfall in the river,
> A moment white—then melts forever;
> Or like the Borealis race,
> That flit ere you can point their place;
> Or like the rainbow's lovely form
> Evanishing amid the storm.

That is pleasure. You may experience it, but you may experience, too, the aftermath; and, unfortunately, nearly all the world is seeking pleasure, not discriminating between it and happiness.

So this morning I am going to follow the suggestion about married life and courting and approach it with this idea. Agree with it or disagree with it, as you may, but the truest source of happiness is found in the home. We have operating in the world today one of the most potent forces against the home that we have ever had, I believe, in the history of the world. We sensed it recently as we approached the Iron Curtain, got within the shadow of the Russian sector in Berlin, and moved about in the Russian zone in Germany.

It is a force which is not only trying to substitute the

state for the home, but trying to dissuade the minds of youth from believing in the existence of God himself! So I am pleading for homes and appealing to the Latter-day Saint home, not only for your own happiness, but for the salvation of the human family.

Way back, hundreds of years ago, Leonidas said:

Cling to thy home. If there the meanest shed
Yield thee a haven or hearth and shelter for thy head,
And some poor plot with vegetables stored
Be all heaven allots thee for thy board,
Unsavory bread and herbs that scattered grow
Wild on the river brink or mountain brow,
Yet in this fearless mansion shall grow
More heart's repose than all the world beside.

I think the old philosopher was right.

The Home

It is important for young people to realize that intelligent home building begins with a young man and a young girl in their teens. Often the health of children, if a couple be blessed with such, depends upon the actions of parents before marriage. In the press, from the pulpit, and particularly in the home, there should ring more frequently the message that in their youth boys and girls are laying the foundation for their future happiness or misery. Every young man, particularly, should prepare for the responsibility of fatherhood by keeping himself physically clean, that he might enter into that responsibility not as a coward or deceiver, but as one honorable and fit to found a home. The young man who, in unfitness, takes upon himself the responsibility of fatherhood is worse than a deceiver. The future happiness of his wife and children depends upon his life in youth.

Let us also teach girls that motherhood is divine, for when we touch the creative part of life, we enter into the realm of divinity. It is important, therefore, that young womanhood realize the necessity of keeping their bodies clean and pure, that their children might enter the world unhampered by sin and disease. An unshackled birth and an inheritance of noble character are the greatest blessings of childhood. No mother has the right to shackle a child through life for what seems in youth to be a pleasant pastime or her right to indulge in harmful drugs and other sinful practices. Those who are to be the mothers of the race should at least so live as to bear children who are not burdened from birth by sickness, weakness, or deformity, because the parents, in fiery youth, as Shakespeare said, "with unbashful forehead woo the means of weakness and debility."

A dominant evil of the world today is unchastity. I repeat what appeared over the signature of President Joseph F. Smith while he was living: "No more loathsome cancer disfigures the body and soul of society today than the frightful affliction of sexual sin. It vitiates the very fountains of life, and bequeaths its foul effects to the yet unborn as a legacy of death." (The Improvement Era, Vol. 20, p. 739.) He who is unchaste in young manhood is untrue to a trust given him by the parents of the girl; and she who is unchaste in maidenhood is untrue to her future husband and lays the foundation of unhappiness, suspicion, and discord in the home. Keep in mind this eternal truth that chastity is a virtue to be prized as one of life's noblest achievements. It contributes to the virility of manhood. It is the crowning virtue of womanhood, and every red-blooded man knows that is true. It is a chief factor to a happy home. There is no loss of prestige in maintaining in a dignified way the standards of the Church. You can be "in" this world and not "of the world." Keep your chastity above everything else! God has commanded that we be chaste: "Thou shalt not commit adultery!" said the Lord at Sinai. (See Exod. 20:14.)

Degenerating forces in the world are rampant, but they can be resisted if youth will cherish right thoughts and aspire to high ideals. The age-old conflict between truth and error is being waged with accelerating fury, and at the present hour error seems to be gaining the upper hand. Increasing moral turpitude and widespread disregard for the principles of honor and integrity are undermining influences in social, political, and business life.

The exalted view of marriage as held by the Church is given expressively in five words found in the forty-ninth section of the Doctrine and Covenants: "marriage is ordained of God."(D&C 49:15.) That revelation was given in 1831 when Joseph Smith was only 25 years of age. Considering the circumstances under which it was given, we find in it another example among hundreds of others corroborative of the fact that he was inspired of the Lord. Before us are assembled thousands of presiding officers in stakes, wards, quorums, and auxiliaries, to whom we say, it is your duty and mine to uphold the lofty conception of marriage as given in this revelation, and to guard against encroaching dangers that threaten to lower the standard of the ideal home.

It is said that the best and noblest lives are those which are set toward high ideals. Truly no higher ideal regarding marriage can be cherished by young people than to look upon it as a divine institution. In the minds of the young, such a standard is a protection to them in courtship, an ever-present influence inducing them to refrain from doing anything that may prevent their going to the temple to have their love made perfect in an enduring and eternal union. It will lead them to seek divine guidance in the selection of their companions, upon the wise choice of whom their life's happiness here and hereafter is largely dependent. It makes their hearts pure and good; it lifts them up to their Father in heaven. Such joys are within the reach of most men and women if high ideals of marriage and home be properly fostered and cherished.

The signs of the times definitely indicate that the sacredness of the marriage covenant is dangerously threatened. There are places where the marriage ceremony may be performed at any hour of the day or night without any previous arrangement. The license is issued and the ceremony performed while the couple wait. Many couples who have been entrapped by such enticements have had their marriages end in disappointment and sorrow. In some instances these places are nothing more than opportunities for legalized immorality. Oh, how far they fall below the true ideal! As far as lies within our power, we must warn young couples against secret and hasty marriages.

It is vital also to counteract the insidious influences of printed literature that speaks of the "bankruptcy of marriage," that advocates trial marriages, and that places extramarital relations on a par with extramarital friendships.

Parenthood, and particularly motherhood, should be held as a sacred obligation. There is something in the depths of the human soul which revolts against neglectful parenthood. God has implanted deep in the souls of parents the truth that they cannot with impunity shirk the responsibility to protect childhood and youth.

There seems to be a growing tendency to shift this responsibility from the home to outside influences, such as the school and the church. Important as these outward influences are, they never can take the place of the influence of the mother and the father. Constant training, constant vigilance, companionship, being watchmen of our own children are necessary in order to keep our homes intact.

There are three fundamental things to which every child is entitled: (1) a respected name, (2) a sense of security, (3) opportunities for development. The family gives to the child his name and standing in the community. A child wants his family to be as good as those families of his friends. He wants to be able to point with pride to his father, and to feel an inspiration always as he thinks of his mother. It is a mother's duty to so live that her children will associate with her everything that is beautiful, sweet, and pure. And the father should so live that the child, emulating his example, will be a good citizen and, in the Church, a true follower of the teachings of the gospel of Jesus Christ.

A child has the right to feel that in his home he has a place of refuge, a place of protection from the dangers and evils of the outside world. Family unity and integrity are necessary to supply this need.

He needs parents who are happy in their adjustment to each other, who are working hopefully toward the fulfillment of an ideal of living, who love their children with a sincere and unselfish love—in short, parents who are well-balanced individuals, gifted with a certain amount of insight, who are able to provide the child with a wholesome emotional background that will contribute more to his development than material advantages.

Divorce almost invariably deprives children of these advantages. Just recently I received a heartbreaking letter from a boy nearly eight years of age whose parents are divorced, from which I quote: "Dear David O. McKay: I am having a problem and it is about Mom and Dad. They are divorced and we (meaning his brother and sister) want to be back together. Can you solve my problem? I love you." What a tragedy for that child, and what unhappiness this separation has caused the children.

The increasing divorce rate in the United States today is a threatening menace to this nation's greatness. The increase throughout the United States, and in our own state, in the percentage of divorces is alarming.

In the light of scripture, ancient and modern, we are justified in concluding that Christ's ideal pertaining to marriage is the unbroken home, and conditions that cause divorce are violations of his divine teachings. Except in cases of infidelity or other extreme conditions, the Church frowns upon divorce, and authorities look with apprehension upon the increasing number of divorces among members of the Church.

A man who has entered into sacred covenants in the house of the Lord to remain true to the marriage vow is a traitor to that covenant if he separates himself from his wife and family just because he has permitted himself to become infatuated with a pretty face and comely form of some young girl who flattered him with a smile. Even though a loose interpretation of the law of the land would grant such a man a bill of divorcement, I think he is unworthy of a recommend to have his second marriage solemnized in the temple. And any woman who will break up her home because of some selfish desire, or who has been untrue to her husband, is also untrue to the covenants she has made in the house of the Lord. When we refer to the breaking of the marriage tie, we touch upon one of the saddest experiences of life. For a couple who have basked in the sunshine of each other's love to stand by and see the clouds of misunderstanding and discord obscure the love-light of their lives is tragedy indeed. In the darkness that follows, the love sparkle in each other's eyes is obscured, and to try to restore it is fruitless.

To look upon marriage as a mere contract that may be entered into at pleasure in response to a romantic whim, or for selfish purposes, and severed at the first difficulty or misunderstanding that may arise, is an evil meriting severe condemnation, especially in cases wherein children are made to suffer because of such separation. Marriage is a sacred relationship entered into for purposes that are well recognized—primarily for the rearing of a family. A flippant attitude toward marriage, the ill-advised suggestion of "companionate marriage," the base, diabolical theory of "free sex experiment," and the ready-made divorce courts are dangerous reefs upon which many a family bark is wrecked.

In order to lessen the breaking up of homes, the present tendency toward a low view of marriage should be substituted by the lofty view of marriage that Jesus the Christ gives it. Let us look upon marriage as a sacred obligation and a covenant that is eternal, or that may be made eternal.

Teach the young of both sexes in the responsibilities and ideals of marriage so that they may realize that marriage involves obligation and is not an arrangement to be terminated at pleasure. Teach them that pure love between the sexes is one of the noblest things on earth, and the bearing and rearing of children the highest of all human duties. In this regard it is the duty of parents to set an example in the home that children may see and absorb, as it were, the sacredness of family life and the responsibilities associated therewith.

The number of broken marriages can be reduced if couples realize even before they approach the altar that marriage is a state of mutual service, a state of giving as well as of receiving, and that each must give of himself or herself to the utmost. Harriet Beecher Stowe wisely writes: "No man or woman can create a true home who is not willing in the outset to embrace life heroically, to encounter labor and sacrifice. Only to such can this divinest power be given to create on earth that which is the nearest image of heaven."

Another condition that contributes to the permanence of the marriage covenant is marriage in the temple. Before such a marriage is performed, it is necessary for the young man and young woman first to obtain a recommend from the bishop. They should go to him in person, and the bishop who does his duty will instruct the couple regarding the sacredness of the obligation that they as young people are going to assume, emphasizing all the safeguards that have been named before. There, in the presence of the priesthood, before taking upon themselves the obligation of marriage, the young people receive instructions upon the sacredness of the duty that is before them; and, furthermore, they determine whether or not they are prepared to go in holiness and purity to the altar of God and there seal their vows and love.

Finally, there is one principle that seems to me to strike right at the base of the happiness of the marriage relation, and that is the standard of purity taught and practiced among true members of the Church. In The Church of Jesus Christ of Latter-day Saints there is but one standard of morality. No young man has any more right to be unchaste than has a young girl. That young man who asks for a recommend to take a pure girl to the altar is expected to give the same purity that he expects to receive.

For the proper solution of this great problem of the mounting divorce rate, we may turn with safety to Jesus as our guide. He declared that the marriage relation is of divine origin, that "marriage is ordained of God" (D&C 49:15), that only under the most exceptional conditions should it be set aside. In the teaching of the Church of Christ, the family assumes supreme importance in the development of the individual and of the society. "Happy and thrice happy are they who enjoy an uninterrupted union, and whose love, unbroken by any complaint, shall not dissolve." The marriage ceremony when sealed by the authority of the holy priesthood endures, as do family relationships, throughout time and all eternity. "What therefore God hath joined together, let not man put asunder." (Mark 10:9.)

Safeguards Against the Delinquency of Youth

"I charge thee," wrote Paul to Timothy,—"I charge thee before God and the Lord Jesus Christ to preach the Word, be instant in season and out of season, reprove, rebuke, exhort with all long-suffering."

In the same letter he prophetically declared "that in the last days perilous times shall come, for men shall be lovers of their own selves, . . . lovers of pleasure more than lovers of God, having a form of Godliness but denying the power thereof."

It is in the spirit of Paul's charge and prophecy that I approach the subject of safeguards against delinquency of youth. I have nothing new to offer in naming these safeguards. You have heard them mentioned frequently, but I think as with the Gospel principles, it is fitting that we be active in season and out of season, that we reprove, rebuke, exhort, admonish with all long-suffering as we contemplate the rising crimewave and bring home to each of us, if possible, the realization that greater diligence is needed.

Few will question that we are living in perilous times, that many people have lost their moorings and are being "tossed to and fro by every wind and doctrine, by the slight of men, and cunning craftiness, whereby they lie in wait to deceive."

A short time ago, a commission on evangelism, appointed by the Archbishops of Canterbury and York, made a report revealing some astounding facts on the present-day status of "Christian" England. The report said:

"The present irrelevance of the Church in the life and thought of the community in general is apparent from two symptoms which admit of ńo dispute. They are (1) the widespread decline in church going; and (2) the collapse of Christian moral standards." Associated with this was the statement that only from 10% to 15% of the population are closely linked to any Christian church.

Commenting upon this report, one of the daily papers in England said, among other things:

"Youth is largely indifferent to Christianity—finding in religion no relevance to life, and in life itself no meaning. If we inquire what it is that has caused these alarming symptoms of national decline and fall, the answer is that our generation has succumbed to the age-long delusion of a self-sufficient humanism which puts man (not God) in the centre of his world, and regards man (not God) as the standard of reference. The worst, however, is not yet told, for the church itself has become infected with the spirit of the age, and has thereby lost its vision, its vitality and its spiritual authority. The real problem is not the 90% which stand outside the churches, but the 10% inside the churches, so many of whom are only half converted and ill-instructed."

Truly it would seem that men and women are either groping blindly for the truth, or have become lovers of pleasure more than lovers of God, having a form of godliness, but denying the power thereof.

Preserving Christian Ideals

Among the glaring evil products of the war and post-war periods are two which seem to be most portentous and which should be curbed if we would preserve true Christian ideals.

These are:

(1) An increasing tendency to dishonor the marriage vow, and,

(2) The upswing in juvenile delinquency.

Careful research would undoubtedly disclose a close relationship between these two unwholesome social conditions.

Marriage Looseness and Infidelity

As evidence of the first, we need only to glance at the number of divorces even among Temple marriages. In the country at large one out of every five marriages are separated by the ever-grinding divorce mill. Latest reports indicate one out of three.

Bearing tragic witness to the lessening regard for purity in marriage is the large number of so-called warbrides whose husbands have returned to face broken promises and gross infidelity.

But it is to the ever-increasing crimewave that I desire to call attention this morning. Children are being corrupted by it; youth are caught in its whirlpool, and are being contaminated overwhelmingly by it. According to the director of the Federal Bureau of Investigation, "It is mounting in intensity. It is growing in severity. It is not isolated. It is nation-wide." Referring to conditions during the war, he comments: "There was the spirit of wartime abandon (for example) with its last-fling philosophy, which provided justification to less resolute wills to violate the conventions of society. Lessons in school became secondary. Girls sacrificed virtue on a false shrine of patriotism. Arrests for prostitution increased 35 per cent, disorderly conduct 357 per cent, and drunkenness and driving while intoxicated 174 per cent among girls under eighteen in the wartime years. To those who were not grounded in fundamentals, established values disappeared, and an attitude of impermanence superseded individual responsibility. Conflicts between liberty and license manifested themselves in wrong-doing. Personal responsibility in too many homes has become archaic and old-fashioned."

In calling attention to these conditions, and in my comments later, I would not have you think that young people generally do not merit our confidence. It is the few, not the many of whom we now speak.

When, a few years ago, a little four-year-old lad wandered into the bad lands of North Dakota, the whole aroused country-side organized for the rescue. They gave no thought, however, to the hundreds of four-year-olds who were safe in their mothers' keeping. A train wreck or an airplane disaster shocks us to attention, awakens sympathy and a demand for more safeguards, while to the hundreds of trains and airplanes carrying millions to safety, we give scarcely a passing thought.

So while we solicitously call attention to the tragedies in the stream of human life, let us not be unmindful of the much greater group who move steadily and successfully along, avoiding the sandbars and rapids of sinful indulgence and spiritual decay, whose noble lives confirm and increase confidence in the growing generation. As we seek the lost sheep, let us be appreciative of the "ninety and nine" that have not strayed.

But no matter how firm our confidence in the majority of the young, we must not close our eyes to the fact that the number of delinquents and youthful criminals is increasing. In the interest of the moral atmosphere of our communities, the welfare of the state, the perpetuity of our democratic form of government, we must search for the causes of this upswing in crime, and, if possible, remove them and apply the proper remedies.

The Home the First Safeguard

One cause of the increase in child delinquency is a let-down in home ideals. The exigencies of war induced many mothers to take up war work, and to leave their children in the care of others, or, too often, to let them shift for themselves. A growing desire for economic independence, or a too eager willingness to improve financial circumstances, have influenced some mothers to neglect the greatest of all responsibilities—the rearing of a family. The national director of the Federal Bureau of Investigation makes the definite statement that "in the background of these youthful offenders lies the story of shocking neglect. Boys and girls are being deprived of the care and guidance necessary to the proper foundation of their characters. Their lawlessness had its roots in every instance in broken homes, in homes where mothers and fathers because of their neglect, misunderstanding, or irresponsibility had failed in their primary obligation. More often than not, God was unknown, or, more important, was unwelcome in their homes.

"On the other hand, in nearly every instance the youthful offender would have been a strong, upright citizen had he been given a chance. If his pent-up energies and desires had been directed along wholesome channels; if his problems—the problems that made him a problem child—had been solved by patient and attentive parents, he would have proved to be an influence for good in his community."

Parental Responsibility

A married woman who refuses to assume the responsibilities of motherhood, or who, having children, neglects them for pleasure or social prestige, is recreant to the highest calling and privilege of womankind. The father, who because of business or political or social responsibilities fails to share with his wife the responsibilities of rearing his sons and daughters, is untrue to his marital obligations, is a negative element in what might be and should be a joyous home atmosphere, and is a possible contributor to discord and delinquency. A president of the United States once said: "Our country has a vast majority of competent mothers. I am not so sure of the majority of competent fathers!" Fathers may and should exercise a helpful, restraining influence, where a mother's tenderness and love might lead to indulgence. In this respect, however, every father should keep in mind that he was once a mischievous youngster himself, and deal with his boy sympathetically.

The home is the best place in the world to teach the highest ideal in the social and political life of man; namely, *perfect liberty of action so long as you do not trespass upon the rights and privileges of another.*

The great need in the American home today is more religion. Parents should make it obvious both by their actions and their conversation that they are seriously interested if not in outward forms in the *fruits* of true religion. Example of parents should emphasize the need of honesty in our dealings with our family, our neighbors, and all with whom we come in contact; of kindness to our employees, of fair play to our employers, or good measure to our customers. "Talk about these intangibles should become as common practice in our homes and offices as talk about golf, parties, and profits if we want to succeed in solving the family problem."

The Lord places the responsibility directly where it belongs, wherein he says that it is the duty of parents to teach their children the principles of the gospel and to walk uprightly before the Lord.

The Church

Next to home, the church should be a dominant force in reducing delinquency. In the Church of Jesus Christ every child should be more or less safeguarded; first, by the ward teacher, whose duty it is to "watch over the Church always, (the "Church" meaning members), to be with and to strengthen them." Today the perfunctory obligations of the ward teacher are fairly well performed, but the looking after of individuals is woefully neglected.

If every teacher, as an appointed representative of the bishopric of his ward, were properly and fully to perform his duty, he would be aware of the activity or inactivity of every child, and of every youth in the Church.

In more direct contact with individuals are the quorum officers and instructors. It is the duty of these officers and instructors to know the status of every youth from twelve years to twenty, and to take personal interest in each.

A third dominant force are the auxiliary associations, comprehending in their enrollment every child and youth from six years of age and upward.

Indifference manifest in the world generally towards church should tend only to spur men of the priesthood and teachers in the auxiliaries in the Church of Christ to more earnest and diligent activity.

The School

If the reports be true with reference to the indifference of the country as a whole toward Christian churches, we shall have to place next to the home not the church but the public school, as the most influential factor in lessening delinquency.

Present-day conditions emphasize the fact (and I believe it with all my heart) that the most paramount objective of the public school system from kindergarten to the university should be character building; the evolving of true, loyal citizens of the republic. The teaching of the three "R's," of the arts, and the sciences, even the delving into research work, should be but a means to the development of true manhood and noble womanhood. Education for loyal citizenship! Ralph Waldo Emerson (sometimes referred to as the wisest American) truly said: "Character is higher than intellect; a great soul will be fit to live as well as to think."

A few years ago inquiry made into the school status of juvenile delinquents in one of our Utah school districts revealed the fact that 81% of the offenses were found committed by the 5% of the school pupils who were out of school. A committee appointed to deal with this situation made the following report:

(1) Since the school offers one of the best resources in the state to prevent and treat delinquency, every effort should be made by both school and court to help the delinquent make a satisfactory school adjustment. In order to accomplish this result, cases which come to the court should be immediately referred to the school coordinator or attendance department of the school district in which the juvenile resides in order to determine whether or not the delinquent has a satisfactory school or work record. If he has not, the court and schools should not cease their efforts until the delinquent is either in school full time on a satisfactory program, or is employed and under proper supervision.

(2) That immediately after the juvenile court has disposed of a case, the school coordinator should be notified of the disposition made.

(3) That the industrial school notify the proper school authority when it releases a boy or girl to his or her own home.

The Community Atmosphere

A fourth and final safeguard against delinquency of youth is the moral atmosphere of the town or community. This is determined by the ideals and actions of adults, and particularly of civic officers and those who are entrusted to enforce the law. The following from one of our leading columnists, referring to the "pervasive example of the behavior of adult civilization," is pertinent:

"As long as we publicize and condone violence; reward profiteering; intensify civil strife; glorify personalities with the sexual morals of rabbits; teach in our high schools and colleges a cheap relativism which denies personal responsibility and places all our sins upon the 'economic system' or 'infantile conditioning,' so long will we have juvenile criminals. Our children are reflections of our-selves, or of the things in our communal life that we toler-ate. England, now, is making special films to be shown in special theaters for teen-agers—films which are partly educational and partly pure entertainment, made by first-rate artists, and frankly designed to magnify and make at-tractive virtue." This writer refers to Thomas Jefferson who "did not believe that you can get a good society ex-cept through good, honest, well-mannered, considerate, law-abiding, clean-living citizens. He thought, in fact, that if education concentrated in the first line on creating those, society and the state would take care of themselves."

Yes, we are living in perilous times, but let us hope that they may be to the present generation as the fiery furnace that consumes the dross but purifies the gold. "A clean man is a national asset. A pure woman is the in-carnation of true national glory. A citizen who loves jus-tice and hates evil is better than a battleship. The strength of any community consists of and exists in the men who are pure, clean, upright and straight-forward, ready for the right and sensitive to every approach of evil. Let such ideals be the standard of citizenship," (Gordon). Such ideals are the fundamentals in the Church of Jesus Christ.

God bless the workers in the priesthood and auxiliary organizations that they may search out the young, be con-stant in season and out of season, guarding well those boys and girls who are not bad but who lack proper guarding. Victor Hugo was not far from the truth when he said: "There are no bad boys and there are no bad men; there are only bad cultivators."

God give us power to be good cultivators of youth, I pray.

The Responsibility of Youth

One hundred years ago, there was not a settlement of civilized man in the Sevier Valley.

It took brave men and women with staunch and loyal hearts to erect the first forts and build the first log houses in this wild unsettled country.

Ten men and two women fell as martyrs to pioneer life.

In imagination tonight I hear the voiceless lips of the young man *Peter Ludvigsen* say to the young men of to-day—BE TRUE.

If *Jens Petersen*, his trusting, heroic wife, and Mary Smith, who were martyred on the morning of March 21, 1867 while on their way from Richfield to Glenwood, could speak to you tonight, they would say—BE TRUE.

Young men and women, yours is not the call to fight the hostile Indians, to build stockades, nor to point the plow for the first time into the sterile, stubborn glebe, but you face problems equally great and stupendous in their effect upon the future welfare of humanity.

In the recent world war, when dictators, drunken with power and intoxicated by desire for conquest, conquered peaceful nations and murdered millions of their fellow beings—who was it that threw themselves in the invaders path and saved humanity from destruction? It was the youth of freedom-loving nations who, many of them with their bodies piled high as an impregnable wall blocked the maddened hordes and drove the would-be destroyers of the rights of man back to a merited, ignominious defeat.

Who is it who now must send out the lifeline to stranded nations and carry forward the banner of peace, liberty and good will as a guide for baffled nations to follow? It is the youth of today who, taught in the ways of morality and in the strength of spiritual attainment, must stand adamant against the false idealogies that would undermine the tried and tested ideals and truths of the pioneers who worshipped the God of truth, and chose the gospel of Christ as their philosophy of life.

The leadership demanded of youth today is not attained by chance, not fostered by indulgence—it demands careful preparation—a preparation that should constantly be impregnated, if you please, by the sweet spirit of four loyalties.

I. *Loyalty to Self*

By conserving physical strength and youthful vigor.

II. *Loyalty to Parents*

Our debt to our parents is unpayable except in one way—and that is in emulating their ideals and bringing joy to them in their old age, and satisfaction to those who have gone before in seeing that we keep ourselves clean and wholesome.

III. *Loyalty to Country*

A great writer has said that "The destiny of any nation at any given time depends on the opinions of its young men under five and twenty."

IV. *Loyalty to God and Truth*

Our belief in equality and brotherhood is a Christian heritage, and it fades out of the picture when Christian belief is forgotten. We have to educate a race to realize that no man is unwanted, that every soul is unique and has a life to live made up of momentous choices which will make or mar his own life and the life of the community and the universe.

Conclusion

To cherish these loyalties to make popular these ideals, the world needs men and women of unimpeachable character. In the words of Riddell:

"The crying need of the hour is manhood; not legislation, not organization, not agitation, but *men*, men who can stand in the presence of Christ and truthfully say, 'The place that I occupy does not need reforming.' Men, who are ready and willing to begin the reformation of the world in their own hearts. Men who can say to the struggling brother, 'Follow me.' "

"If I were a voice—a persuasive voice
That could travel the wide world through,
I would fly on the beams of the morning light
And speak to men with a gentle might,
And tell them to be true.
I'd fly o'er land and sea,
Wherever a human heart might be,
Telling a tale, or singing a song,
In praise of the Right and in blame of the Wrong."

What is your answer?

A Plea for Better Environment

It is my purpose this morning to say a few words about the effect of environment upon youth, and the responsibility of adults to make home and civic environment a contributing factor to their right living.

The following is pertinent to what I have in mind:

It is the age that forms the man, not the man that forms the age. Great minds do indeed react on the society which has made them what they are, but they only pay with interest what they have received. (Macaulay.)

So also is this ancient proverb applicable:

If there is righteousness in the heart, there will be beauty in the character. If there is beauty in the character, there will be harmony in the home. If there is harmony in the home, there will be order in society. And if there is order in society, there will be peace in the world.

From the pulpit and public press, even in homes and social circles, we hear discouraging comments on the delinquency of youth.

If there is concern about the recalcitrance of boys and girls, this generation is no exception to those which have preceded it. Our great-grandfathers and their great-grandfathers worried about the forwardness and recklessness

of their children, and the bleakness of their future just as
we do today.

Speaking generally, I have confidence in our young
people. This confidence springs primarily from my inti-
mate associations with hundreds of returned soldiers and
others who have gone on missions, particularly during the
last three years. While our young men were in the army,
most of them (there were exceptions, of course) conducted
themselves creditably. They met as regularly as possible
for sacred service. As an illustration: During the war in
the Pacific when the conflict was at its height, a chaplain
one day accosted a colonel, saying, "Are you going to conference tomorrow?" "What do you mean, conference?"
answered the colonel. "The Mormon soldiers in New Britain are holding a conference tomorrow."

I heard that same colonel say, upon his return from
the army, "Those soldiers are among the best missionaries
that the Church has ever had."

Many of these young men saved their money to pay
the expenses of missions which they are now filling in
various parts of the world, some of them in lands where
they fought as soldiers.

I tell you, so long as there is an indication of that spirit
among our youth, I am going to uphold them and have
confidence in them.

I know that it is hardly fair to judge the group by
those especially selected as missionaries, but I have been
in touch with other groups whose lives tip the scales
against delinquency. Recently there was held in this city
a convention of one of the national college fraternities.
For dignity, temperance, brotherhood, and other commendable virtues, it was one of the choicest conventions
if not the choicest convention, ever held by such an organization, and that was said by one who had attended
fifty of them. In nearly every detail, it was planned and
carried out by our local youth.

A recent outing by that same group, one hundred twenty strong, was characterized by actions most creditable.

That there is a threatening increase in delinquency in our communities, particularly among boys and girls of high-school age, is all too apparent to anyone who will open his eyes to see, and his ears to hear; and steps should be taken to curtail this delinquency.

It is with this purpose in mind that I refer not to the delinquency of youth, but to the delinquency of adults.

Youth is influenced by example and environment. Dominating groups exerting this influence are the home, the church, the school, social circles, and civic conditions.

There are too many delinquent fathers and mothers. Our homes are the centers that determine the type of our citizenry. To dignify home and parenthood is one of the noblest aims of human society. The greatest responsibility given to women is the divine gift to be a mother. She thus blessed, who has health and opportunity, and shirks the responsibility for social prestige and pleasure, is recreant to her duty as wife and mother. The father particularly, if he be a member of the Church and holds the priesthood, who fails to set a proper example before his children is a delinquent, and is a contributor to child delinquency.

Upon the responsibility of parents to have proper home environment, modern revelation is most explicit:

And again, inasmuch as parents have children in Zion, or in any of her stakes which are organized, that teach them not to understand the doctrine of repentance, faith in Christ the Son of the living God, and of baptism and the gift of the Holy Ghost by the laying on of the hands, when eight years old, the sin be upon the heads of the parents.

For this shall be a law unto the inhabitants of Zion, or in any of her stakes which are organized.

And their children shall be baptized for the remission of their sins when eight years old, and receive the laying on of the hands.

And they shall also teach their children to pray, and to walk uprightly before the Lord. (D&C 68:25-28)

Quarreling among parents and children, faultfinding, backbiting, smoking cigarettes, drinking intoxicating liquors, using profane language, make a home environment that contributes to delinquency. No parent can consistently teach faith in Christ who profanes the name of Deity. Profanity is never heard in the well-ordered home. Swearing is a vice that bespeaks a low standard of breeding. Blasphemous exclamations drive out all spirit of reverence. Irreverence is always a mark of delinquency.

Profanity is a vice all too prevalent in America, and though we say it with embarrassment, all too frequently used in the Church.

The great Chinese philosopher, as a minister of crime, is reported to have set free a son who had offended against the canon of filial behavior, on the ground that the father who had so ill-taught him was the one to blame. Said he:

When superiors fail in their duty, should inferiors die? This father never taught his son to be filial. To act upon this charge would be to kill the innocent.

But until the millennium there will be delinquent parents and delinquent homes, and as a result from out of these there will come children inclined to delinquency.

It is the duty of the Church to render such assistance as is possible. First, to find these delinquents, and then to awaken higher ideals in daily living and to inspire faith in the gospel of Jesus Christ.

But only a small percentage of children and youth ever come in contact with the church. In New York City alone, fifty thousand children are unaffiliated with any church. A potent factor, therefore, in character development is the public school.

To these democratic institutions come children from all kinds of homes, including the delinquent. All I can say this morning is that every teacher in church and in school should realize that he has the moral as well as the assigned responsibility to impress upon his students the true value of the highest and noblest things in life.

More concern, it is now apparent, should be given to the influences outside the home, the church, and the school. One of the most important conferences ever held in this country was the White House Conference on Child Health and Protection held during President Hoover's administration. Governor George Dern followed the matter up in Utah. As a result, hundreds of progressive people, forward-looking citizens, participated in the Utah State White House Conference, and considered influences that affect the child. From one of these reports I quote as follows:

> The decadence of the old-time home with its wide physical arena of family life, its home with genius industry, its concern in the individual welfare and control over the child, yields to community influences which now have a larger part in the life of the child.

With the great masses of sensationalism and artificial stimulation to which the child of today is subjected in this age of mechanical wonders, it is of the gravest importance that society realize that it is only in the example of sincere living upon the part of the individual members of society that the child finds a dynamic impulse for his own wholesome development.

If we are sincere in our desire to reduce this delinquency among youth, let us look to ourselves as members of the community and as leaders and officials in civic circles. I continue to quote:

> A nation that has conquered great material difficulties, and harnessed its physical powers must have some more effective means of combatting the cynicism of its youth—the cynicism born of widely flaunted dishonesty of those in high places, insincerity of leadership, and gaudy pageantry of crime.
>
> We have been termed the most lawless nation in the world. This is not merely that we have so many laws that any one enactment loses sanctity. This is not merely that the administration of criminal law has failed to keep pace with our urbanization. This is not merely that we feel that individual rights stand above the law. Deeper

than all this lies a form of lawlessness that pervades our whole people, that infects our children—the tragic result of our unlimited natural resources, the facility of their wealth and the apparent omnipotence of our machinery—the heritage in our generation of the vicious belief that somehow more can be gotten out of life than one puts into it. This is truly in its deepest and most devastating sense a belief in lawlessness.

Recently a delinquent adult, a prominent movie actor, was caught with others in an illegal "dive." A few days later, a columnist published in the public press, the following:

I don't quite savvy all this sudden bleeding over the plight of a droopy-eyed young movie actor who seems to have been caught by the cops on a reefer binge with a couple of blondes. For one thing, it is not an unusual offense in Hollywood. Dragging the weed ranks roughly in the film colony with taking benzedrine as a substitute for sleep and sobriety.

I ask you, I ask the American public, to consider, what effect such comment would have upon young people who are already inclined to yield to the urge of new experience. More shame to the adult delinquent than to the youth!

It is the duty of every law-abiding citizen to see to it that our children have a wholesome community environment in which to live during their tender and impressive years.

The secret, illegal selling of bawdy literature and obscene pictures, the drinking of intoxicating liquors in public, the harboring of gambling devices, and particularly of "one-armed bandits" in "joints" throughout the state, and I speak advisedly, lure the youth into an atmosphere of criminality. Sale of liquor by the drink would only increase the danger and make more readily accessible to young people a demoralizing environment.

I am throwing out these two thoughts to emphasize the need of keeping our young people, as far as possible, in a wholesome and not a demoralizing environment.

In conclusion, let me say:

Let us here and now express gratitude for the Church of Jesus Christ with quorums and auxiliaries specially organized to combat these evils. It was established by divine revelation of God the Father and his Son Jesus Christ. Its glorious mission is to proclaim the truth of the restored gospel; to uplift society that people may mingle more amicably one with another; to create in our communities a wholesome environment in which our children may find strength to resist temptation and encouragement to strive for cultural and spiritual attainment; to make ineffective the influence of designing men who would make profit out of their fellows who are fallen so low as to be slaves to their appetites and passions—and who would fill their purses through the weaknesses of addicts to gambling, and the pitiable courtesan outcasts. The gospel is a rational philosophy that teaches men how to get happiness in this life, and exaltation in the life to come.

The mission of the Church is to establish the kingdom of God upon the earth, which, in the words of Thomas Nixon Carver, is not a mystical but a real kingdom. It is a body of people dominated by ideals of productivity, which is mutual service. We do not strive for the things which satisfy but for the moment and then leave a bad taste. We strive for the things which build us up, and enable us and our children to be strong, to flourish, and to conquer. We strive to make ourselves worthy to receive the world more productively than others. We believe that obedience to God means obedience to the laws of nature, which are but the manifestations of his will; and we try by painstaking study to acquire the most complete and exact knowledge of that will, in order that we may conform ourselves to it.

We believe that reverence for God is respect for these laws, that meekness is teachableness and willingness to learn by observation and experience. By practicing this kind of meekness, or teachableness, we believe that we shall inherit the earth; whereas the unmeek, the unteachable, the pigheaded, who are dominated by pride of tradition, shall not. We offer you hard work, frugal fare, severe discipline, but a share in the conquest of the world for the religion of the productive life.

God help us to discharge our responsibilities to our youth by making an environment in home, in school, in church and in our communities that will be uplifting, wholesome, faith-inspiring, I pray.

Home Building

At the turn of the century in 1901 there was distributed throughout the Church with the approval of the presidency and general board of the Relief Society, a book entitled *Woman*, one paragraph of which I think is so applicable I am going to read it:

"As for woman, wherever she goes and whatever her mission—for travel or for service—her native instincts draw her homewards.

"She may have unusual power and be distinguished for versatility; she may have artistic ability and attain distinction on the stage or in the studio; she may make bargains behind the counter or 'be mighty in ledger and great upon change,' she may serve as shop-girl, toil as fieldhand or in factory, be typist, ticket agent, street car conductor; she may write with the power of George Eliot and Elizabeth Barrett Browning; she may skillfully wield the pen and prove a very magician in journalism and in the nobler literatures; she may possess great persuasive power in the pulpit or on the platform; she may display diplomatic ability in the lobby or cabinet; she may fill the professor's chair or preside over college or university; she may, like Joan of Arc, be the heroine of many battlefields, or, like Victoria, reign with 'all the royal markings of a queen,' but wherever a woman is, or whatever a woman does, she is at her best, her

divinest best, at home! There is the center of her power.
Amiel says, 'Woman is the salvation or destruction of the
family. She carries its destiny in the folds of her mantle.' "

It is wonderful what a responsibility each wife and
mother carries. A successful wife and mother is responsible,
first, for the physical welfare of her children. Second, she
must have the qualities of a teacher. She should be, indeed
is expected to be, not only a disciplinarian but one who
wisely guides her children in their quest for truth and
knowledge. In this she becomes a confidant—she warns—
she protects. Third, she must be a business woman. Fourth,
upon her, even more than upon the father, depends the
child's guidance in spirituality.

For me to comment even briefly upon these responsibilities would occupy more time than I have at my disposal,
so I shall confine my remarks to the second named responsibility—woman's influence as teacher, disciplinarian, guide,
protector.

After a lecture by the late Francis Wayland Parker, a
great Chicago educator, a woman asked:

"How early can I begin the education of my child?"

"When will your child be born?" asked the educator.

"Born?" she gasped. "Why, he is already five years
old."

"My goodness, woman," he cried, "don't stand here
talking to me—hurry home; already you have lost the best
five years."

Do you know, I believe that it is absolutely true. If
mothers would get control of their children throughout
childhood and youth, they should get control of the child
before he is five years of age. That is fundamental, and it
can be done in kindness and in love.

Now, so much for influence, so much for the responsibility and opportunity of mother. I do not want to be a
pessimist, but I must speak as I feel, and warn if necessary,
and I am going to take you into confidence and speak,

however, of something which is just as apparent to you as
to anybody.

> She of whom you speak,
> My mother, looks as pure as some serene
> Creation minted in the golden moods
> Of sovereign artist; not a thought, a touch,
> But pure as lines of green that streak the white
> Of the first snowdrop's inner leaves.

I love to think of my mother just that way. I may be
old fashioned, but I think I could not if I felt she had the
stain of nicotine in nerve, or sinew, or muscle.

I do not wish to be understood as implying that woman's ability to occupy and to reign in the domestic realm
precludes the occupancy of other spheres and the discharge of other duties.

"Other than purely domestic engagements may and
indeed must occupy her attention. She must attend church
and contribute to the charms of social entertainments. She
must be interested in local philanthropic reform. She must
pursue courses of reading and research. She may use pen
and brush or chisel in the worlds of literature and art. She
must examine, according to her endowment, opportunity,
and responsibility, political, social, and scientific questions,
and according to her ability render service in all. But she
must account every other thing as beneath the domestic in
importance and power. She must feel that in passing from
any one or all of these she ascends when she enters or re-
sumes the domestic life."

"And parents shall also teach their children to pray,
and to walk uprightly before the Lord." (D&C 68:28.)

This command leaves no question as to the responsibility of parents to teach their children—a responsibility too
frequently shifted to the shoulders of the Church, the public schools, and officers of the law.

In the present world-wide struggle there are four essential bulwarks, viz.,

1. The *battle front*, where men in uniform are facing the enemy in death-dealing conflict.

2. The *essential industries front*, where men and women are furnishing tanks, airplanes, bombs, bullets, and all other necessary war equipment and weapons for their sons, brothers, and sweethearts fighting on land, on sea, and in the air.

3. The *agricultural front*, upon the success of which depends not only the morale, but the very life of our armed forces, and the subsistence of millions of non-combatants.

4. The *home front*, the stabilizing force of the world in war and peace.

The stupendous accomplishments of the United States industries in the short space of two years in building ships, airplanes, manufacturing munitions, and in shipping supplies to allied countries, are little short of miraculous—a record unparalleled in the history of the world!

The home front seems to be cracking! It is of this I am going to speak.

Out of the homes of America go the future citizens of the republic. Upon properly ordered households and the uplifting moral atmosphere of home life depend more than upon any other phase of social life the happiness of the human family. Home, not the state, is the natural protector of childhood. Parents more than teachers, more than officers of the law, are molders of children's moral natures.

One of the foreboding indications of the weakening of the home line is the waning influence of parenthood as shown in the increasing delinquency among the young. Too many parents seem to be neglecting to teach their children "to walk uprightly before the Lord." A few weeks ago Inspector Rolf T. Harbo, of the Federal Bureau of Investigation, told national officers, chairmen, and state presidents of the National Congress of Parents and Teachers that "delinquency among girls under 21 has risen 64% in the first half of [the year past];" and "this increase comes on top of an increase of 95% for the [year past]. . . . They blame the rise of youthful crimes on the breakdown of family ties, the irregular working hours of adults with the resultant lack of supervision, the gangs of juveniles formed for unwholesome acts, and a general laxity on the part of adults."

In Utah, as well as throughout the United States, delinquency, particularly among young girls, is increasing. Fifty-two per cent of the delinquents are from broken homes!

For much of this delinquency, we must hold parents responsible. True, the wisest parents sometimes lose control of one or more of their children. Secret indulgences in sinful practices, false teachings, and ideals inculcated by pseudo-philosophers, sometimes counteract wholesome home influences. Even the Lord himself had one-third of his family on one occasion reject the divine Plan of Salvation. But after recognizing all this, the fact remains that "homes are the nursery of all domestic virtues, and without a becoming home the exercise of those virtues is impossible."

How apt, then, the divine admonition: "And they shall teach their children to pray, and to walk uprightly before the Lord."

A man who has entered into a sacred covenant in the House of the Lord to remain true to the marriage vow is a traitor to that covenant if he separates himself from his wife and family just because he has permitted himself to become infatuated with a pretty face and comely form of some young girl who flattered him with a smile.

When we refer to the breaking of the marriage tie, we touch upon one of the saddest experiences of life. For a couple who have basked in the sunshine of each other's love to stand by daily and see the clouds of misunderstanding and discord obscure the lovelight of their lives is tragedy indeed. In the darkness that follows, the love sparkle in each other's eyes is obscured. To restore it fruitless attempts are made to say the right word, and to do the right thing; but the word and act are misinterpreted, an angry retort re-opens the wound, and hearts once united, as two dewdrops that slip into one, become torn wider and wider asunder. When this heart-breaking state is reached, a separation is sought. But divorce is not the proper solution, especially if there are children concerned. Far better to follow the wise admonition of William George Jordan:

"Life is too short and love too great to sacrifice one hour through pettiness. What matters it whose the fault or whose the forgiveness? It is a very poor brand of personal dignity that dares to throw its desecrating shadow between them and the joy of reconciliation and new bonds of love.

"When the realization of the waning of love comes, the two should seek to forget for a moment the differences, the saddening changes, the cemetery of dead memories and buried emotions, and try to get back somehow to some common ground of unity and understanding. They should seek to gather together the trifles of sacred things not yet lost. In the thought of these there may be a vitalizing flame of old love flashing out from the dull gray of the ashes that will burn away the dross of discord and misunderstanding. . . .

"Love is the most valuable cargo on the ship of life. It is the greatest thing in this world, and the only thing that will make the next worthy of the living. The ebb-tide of love is the saddest thing in a true individual life. It is a life's folly to let love die if aught we can do will keep it real and living."

To make home life more stable:

(1) Instruct the youth of both sexes that the foundation of a happy home is laid during pre-marital days. Teach young men as well as young women to keep the spring of life pure by conforming their youthful lives to the single standard of morality. When that is done, the bride comes to the man she loves a stainless, priceless jewel. He in turn

receives her not as a cheat, but as a man who can meet his bride on the high plane of moral integrity.

I know there are people in the world, some perhaps who are listening to what I am saying, who consider such an ideal old-fashioned, behind the times! They dub those who entertain such ideas as "reactionaries," "standpatters," and "anti-progressives," etc. Well, all I can say is that nature herself is "old-fashioned," as old as love itself; for since history began man has wanted the woman he loved to be his and his alone. But aside from this, the couple who come to each other as true lovers should have no hidden secrets to break forth at a future time to cause embarrassment and perhaps to destroy the temple of love that has been in process of building for years.

(2) Teach the young people that marriage is not merely a man-made institution, but that it is ordained of God, is therefore a sacred ceremony, and should receive their gravest consideration before they enter upon a contract that involves either happiness or misery for the rest of their lives. Marriage is not something which should be entered into lightly, terminated at pleasure, or ended at the first little difficulty that might arise. The least young people can do is to approach it with honest intentions of building a home that will contribute to the bulwark of a noble society.

(3) The ceremony should be consummated not in secret but in the presence of friends and loved ones. Let marriage be solemnized as far as possible at the place of residence, which will minimize the evils of runaway marriages. For members of the Church the temple should be the chosen place in which this sacred obligation is assumed. For the future of Latter-day Saint homes, young men and young women should so live as to be worthy to consummate their union for time and all eternity in the House of the Lord. Regarding this any intelligent person who believes in the persistence of personality after death, in the immortality of the soul, will recognize at once that love, the divin-

est attribute of the last, will also persist. Death cannot dissolve the union formed by love when that union is sealed by the power of the holy priesthood. Couples having sealed upon them the blessings of the new and everlasting covenant may continue in joy and exaltation throughout the eternities to come.

Under the present stress and strain manifest among social and political groups today, because of the exigencies and horrors of war, the home front does seem to be somewhat unstable, yet the divine institution of marriage must and shall be saved.

Would you have a strong and virile nation?—then keep your homes pure. Would you reduce delinquency and crime?—then lessen the number of broken homes. It is time that civilized peoples realize that the home largely determines whether children shall be of high or low character. Home-building, therefore, should be the paramount purpose of parents, and of the nation.

Peace from Within

There is no happiness without peace. Today, the president of the United States, his cabinet, Congress, the Senate, the House of Representatives, the judiciary, are all seeking peace in the world. Nations are longing for it. Mothers and fathers, grandmothers and grandfathers who have children and grandchildren in the armed forces are praying daily that we might have peace.

Peace is the message that came when the Savior was born a babe in Bethlehem. It was heralded by the angel choir, singing, "Glory to God in the highest, and on earth peace, good will toward men." (Luke 2:14.)

"Peace," he said to his disciples toward the close of his ministry, "These things I have spoken unto you, that in me ye might have peace. In the world ye shall have tribulation: but be of good cheer; I have overcome the world." (John 16:33)

After his resurrection, when the doors were closed and the ten disciples were in session, as he greeted them, his first salutation was, "Peace be unto you." (John 20:21) And eight days later, when the eleven were there, the same salutation, "Peace." (See John 20:26)

What a glorious thing it is, brethren and sisters, and this is my message: Peace cannot be found in external things. Peace comes from within. "There is no peace except by the triumph of principles," said the wise Emerson. Peace is within the individual soul. There is no peace when one's conscience is seared or when one is conscious of having committed some untoward act.

Peace springs from righteousness in the soul, from upright living. If we are going about in the world to establish peace, let us begin at home, first with each individual. If you want peace tonight, remember yours is the responsibility to obtain it, and it is my responsibility, and it is your privilege and mine to attain it.

May our homes become warm nests where children may be protected and grow into noble men and women; where love may find privacy, old age repose, prayer, an altar, and the nation a sure source of strength and perpetuity.

Some Principles of a Happy Home

"And again, inasmuch as parents have children in Zion, or in any of her stakes which are organized, that teach them not to understand the doctrine of repentance, faith in Christ the Son of the Living God, and of baptism and the gift of the Holy Ghost by the laying on of hands, when eight years old, the sin be unto the heads of the parents.

"For this shall be a law unto the inhabitants of Zion . . .

"And they shall also teach their children to pray, and to walk uprightly before the Lord." (D&C 68:25-26, 28.)

We are living in a most momentous age. We see on every hand manifestations of commotion. Political institutions are crumbling. Old forms and methods are fast giving way to new ones. Political organizations are being revolutionized, some for better and some for worse. Old fundamental principles of government are tottering. Some have been replaced by theories that are not tenable, others are not practicable, and some that are infamous. In the midst of this world commotion, the home, the fundamental institution of society, is also threatened. Some, inbued with false philosophies, have attempted to strike at the sacredness and the perpetuity of family life. And wherever we find the evidence of these undermining false philosophies, the responsibility of saving this sacred institution, the home, devolves largely upon us—for we know that the family ties are eternal.

There is nothing temporary in the home of the Latter-day Saints. There is no element of transitoriness in the family relationship. To the Latter-day Saint the home is truly the basic unit of society; and parenthood is next to Godhood. The secret of good citizenship lies in the home. The secret of instilling faith in God, faith in his Son, the Redeemer of the world, faith in the organizations of the Church, lies in the home. There it is centered. God has placed upon parents the responsibility of instilling these principles into the minds of children. Our schools, our Church organizations, and some worthy social institutions are all helps in the upbuilding and guidance of the youth, but none of these—great and important as they are in the lives of our youth—can supplant the permanence and the influence of the parents in the home.

There are a few fundamental principles which we should ever keep in mind; first, the eternity of the marriage relation. Oh, may our youth throughout the land realize that they have within their grasp the possibilities of that form of marriage which will contribute more to their happiness in this world and to their eternal union and happiness in the world to come than can be obtained anywhere else in the world. Let our young men and women look forward with pride, with eagerness, to the time when, in worthiness, they may go to the House of God and have their loved ones sealed by the bonds of the eternal priesthood for time and all eternity.

Second, let us hold to that first word in the second part of the fundamental law of humanity, the Ten Commandments. Those first few commandments refer to our relationship to God; the last few to our relationship to humanity. The second part begins with the word honor—"Honor thy father and thy mother." (Exodus 20:12.) Let us cherish in our homes as we cherish the lives of our children themselves, that word honor with all the synonyms—respect, reverence, veneration; honoring mother, honoring father, seeking to have our children honor us as we honor and revere God, our Eternal Father. Let the element of honor, devotion, reverence permeate the home life.

Third, let us never lose sight of the principle of obedience. Obedience is heaven's first law, and it is the law of the home. There can be no true physical force, but through the element of love. There is no "home" without love. You may have a palace and yet not have a home, and you may live in a log house with a dirt roof, and a dirt floor, and have there the most glorious home in all the world, if within those four log walls there permeates the divine principle of love, love that draws from husband to wife and from children to parents that blessed obedience and compliance that makes life worthwhile.

I believe firmly that parents fail to get obedience from their children during the first five years of childhood. I believe that during that most important period of child life the parents sow the seeds of obedience or disobedience. Some of us fill that period of child life with too many don'ts, failing to make the child realize that a request from father, a request from mother should be complied with. Mother says: "Don't touch that," to the little child. The little child toddles along and touches it. What is the result? The seeds of disobedience are sown. You don't have to punish the little child. Lovingly, kindly, but firmly, teach the child that there are rules in the house which should be obeyed. Mothers, fathers, treasure sacredly and sense keenly your responsibility to the child during those first five plastic years of its life.

With these home elements I desire to mention another, and that is mutual service, everyone working for the others. If some pernicious theories were permitted to prevail and take out from the home the relationship of parents to children and children to parents, and children to each other, they would deprive humanity of one of the greatest means of teaching the true spirit of Christ—sacrifice for one another, salvation through service. Oh, that home is most beautiful in which each strives to serve the other in unselfish service.

Honor, obedience, mutual service, eternity of the marriage relation—these spell home, and they comprehned the spirit in which the principles of life and salvation should be taught to children.

Three Realms in Which Woman's Influence Should Ever Be Paramount

We are living in a changing world. We are in the midst of it, so near us that many of us fail to realize or discern while changes are being brought about. I noticed this recently when we were being driven from the airport in London to our hotel, about twenty or twenty-five miles distance. I noticed the difference in transportation. Sixty years before this recent visit, I crossed on a steamboat to Great Britain. It took, as I remember, about seven-and-a-half days. That morning we had been only fourteen hours from New York, and we were delayed by head winds and the pilot thought it best to land at Shannon, Ireland, to refuel. As I say, it took fourteen hours. Think of the progress during those sixty years! Then another thing, as we were being driven to the hotel, I was surprised at the number of autos, or rather, at the absence of the fine Clydesdale horses that I saw sixty years before, drawing heavily loaded lorries. Not one did we see during that entire trip that morning. All had given way to the advance in building and driving of automobiles, trucks, etc. Another thing, I was surprised to see a lady policeman—women policemen. Sixty years before that, even thirty years so far as I was concerned, we hadn't thought that was a field for women to enter. And I learned, while I was in London, of the efficiency of women as women policemen. In 1930, there were over eight million women workers gainfully employed. Today, as we have learned, there are twenty-eight million. There has been a vast increase in women workers during the last twenty-five years in various occupations in which, formerly, only men participated. And this great increase is particularly among married women.

Now I don't know that there is any objection to women entering the fields of literature, science, art, social economy, study and progress, and all kinds of learning, or participation in any and all things which contribute to the fullness of her womanhood and increase her upbuilding influence in the world; but I do know that there are three areas or realms in which women's influence should always be felt. No matter what changes take place, these three realms should be dominated always by the beauty, the virtue, and intelligence of womankind.

I should like to refer to those three. The first has been covered impressively by Sister Spafford, and that is the realm of home building. Next to that is the realm of teaching, and the third, which has already been emphasized, the realm of compassionate service. "Someday," writes one of our leading columnists, "when women realize that the object of their emancipation is not to make them more like men, but more powerfully womanly, and therefore of greater use to men and themselves, and society, this implicit demand and need of women for a world based, not on mechanical but on human principles, may break through as the most important influence upon history, and bring with it a renaissance of liberalism and humanism."

Nor is it necessary to convince us of the potency of home influence in shaping character. There are certain trusts to which it is only necessary to call attention and minds instinctively assent to them. Some of these trusts are that the home sentiment is second only to religion in influencing the human mind, and all else may be forgotten, but the experiences of childhood will remain undimmed on the walls of memory. "Napoleon understood well the nature of home and its influence, when he said, 'The great need of France is mothers.'

"In democratic countries like the United States and Canada, where the fate of the nation is in the hands of the people, the future of the nation is in the hands of the children. They must be fitted for their high responsibilities by the influences of home. These countries should fear the disloyalty and contention of the fireside more than nefarious plots of scheming politicians. If boys wrangle and contend at home, if they cannot discuss with dignity the little questions that arise in their daily intercourse with one another, be sure they will not honor the nation when they take their places in Senate, Parliament, or Congress to discuss the great problems that confront the civilization of the twentieth century.

"Now, if home may be so powerful an influence for good, how important becomes the cultivation of the home sentiment. To be destitute of this sentiment is almost as great a misfortune as to be destitute of the religious sentiment. Indeed, we believe that one cannot possess a true exalted love of home while there is wanting in his character that which unawakened may yield the fruit of a godly life." (And I cannot think of a member of this Church, particularly one who holds a prominent position, being cruel to his wife, especially before children. I think he is not a good member of the Church; he is not a good Christian. And for a man to strike a woman, as I have heard recently, is just beastly.) "What a mighty responsibility rests upon him who assays to make a home, for the founding of a home is as sacred a work as the founding of a Church. Indeed, every home should be a temple dedicated to divine worship, where human beings through life should worship God through the service of mutual love,—the highest tribute man can pay to God." (Our Home, page 38.)

One of the greatest needs in the world today is intelligent, conscientious motherhood. It is to the home that we must look for the inculcation of the fundamental virtues which contribute to human welfare and happiness.

Womanhood should be intelligent and pure, because it is the living, life-fountain from which flows the stream of humanity. She who would pollute that stream by smoking tobacco, using poisonous drugs or by germs that would shackle the unborn, is untrue to her sex, and an enemy to the strength and perpetuity of the race.

The laws of life and the revealed word of God combine in placing upon motherhood and fatherhood the responsibility of giving to children, not only a pure, unshackled birth, but also a training in faith and righteousness. They ought to be taught "to understand the doctrine of repentance, faith in Christ the Son of the living God, and of baptism and the gift of the Holy Ghost by the laying on of the hands, when eight years old." To those who neglect this in precept and example, the Doctrine and Covenants says, "the sin be upon the heads of the parents." (D&C 68:85.)

There seems to be sweeping over the nations of the earth at the present time a wave of disbelief in God, of disregard for agreements, of dishonesty in personal as well as in civil and international affairs. There is a reversion to the rule and law of the jungle in which might makes right. David Harum's silver rule, "Do unto the other fellow what the other fellow wants to do to you, and do it first," too often supplants the Golden Rule, "Do unto others as you would have others do unto you."

Political poison is being administered to the youth of America by advocates of communism professedly interested in fostering liberty, peace, and democracy, but who insidiously attempt to influence youth associated with what they call the National Youth Administration, or American Student Union, and various other organizations, as some other poison being administered, secretly, as we have learned recently, even in the mission field by cultists who do not hesitate to lie and misrepresent supposed principles of the gospel.

In an article recently printed in a current magazine appears this statement: "There are a great many more young communists in universities in this country than most of the adult population even dares to realize. That is because," continues the quotation, "parents do not bother to ask their children what their beliefs are."

There is one effective source which can counteract such teaching, and that is the teaching of an intelligent, Christian mother. The times cry for more true religion in the home.

Now I should like to say a word about teaching. Every mother is a teacher, she cannot help it. Either good or bad, the mother's image is the first that stamps itself on the unwritten page of the young child's mind. It is her caress that first awakens a sense of security; her kiss the first realization of affection; her sympathy and tenderness, the first assurance that there is love in the world. Her influence, either good or bad, implanted during the first years of his childhood, lingers with him and permeates his thoughts and memory as distinctively as perfume clings to each flower. In her office as mother, she holds the key to the soul, and she determines his character.

But mother is not the only one who exerts an influence as teacher. Often it is a maiden aunt who many times exerts a greater influence than the mother; yet her labors, "gleaming hopes, and obscure sacrifices, her solitary broodings and vicarious ambitions, have seldom received attention from the historian or the biographer. As a molder and shaper of the unpromising material of nephews and nieces, she has been allowed to live, toil, and die unpraised."

Read Emerson's life and see how his aunt's influence shaped his course and made a sickly boy one who is recognized as the greatest thinker in America.

And now I should like to say a word about the young girls as teachers. If we can make our girls think that they are living in a realm where they have power to shape the destiny of teen-agers, it would be a wonderful thing in society. I do not know whether we can, but I shall give a hint. One of the greatest safeguards for a teen-age girl is a consciousness that by her words and acts, she contributes to the betterment or degradation of society—that in protecting or defending herself from the questionable advances of a scheming young man, she honors herself and womankind by resistance rather than by indulgence. She can do this by answering his flattering words of pretended love by saying in her own words, "No man will injure one he loves." Thus, in her early career, she becomes not an enticer but a teacher, her natural and noble calling.

Next to motherhood and teaching, woman attains her highest glory in the realm of compassionate service. One of the most impressive instances in the Bible is the history told by one or of one to whom I apply the title, "A Relief Society of the Ancient Church" whose life was full of "good works and almsdeeds which she did." Her name was Tabitha, "which by interpretation is called Dorcas" (which means gazelle, beautiful).

Marriage—a Sacred Relationship

It is possible to make home a bit of heaven. Indeed, I picture heaven as a continuation of the ideal home. Some man has said: "Home filled with contentment is one of the highest hopes of this life." He is not far from it.

> I could not find the little maid Content,
> So out I rushed, and sought her far and wide;
> But not where Pleasure each new fancy tried,
> Heading the maze of rioting merriment,
> Nor where, with restless eyes and bow half bent,
> Love in the brake of sweetbriar smiled and sighed,
> Nor yet where Fame towered, crowned and glorified,
> Found I her face, nor wheresoe'er I went.
> So homeward back I crawled, like a wounded bird,
> When Lo! Content sat spinning at my door;
> And when I asked her where she was before—
> 'Here all the time,' she said; 'I never stirred;
> Too eager in thy search, you passed me o'er,
> And, though I called, you neither saw nor heard.'
> (Alfred Austin)

Yes, truly the "Maid Content" is in the ideal home. Thinking men generally have come to that conclusion today. Scientists say that civilization is to be measured at different stages largely by the development of the home. Historically they tell us about practices of different forms of marriage among early peoples and races. Most of them are united in the conclusion that the family stands forth as the highest form of associated life. It is the natural unit of all future civic development, for in the home we find content.

"There is something wrong," said one man, "with our present-day marriages." The fault, he thinks, lies in the fact that men marry without any thought of fatherhood. They choose their mates from the "pin-up" girls rather than ask the question, "Will she be a good mother to my children?" and she, looking for a hero instead of thinking "Will he make a good husband and father?"

This author continues: "One current fundamental thing becomes plain: Nobody teaches fatherhood in America. And yet it is the basic reason for the very existence of males! . . . To take the place of fatherhood and, to some extent, of motherhood also—our society has invented endless forms of child appeasement: radio programs and comic books, movies and kindergartens and summer camps— parent substitutes of every possible sort. . . .

"If the home is the foundation of the nation and of society, which it is, we as a people had better begin making real homes and real families. It has become increasingly popular to regard youngsters as a bore and to seize every possible means to escape their company. Children raised by such couples will inevitably be bored by everything in marriage except pleasure. But the good life is not a pleasure hunt. If we want to be happy, we must pursue happiness, not pleasure. And the measure of a happy person is his ability to be tough with himself and tender with others.

"If we are to give marriages their proper start, we must change the ideas and values of those who are to marry. The question of the young man must not be: Who's the cutest number I know? The young woman must not ask: Who will treat me like a bride forever? The question most likely to yield the right lifetime answer is this:

"Is she the best mother I can find for my children? He the best father?

"Or phrase it: Would I want to be her child? His?"

Such is the expression of one who senses the responsibility of the home as a place in which to rear children. That is the point I am asking, and if we keep that in mind—not look upon marriage as a means of selfish indulgence—we are going to save many misunderstandings, for father and mother lose themselves in the lives of the little babes that come. In the lives of little children they find content and true happiness.

Here, to young folk particularly, and to all of you, and to the nation, I should like to say a word about divorce because there are too many who are wrecking their lives upon the shoals of broken homes. I used to think that the man was entirely to blame. I grew to manhood thinking there was no unfaithful woman. My mother was my ideal, my sisters, and my wife. And for all marital troubles in life, I blamed the man. I am deeply sorry that during my schooldays I had to change that ideal. Here are some of the usual causes for divorce: infidelity on the part of one or the other, habitual drunkenness, physical cruelty or violence, union of an innocent girl with a reprobate. I mention these as conditions which seem to justify in some cases a separation. If we could remove them I would say there never should be a divorce. It is Christ's ideal that home and marriage should be perpetual—eternal. To the Pharisee's question, "Is it lawful for a man to put away his wife" the Savior answered: "Have ye not read, that he which made them at the beginning made them male and female.

"And said, for this cause shall a man leave father and mother, and shall cleave to his wife: and they twain shall be one flesh?

"Wherefore they are no more twain, but one flesh. What therefore God hath joined together, let not man put asunder." (Matthew 19:3-6.)

Marriage is a sacred relationship entered into for purposes that are well recognized. It is claimed by some observers that our present modern marriages tend to frustrate these purposes. Modern living conditions, writes one, contribute to these frustrations.

"Formerly a married woman had a home to care for, often several children. Today, in many parts of our country, a married woman continues either to follow her vocation or to spend her time seeking new stimulations—no children to care for—no house to clean—no meals to cook. Under such conditions her leisure-time activities become her all-absorbing interests—interests which often lead her away from her husband rather than to him."

Here is a paragraph from a letter I received only last week: "The first year of our marriage seemed to go very well, but after our baby was born, it seemed like things started going on the rocks. My husband seemed to resent the attention I paid to the baby. When the baby was cross, instead of trying to make things easier for me by helping me with what I was doing so I could go and take care of the baby, or care for the baby himself, he would lose his temper, yell at the baby, shake the baby basket and scare the child."

After reading that, I rode to Ogden and entered a business store. An old friend came up and said, "I should like to ask you a question. My daughter is having trouble with her husband. They have three children, three boys. He has fallen in love with an 18-year-old girl."

"Were they married in the temple?" said I.

"Yes."

"Well, if I were you I would see her parents and tell them the danger that the girl is in. She and your daughter's husband are standing on a precipice."

I will not relate the entire circumstance, but I am going to say this: that that condition with that couple is one in which a husband has an opportunity to prove himself either a man or a monkey; one in which he proves whether his character is that of a lion or a rat.

A married man's trifling with a young girl's affections, a flippant attitude toward marriage, the ill-advised suggestion of "companionate marriage," the base, diabolical theory of "free sex experiment," and the ready-made divorce courts are dangerous reefs upon which many a family bark is wrecked.

Temple Marriage

Before dwelling upon the significance of the temple marriage, I should like to make a few remarks about marriage in general. We read in the Doctrine and Covenants that "marriage is ordained of God for man." Note that expression. "Wherefore it is lawful that he should have one wife and they twain shall be one flesh, and all this that the earth might answer the end of its creation." (D&C 49:15, 16.)

In this revelation is set forth clearly the significance of marriage in the Church of Jesus Christ. Marriage is not something to be entered into lightly, terminated at pleasure, or ended at the first difficulty that might arise.

To the Latter-day Saint, marriage is a divine ordinance, and we look upon the home as the best security of civilization, and upon properly conducted homes in which intelligent parenthood directs, as the best means of the improvement of mankind. I think we make no exception. It is in such homes that the virtues that produce true manhood and beautiful womanhood are fostered. That, my dear young people, is the kind of marriage and the kind of home that we shall have in mind as we consult together this evening.

Marriage, therefore, in the light of revelation is an institution with the stamp of divinity upon it, and no person and no state can deprecate that institution with impunity. When Jesus referred to marriage, he associated with it the eternal idea: "What God hath joined together let no man put asunder."

One writer said, "In this human life, changeable, ephemeral, evasive, failing, frail, there is only one thing that ought to last forever, till death," then he adds, and beyond death—marriage, the only link of eternity in the perishable human chain." (Papini)

Marriage is almost a universal desire. Every young person at one time or another, particularly when he or she is in the later teens, is looking forward to the consummation of that ordinance. Hency C. Link, psychologist, corroborates this idea in these words: "Within the past three years I have, in connection with certain nationwide studies among college students, asked the young women such questions as: 'What career in life is most important to you? Do you consider marriage and helping a husband in his career more important, less important, or equally as important as an independent career of your own?'"

I wonder how you girls would answer that tonight.

"From ninety to ninety-five per cent of the college women have answered that a career as a wife and mother was their primary aim, and that helping a husband in his career was more important than a career of their own. The growing belief among college women that the making of a home, the raising of a family, and furthering the career of a husband were in themselves a career of major importance indicates a wholesome return to fundamentals."

The same author quoted in an article in a current magazine, asked this: "If you had to choose one of the following: An interesting job, an independent income of $500 a week, a happy family and home life—which would you choose?

"Eighty per cent answered: A happy home and family life."

I offer that as encouragement under present conditions, when our great economic changes are threatening the home, necessitating wives to work, mothers to leave their children with baby-sitters or groups organized to take care of babies. We must not get away from the fundamental facts that the home is the basis of civilization, and Latter-day Saints have the obligation to build ideal homes and rear exemplary families to the world.

I am happy to greet you young men and young women who are now just entering your later teens, and who cherish, I hope, the ideals to which I now briefly refer.

The problem of choosing a proper, congenial mate is very vital. In regard to this I suggest in general that you follow the advice of Sandy, the Scotchman, but not his example. His friend MacDonald came to Sandy and said, "I'm verra much worried, Sandy. I dinna ken whether to marry a rich widow, whom I do not love, or marry a puir lass of whom I'm verra fond."

And Sandy said, "You'd better follow the promptins o' yer heart, MacDonald."

"All right," said MacDonald, "I'll do it. I'll marry the puir lass."

"In that case," said Sandy, "would you mind giving me the address of the widow?"

Young men and young women, the achievement of a happy marriage begins in childhood and youth. The opportunity of marriage begins in your early days in school. The young girl who learns to play the violin is more likely to find a good mate than one who sits at home, refusing to go out in society.

The boy who participates in athletics is more likely to find a mate than one who sits by the radio. In other words, associations are conducive to happy marriages, because you become acquainted, one with another. You have more opportunities for choice.

In this connection, think for a moment what the

Church offers to its members, particularly to the young boys and girls.

I was riding on a steamer that left Australia about 20 years ago, and a couple from California who had learned from the purser that there were two Mormons aboard — introduced themselves to President Cannon and me.

After asking a few questions, the woman said, "Will you pardon me if I ask you a personal question?"

"Certainly, and I answer without your asking. I have only one wife."

She said, "How did you know I was going to ask that?"

"Oh, I could see from your expression, and apologetic approach."

Well, we soon explained our attitude toward plural marriage, and then to my surprise she said, "Well, if that is not a fundamental tenet of your religion, what is?"

"Why," I said, "we are Christians."

She said, "Well, so are we." Then she made an important query: "In what way does your teaching differ from the teaching of other Christian churches?"

I am glad you are attending seminary so that you can answer that question intelligently. It is not so easy as at first it seems. If you say "Baptism," that is not a distinguishing feature. "Laying on of hands?" That is not a distinguishing feature. "Teaching of faith?" That is not a distinguishing feature. "Repentance?" No.

"Book of Mormon?" Yes. That is a distinguishing feature. Time will not permit to tell you about the conversation carried on during the next two or three hours. But one distinguishing feature of the Church we said, is divine authority by direct revelation. There are two other great churches who claim divine authority but not by direct revelation.

Then the gentleman said, "If your Church is guided by direct revelation then we have the right to expect to find in your organization the answer to the spiritual needs, social needs, and other needs of the human soul."

I said, "That is right. Name a need."

He hesitated. He wore in the lapel of his coat a button that indicated his membership in a secret order. I said, "What does that signify?"

"Brotherhood and fraternity."

"Is that a need?"

"It is."

"All right, if so we should find it in the Church of Christ." Then I mentioned the quorums, and contrasted his group with the groups and opportunities offered by the quorums. After that, "Name another need."

After hesitating a moment, he named education, saying "There should be every opportunity for education in your Church."

"That is right." Then we named quorums as educational groups as well as opportunity for fellowship and fraternity, for boys and men from 12 to 100 years of age. We mentioned all the auxiliaries as opportunities of education for every man, woman and child in the Church, with 50,000 teachers devoting their time every week free of charge and books furnished at minimum cost to the students—courses of study given, to over 500,000 men and women with an opportunity to meet every week, and have instruction free of charge. Where can you duplicate it?

All this in addition to the public school; and public schools in Utah rank second, third, and fourth among all other states in the Union. In addition to that the Church fosters an educational system, in which there are seminaries, institutes, colleges, and a central university.

Think of it, young men and women! Notwithstanding all this there are hundreds of young people in our Church who hesitate to take advantage of those opportunities for education. And there are hundreds of parents who fail to realize what the Church offers for the cultural development of their sons and daughters.

That is one reason for my asking how many miles you have traveled tonight to commend you and that young man particularly who rises at three in the morning to do his work and get to his seminary class, and the young girl who leaves her home at six or seven o'clock in the morning. I congratulate you, and commend you, and commend the parents. If only from the standpoint of education our parents should see that their children attend seminaries and institutes because students get training in spirituality along with their day school training. Parents are recreant who neglect to take advantage of opportunities thus afforded. But that is another theme. I mention it tonight, because of the opportunity seminaries and auxiliaries furnish young men and young women to choose their future mates.

Regarding the value of such, may I repeat: "The girl who learns to play tennis is more likely to find a husband than the girl who does not. The boy who takes part in school dramatics is more likely to find a wife than the boy who prefers listening to the radio or reading about romance. Children who practice musical instruments and get into school orchestras or are able to amuse their friends will have wider opportunities for selecting mates than do those who only listen.

". . . Those who are active in scout groups, go to Sunday School, belong to young people's societies, and who obligate themselves to groups of people, even though they do not like all the individuals, are more likely to marry than are the stay-at-homes."

That is the idea of a man who approaches the subject of marriage purely from a psychological standpoint.

Yes, I believe in seminaries, and auxiliary associations, and particularly priesthood quorums, merely as an adjunct to this question of marriage.

One more thought before I come to the real theme: How may you know when you are truly in love? That is a question which worries you. A young boy, thinking that he is in love with a girl, will dream about her, and piningly yearn for her company. Six months later, however, he may meet another young lady with whom he is sure he is in love. Girls also have their "Prince Charmers," and wonder with which ones they are truly in love.

Just in passing I will say if you think a girl is the sweetest, most beautiful creature on earth, ask yourself the question, "Does she inspire me to do my best? Do I feel that I want to accomplish something in life in order to be worthy of her; or does she appeal only to my baser nature? If the latter, you are not in love. You are infatuated. If the first, she is probably worthy of your closer attention. Young lady, does he inspire you to wish, with Portia, that you were 170 times more beautiful, a thousand times richer? That is what Portia wished when Bassanio chose the casket that held Portia as the prize. In other words, you distinguish between the one who just arouses your baser nature, and the one who inspires you to do your best.

Second, look for distinguishing qualities. First, note whether he or she is unselfish. Be careful not to choose a selfish person. Marriage is a state in which each must give, not take entirely. You have heard sometimes about the introvert. Avoid him, or avoid her. It is best to choose the extrovert, or one who is willing to serve, to give.

Third, see whether he controls himself, whether or not he has mastery over his temper, whether he has mastery over his tongue. Self control is a great virtue. It is a contributing factor to a happy home. There will be many times after you marry when you will be provoked to say something with passion and condemnation. If you have self-control you will not speak the condemnatory word, because there may be a retaliatory reply, which may result in a quarrel. Refrain from saying those things which will cause a wound in the heart of the other.

Fourth, I would name reverence. Has he reverence for sacred things? Has he deference for old people? If he is irreverent, if he mocks at that which is sacred, you will be wise not to choose him for a mate. Is he profane? Does he take the name of God in vain? I think I would avoid him. Profanity is a vice, indulgence in which lowers the moral standard of the home.

Next, if I were you, I would look to see whether or not he has the ability to succeed financially. You have to live with him; he has to support a family. You probably have to help him. But the man should be the supporter. The man should be the provider. Girls, you look for the young boy who is ambitious. I use that word in the sense of emulation—that he is going to try to make something of himself, and will do his best.

But young man, don't put off marriage too long simply because you think you cannot supply the young girl with the comforts she had in her own home. You will find the young girls are willing to help.

That brings me to the next point in general, and that is the rearing of a family. Marriage is for the purpose of rearing families, having children. That is fundamental, and I am sorry to note a tendency even among our own people to limit the number of children in the family. I was very much interested in the following from one who has not the ideals that we have:

"Man has concocted many theories and notions about marriage—among them the theory that each couple has the right to decide whether to have children. Regardless of theories, the chief purpose of sex and marriage is children. This is a law of human nature, which cannot be defied with impunity. A couple entering marriage without planning to have children soon is courting disaster from the beginning.

"Having children is a physical process by the experience, but the experience is a spiritual one as well. It involves continuous self-sacrifice of many kinds, possibly even the sacrifice of immediate security. It is through the choice of spiritual values, where they conflict with material values, that true security is to be found.

"Probably the most popular as well as the most dangerous theory about love is that it is something one falls out of as well as in to. This ignores the truth that love, no matter how it starts, is something that must be consciously created. Lasting love depends on permanent sex compatibility, and this in turn depends heavily on having children. When the experience of sex is subordinated to the birth and care of children, it takes on a new spiritual significance. This is the basis for true and lasting love, a continuous process of creation and self-sacrifice centered around raising a family.

"Having a child is the final and strongest pledge of a couple's love for each other. It is an eloquent testimony that their marriage is a complete one. It lifts their marriage from the level of selfish love and physical pleasure to that of devotion centered around a new life. It makes self-sacrifice rather than self-indulgence their guiding principle. It represents the husband's faith in his ability to provide the necessary security, and it demonstrates the wife's confidence in his ability to do so. The net result is a spiritual security which, more than any other power, helps to create material security as well."

Now, what about marriage in the temple? The eternity of the marriage covenant has its base in the eternal truth of the immortality of the soul.

By great thinkers generally, Jesus is recognized as the greatest philosopher, greatest teacher, that ever walked the earth. He accepted the immortality of the soul without question.

To members of the Church, he is God made manifest in the flesh. He lived before he came. He accepted the hereafter as you accept your sleep tonight, or the sunshine tomorrow. He said: "In my Father's house are many mansions: if it were not so, I would have told you." He did not argue it. To him it was an accepted fact. Upon the eternal truth of immortality rests the value, the importance, of marriage in the temple.

Now, will you please name the most divine attribute of the human soul? Without hesitancy you will answer

LOVE. If your spirit lives after death, as it does, then that attribute of love will persist also, just as sympathy, just as reverence, and every other virtue that you have. That is reasonable, is it not?

All right, if love, then, is as eternal as the spirit, and you love that girl whom you take to the altar, do you not want to have her for time and eternity? To that question there is only one answer. And if death comes to separate you, and you look upon the sweetheart as living in the world beyond, do you not have that same love for her that you had here? Whom should you like to meet when you go to the other side? Whom will you love when you go to the other side?

I asked that of some critics one time, and a woman answered, "Why, we should love everybody." Yes, we should love everybody here also, but I love my wife, by whose side I have sat at night watching a little sick child. I love those children for whom we have worked and struggled, and who have reciprocated that love, and if earthly things are typical of heavenly things, when I shall meet those loved ones over there, I shall think more of them than of persons from India or Russia whom I have never met.

Temple marriage is basically appealing; it is scientifically sound, and any young man who takes his sweetheart to a temple should go there with the understanding that their union is to be just as eternal as the love that has brought them to the altar, and there is no question about it.

Before you can get married in the temple, it is required that you have lived a clean life. You have the assurance, young lady, that the man whom you are about to marry is bringing to you a clean body. Each of you has the assurance that the source of life is unpolluted.

To summarize: Young men and young women who would live the happiest lives would do well to prepare themselves to be worthy of that form of marriage which God has ordained—the union of a man and woman worthy to have their marriage consummated in the temple of the Most High. There as true lovers kneel to plight their troth, each may cherish the assurance of the following:

First, that their married course begins in purity. The children who come to bless the union are guaranteed a royal birth so far as inheriting a clean body is concerned.

Second, that their religious views are the same. The difficulty of rearing children properly is aggravated when father and mother have divergent views regarding doctrine and church affiliation. (Another great advantage of seminaries, auxiliaries, Sunday School, etc., you meet those of your own Church.)

Third, that their vows are made with the idea of an eternal union, not to be broken by petty misunderstandings or difficulties.

Fourth, that a covenant made in God's presence and sealed by the holy priesthood is more binding than any other bond.

Fifth, that a marriage thus commenced is as eternal as love, the divinest attribute of the human soul.

Sixth, that the family unit will remain unbroken throughout eternity.

Boys and girls, God bless you to keep your lives unpolluted, that you may go in prayer to God and ask him to guide you in choosing your mates, and when chosen, that you will both so live that you can enter the House of God, and if he were present and asked you about your lives, you could answer him honestly, "Yes, we are clean."

A marriage begun on that basis, will bring you the happiness, the sweetest joy in this life, or throughout eternity.

Section Three —

Holidays

Easter

Ye seek Jesus of Nazareth, which was crucified: he is risen; he is not here: behold the place where they laid him. (Mark 16:6)

Easter—How Designated

One week from today there will be celebrated throughout Christendom the greatest event of all history— the resurrection of Jesus Christ. This event is celebrated at Easter, a spring festival that antedates Jesus' advent on earth. According to the present designation of Easter, it is just as appropriate to celebrate the event this day as one week later. This Christian celebration is an adoption of the Pagan celebration given in honor of Astarte, or Eostre, a Saxon goddess corresponding to the Ashtoreth of Syria. Unlike Christmas, the celebration of Christ's birth, Easter does not come on a specified day of the month, but varies with changes of the moon. Easter is the first Sunday after the full moon that comes upon or next after the 21st of March. If the full moon comes on Sunday, then Easter is the Sunday following, thus making it possible for Easter to occur on any day from March 22 to April 25. It seems to me that there is little or no justification for the continuance of this shifting of the Easter date.

It would be much more sensible if all nations would adopt what is known as the "World Calendar," a twelve-month scheme in which "the year would consist of equal quarters, each having a month of 31 days followed by two months of 30 days. Every quarter would have 13 even weeks, and would begin on Sunday and end on Saturday." There would be an extra day at the end of each year, known as "supernumerary Saturday" or "year end" day. If this new calendar were introduced at the close of this year, next year and every year thereafter would begin on Sunday, and any given date, including July 4, July 24, Thanksgiving, Christmas, and everybody's birthday would invariably fall on the same day of the week. Perhaps then a definite date might be agreed upon for Easter. The representatives of fourteen nations or more have already endorsed this new "World Calendar."

However, as I say, it is not the *day*, but the event itself that is really important. Did Christ take up his body and appear as a glorified, resurrected being? Establish this fact and you prove that man is an immortal being.

Jesus of Nazareth, Though Crucified, Still Lives

Of the lonely, ignominious death of Jesus, Lloyd C. Douglas writes as follows: "Demetrius, a slave and friend to his master Marcellus, forced his unwilling feet to advance slowly towards three crosses where hung three condemned men. The gruesome scene stunned him, and he came to a stop. The two unidentified men were writhing on their crosses. The lonely man on the central cross was still as a statue. His head hung forward. Perhaps he was dead, or at least unconscious. Demetrius hoped so.

"For a long time he stood there, contemplating this tragic sight. . . . The lonely man had thrown his life away. There was nothing to show for his audacious courage. The temple would continue to cheat the country people who came in to offer a lamb. Herod would continue to bully and whip the poor if they inconvenienced the rich. Caiaphas would continue to condemn the blasphemies of men who didn't want the gods fetched to market. Pilate would deal out injustice—and wash his dirty hands in a silver bowl. This lonely man had paid a high price for his brief and fruitless war on wickedness. But—he had spoken: he had acted. By tomorrow, nobody would remember that he had risked everything—and lost his life—in the cause of honesty. But—perhaps a man was better off dead than in a world where such an event as this could happen. Demetrius felt very lonely too."

> For what are men who grasp at praise sublime,
> But bubbles on the rapid stream of time,
> That rise, and fall, that swell and are no more,
> Born, and forgot, ten thousand in an hour?

In Influence Christ Lives Today

To live is not merely to breathe, to eat, to sleep, to gratify appetite and passion. Only to do such things is to exist—but not to live. To live is to have joy, to experience high thoughts, noble aspirations, to sense the happiness in friendship, the ecstacy of true love, the inspiration that comes from the consciousness of communion with God through his divine spirit. Measured by this standard, Jesus, though crucified in ignominy nearly 2000 years ago, is alive today. The memory of his childhood is an inspiration to youth. His teachings guide and comfort millions. His perfect life and godlike character are ideals that uplift the world.

You may say, "Well, so is the life of Buddha, of Socrates, of Plato, of Confucious, and hundreds of other great men whose influence continues to persist throughout the ages."

This I grant you, and in so doing emphasize the fact that death is not victorious in ending the true life of a noble human being who truly lived in a mortal state.

But to live thus is not immortality, nor does it bear directly upon the resurrection of Jesus from the grave. What we celebrate today is the persistence of Christ's personality during the time and following the placing of his body in the borrowed tomb.

That the literal resurrection from the grave was a reality to the disciples who knew Christ intimately is a certainty. In their minds there was absolutely no doubt. They were witnesses of the fact. They knew, because their eyes beheld, their ears heard, their hands felt the corporeal presence of the risen Redeemer. Of the value and significance of such nearness and intimacy Beverly Nichols, author of "The Fool Hath Said," writes:

"The authors of the epistles were within hailing distance, historically, of Christ; at any rate when their ideals, which they afterwards transmitted to paper, were formed. The winds had already had time to efface the sacred print of his steps in the sands over which he walked. The rain had hardly had time to wash away, with its callous tears, the blood from the rotting wood of the deserted cross.

"Yet, these men knew—I can't go on using the word 'believe,' which is far too vapid and colorless—that God had descended to earth in the shape of a certain man, that this man had met an obscene and clownish death, and that the grotesque mode of his dying had redeemed mankind from sin. They knew, moreover, that he had risen from the dead on the third day and ascended into heaven."

At Jesus' death, the apostles were stricken with gloom. When he lay dead their hopes all but died. Their intense grief, the story of Thomas, the moral perplexity of Peter, the evident preparation for a permanent burial, combine to illustrate the prevalence of a fear that the redemption of Israel had failed.

Notwithstanding the often repeated assurance of Christ that he would return to them after death, the apostles did not seem fully to comprehend it. At the crucifixion, they were frightened and discouraged. For two and a half years they had been upheld and inspired by Christ's presence. But now he was gone. They were left alone, and they seemed confused, fearful, helpless; only John stood by the cross.

The world would never have been stirred by men with such wavering, doubting, despairing minds as the apostles possessed on the day of the crucifixion.

The Seal of Genuineness

What was it that suddenly changed these disciples to confident, fearless, heroic preachers of the gospel of Jesus Christ? It was the revelation that Christ had risen from the grave. His promises had been kept, his Messianic mission fulfilled. In the words of one universal writer, "The final and aboslute seal of genuineness had been put on all his claims, and the indelible stamp of a divine authority upon all his teachings. The gloom of death had been banished by the glorious light of the presence of their risen, glorified Lord and Savior."

On the evidence of these unprejudiced, unexpectant, incredulous witnesses, faith in the resurrection has its impregnable foundation.

Let us listen again to the testimony of these eye witnesses, whose honesty is not questioned even by skeptical criticism.

Mark

One of the first to put his testimony in writing was Marcus, whose original Jewish name was John. He was a cousin of Barbarus. There is no record to show that he joined the Church while Christ was living. There is reason to believe that he was a convert of Peter's who affectionately refers to him as "Marcus my son." (1 Peter 5:13). His mother was a believer, and with her the apostles lodged at least soon after the resurrection, if not before, and it is not improbable that Jesus himself was in her house on the night of the betrayal. Mark, then, was old enough to know and to have personal acquaintance with the men who were eye witnesses of the resurrection. It is highly probable that he was the young man who rushed to the Garden of Gethsemane with only a loin cloth wrapped about his naked body. Certain it is that he was closely associated with Peter from whom he heard at the time, not years after, all the details surrounding Jesus' death, burial, and coming-forth from the tomb. His authorship of the second Gospel has never been disputed by the Christian churches, and even the scathing modern, negative criticism is disposed to regard him as the author of at least the main part of the present gospel.

The First Empty Tomb

Mark does not himself recount any appearance of the risen Lord, but he testifies that the angel at the tomb announced the resurrection, and promised that the Lord would meet his disciples. From Mark we hear the glorious proclamation of the first empty tomb in all the world. For the first time in the history of man the words "he is dead" were substituted by the divine message "he is risen." No one can doubt that Mark was not convinced in his soul of the reality of the empty tomb. To him the resurrection was not mythical, not problematical, not questionable—it was real; and the appearance of his Lord and Master among men was a fact established in his mind beyond the shadow of doubt. To the proclaiming of this truth he devoted his life, and if tradition can be relied upon, he sealed his testimony with his blood.

Luke

Another who records the testimony of the eye witnesses was Luke, a gentile, or, as some think, a proselyte of Antioch in Syria, where he followed the profession of physician. (Col. 4:14). Even some of his most severe modern critics have placed him in the first rank as an historian, and his personal contact with early apostles makes his statements of inestimable value.

Acts, eleventh chapter and twenty-eighth verse implies that he was present when the Prophet Agabus delivered his famous prophecy before the Church of Antioch. It is believe that before he joined Paul at Troas (Acts 16:10), he was a convert to the Christian faith, and in all probability already a missionary. His significant expression, "Had called us to preach the gospel unto them," implies that his conversion did not begin when he joined Paul on the latter's second missionary journey.

Luke's Testimony

What he writes was the result of personal inquiry and investigation, and was drawn from all available sources. Particularly, he interviewed and recorded the declarations of those "who from the beginning were eye witnesses and ministers of the Word." He avers that he "accurately traced all things from the very first," so that he might "write them in order." This means that Luke obtained the testimony of these "eye witnesses" directly from themselves, and not from previous narratives.

According to all trustworthy testimony, we have the Gospel of Luke as it came from his hand. In chapter twenty-four, Luke testifies to the divine message: "Why seek ye the living among the dead? He is not here, but is risen."

He records also the visitation of two disciples who were on their way to Emmaus. These returned to Jerusalem and declared: "The Lord is risen indeed, and hath appeared unto Simon." To the reality of the appearance of Jesus to the Eleven, Luke testifies as follows:

"And as they thus spake, Jesus himself stood in the midst of them, and saith unto them, Peace be unto you.

"But they were terrified and affrighted, and supposed that they had seen a spirit.

"And he said unto them, Why are ye troubled? and who do thoughts arise in your hearts?

"Behold my hands and my feet, that it is I myself:

handle me, and see; for a spirit hath not flesh and bones, as ye see me have." (Luke 24:36-39.)

Authorship Admitted

Luke is also the author of the "Acts of the Apostles." His authorship is now admitted even by some who were leaders in doubting it. During the last half century modern criticism has subjected to the severest scrutiny every ancient document that purports to contain any witness of the resurrected Christ. As a result many have been thrown aside as spurious, including the "Acts of John," "Acts of Andrew," "Acts of Peter," but the "Acts of the Apostles" has emerged from that criticism with its authenticity established. Statements and historical references within the book at one time doubted as to their truth and reliability have been proved to be accurate.

With equal assurance as to their accuracy we can accept his statements and witness in regard to Peter's and Paul's, and other apostles' testimonies regarding the resurrection, "to whom also Christ showed himself alive after his passion by many infallible proofs, being seen of them forty days, and speaking of the things pertaining to the kingdom of God." Who can doubt Luke's absolute confidence in the reality of the resurrection.

From Peter, Luke undoubtedly obtained this:

"Ye men of Israel, hear these words; Jesus of Nazareth, a man approved of God among you by miracles and wonders and signs, which God did by him in the midst of you, as ye yourselves also know:

"Him, being delivered by the determinate counsel and foreknowledge of God, ye have taken, and by wicked hands have crucified and slain:

"Whom God hath raised up, having loosed the pains of death: because it was not possible that he should be holden of it." (Acts 2:22-24)

"This Jesus hath God raised up, whereof we all are witnesses." (Acts 2:32)

Paul's Personal Testimony

It is true that neither Mark nor Luke testifies to having personally seen the risen Lord, and therefore, some urge that their recorded testimonies cannot be taken as first-hand evidence. That they do not so testify, and yet are convinced that others did see him shows how incontrovertible was the evidence among the apostles and other disciples that the resurrection was a reality. Let us now consider a document that does give the personal testimony of an eyewitness to an appearance of Jesus after his death and burial. This personal witness also corroborates the testimony not only of the two men whom I have quoted, but of others also. I refer to Paul, whose Jewish name was Saul, a Jew of Tarsus, educated at the feet of Gamaliel, a strict pharisee, and who, before his conversion, was a bitter persecutor of all who believed in Jesus of Nazareth as having risen from the dead. The story of Saul's conversion follows:

"Why should it be thought a thing incredible with you, that God should raise the dead?

"I verily thought with myself, that I ought to do many things contrary to the name of Jesus of Nazareth.

"Which thing I also did in Jerusalem: and many of the Saints did I shut up in prison, having received authority from the chief priests; and when they were put to death, I gave my voice against them.

"Whereupon as I went to Damascus with authority and commission from the chief priests,

"At midday, O king, I saw in the way a light from heaven, above the brightness of the sun, shining round about me and them which journeyed with me.

"And when we were all fallen to the earth, I heard a voice speaking unto me, and saying in the Hebrew tongue, Saul, Saul, why persecutest thou me? It is hard for thee to kick against the pricks.

"And I said, Who art thou, Lord? And he said, I am Jesus whom thou persecutest.

"But rise and stand upon thy feet: for I have appeared unto thee for this purpose, to make thee a minister and a witness both of these things which thou hast seen, and of those things in the which I will appear unto thee." (Acts 26:8-16.)

Reasoning and Analogy

Later Paul gives direct evidence in his letter to the Corinthian Saints. Nobody even questions Paul's authorship of this document. Its genuineness has been attested, and it stands today as the oldest authentic written testimony of the resurrection of Jesus Christ and of his appearance among men. In that immortal chapter, he anchors the faith of the saints to the resurrection of Christ as an historic fact, "shows how all essential it is to the Christian hope, and then proceeds by reasoning and analogy to brush aside certain naturalistic objections to the great doctrine."

His direct and confirmatory testimony of Christ's appearances follows:

"For I delivered unto you first of all that which I also received, how that Christ died for our sins according to the scriptures;

"And that he was buried, and that he rose again the third day according to the scriptures:

"And that he was seen of Cephas, then of the twelve:

"After that, he was seen of above five hundred brethren at once; of whom the greater part remain unto this present, but some are fallen asleep.

"After that, he was seen of James; then of all the apostles.

"And last of all he was seen of me also, as of one born out of due time.

"For I am the least of the apostles, that am not meet to be called an apostle, because I persecuted the church of God." (1 Cor. 15:3-9.)

Time will not permit, nor is it necessary, to quote other witnesses. So impressive and conclusive is the evidence that sincere and upright men declare that—
"The resurrection of Jesus Christ is a certainty. If any fact, not merely of Christianity, but of history, stands on an impregnable foundation, this does."

To summarize: The direct evidence of this may be stated as follows: First, the sudden and marvelous transformation in the spirit and work of the disciples; second, the practically universal belief of the early church as recorded in the Gospels; third, the direct testimony of Paul.

We affirm, then, with Spurgeon that "no fact in history is better attested than the resurrection of Jesus Christ from the dead. It must not be denied by any who are willing to pay the slightest respect to the testimony of their fellow-men, that Jesus, who died upon the cross, and was buried in the tomb of Joseph of Aramathea, did literally rise again from the dead."

How Many Believe?

It would be interesting, this Easter morning, to know just how many who call themselves Christians, and who have attended Christian churches that day, truly and sincerely believe in the literal resurrection of their Lord. Many—too many—do not, and among them are ministers who profess to accept the New Testament as their authority to preach the gospel. They claim that it is not essential to Christianity to believe in the "resurrection story," nor the dogma "of the virgin birth." Some call belief in these, childish.

The Church of Jesus Christ of Latter-day Saints stands with Peter, with Paul, with James and with all the other apostles who accepted the resurrection not only as being literally true, but as the consummation of Christ's divine mission on earth.

Eighteen hundred years after Jesus died upon the cross, Joseph Smith declared: "I saw a pillar of light exactly over my head, above the brightness of the sun, which descended gradually until it fell upon me.

"It no sooner appeared than I found myself delivered from the enemy which held me bound. When the light rested upon me I saw two personages, whose brightness and glory defy all description, standing above me in the air. One of them spake unto me calling me by name, and said, pointing to the other—THIS IS MY BELOVED SON. HEAR HIM!"

Since Christ lived after death, so shall all men, each one taking that place in the next world for which he is best fitted. Since love is as eternal as life, the message of the resurrection is the most comforting, the most glorious ever given to man; for when death takes a loved one from us, we can look with assurance into the open grave and say, "He is not here; he is risen."

Jesus Christ, our Lord, has revealed and made possible the immortality of the soul.

Independence Day

Approximately two weeks ago, I visited the old Pennsylvania State House in Philadelphia, now called Independence Hall—it is the scene of the adoption of the Declaration of Independence, July 4, 1776. About eleven years later the Federal Convention completed its work on the Constitution and referred it through Congress to the individual states for ratification. It was the seat of government for the United States from 1790 to 1800.

I had just reread in the daily press the experiences of Robert A. Vogeler imprisoned behind the Iron Curtain as an American spy. This American business man, after nearly a month of treatment at the Bethesda Naval Hospital, gave the following chronological account of the prison ordeal which began with his arrest November 18, 1949 by communist police:

Thrust into the Secret Police prison at Budapest, his first 78 hours were passed under repeated grilling and without sleep. Then he collapsed.

"Then I was presented with a so-called confession of the sabotage which in fact was a partial statement of normal reasons why the telephone plant had not been up to snuff," Vogeler related. "Before I signed the statement, we argued it word by word, line by line."

Afterward Vogeler said he underwent 12 days of further grilling which lasted 18 hours a day.

Whenever he appeared to approach exhaustion, he
said he was given coffee and cigarettes which "obviously
contained strong stimulants that allowed me to speak, to
protest, or to write again."

For one 10-day period he said he was not allowed to
wash and lived on black bread and water. When he refused to abandon denials, he said he was kept 10 days in a
wet and unheated cell on bread and water under continual
grilling and observation.

One experience included being dumped naked into a
pail of ice water. He said he lost 20 pounds during his imprisonment.

Thanking the American Press for "keeping the case
alive," Vogeler said this was a "case history" of communist
methods, and advised that "it can happen to you."

"I wish everyone could understand this," he said, *"no
price is too dear to pay for our way of life."*

Later I read the harrowing experiences of Elinor Lip-
per during eleven years in Soviet Prison Camps. The following is an account of her arrest by the Soviet secret
police:

I started up. Was it a dream, or had someone knocked? There
it was again, once, twice, three times—a loud, harsh insistent knock-
ing. A man's voice called out, "Open the door!"

I had to get something on—quickly. I could not find the sleeves
of my robe. Why was I trembling so? I had committed no crime.

Again the threatening voice: "Open the door!"

Three officers entered. The stripes on their uniforms showed
that they were members of the NKVD, the Soviet political police.

They handed me a paper. I could make out a few international
words—"Order . . . Arrest . . . "

I was stunned.

Instead of taking the elevator, the men walked me down six
flights. I took my last automobile ride through the streets of Moscow
inside a prison van that carried me swiftly into the unknown. My
stomach contracted with fear; my forehead was wet with cold per-
spiration. Were they going to kill me? If I had been arrested for
nothing, I could be shot for nothing.

I clambered out of the van and entered the huge vaults of Butyrka Prison. The first day of eleven years of imprisonment had begun!

I had read also of the accounts of the arrest and imprisonment of communist spies here in America who would overthrow our government. That morning New York was stirred with the disclosures of the sale of narcotics among the youth, which stunned the nation more than the disclosures of the Kefauver investigation committee on the relation of organized crime with politics. Communist infiltration into key positions in government and in scientific laboratories, have filled loyal citizens with distrust. One United States senator recently remarked that he believes "the evil and insidious materialism of the communists is a greater danger to us than their guns."

A company of tourists following an official guide at Independence Hall left the room, and for a few moments I stood there alone. I let the curtain of the present period drop, and in retrospect I went back to the scenes prior, during, and following the historical year 1776. I tried to get the spirit of those revolutionary times, and noted the principles that actuated the men to resist the tyranny of King George the III. There came to my mind while standing there the question asked James Russell Lowell by the French Historian Guizot—"How long will the American Republic endure?" Lowell's answer was—"As long as the ideas of the men who founded it continue dominant."

Individual Liberty

Basic among those ideas was individual freedom. Prior to the Declaration of Independence, I saw a group of men in the Old State House rise in consternation when a voice shouted: "Caesar had his Brutus, Charles the First, his Cromwell, and George the Third"—"Treason, Treason!" shouted the men in the Assembly. "And George the Third may profit by their example!" Then I recalled Patrick

Henry's speech climaxed by his fervent appeal: "Is life so dear or peace so sweet as to be purchased at the price of chains and slavery? Forbid it, Almighty God! I know not what course others may take, but as for me, give me liberty or give me death!" And, later,—"Yes, were my soul trembling on the wing of eternity, were this hand freezing to death, were my voice choking with the last struggle, I would still, with the last gasp of that voice, implore you to remember the truth. God has given America to be free."

Thomas Jefferson, who wrote the Declaration of Independence, was actuated by that same love of liberty, for later when president of the United States he wrote: "I have sworn upon the altar of God eternal hostility against every form of tyranny over the mind of man."

Fifty-six men signed that document July 4—fifty-six men representing all walks of society. Most of them were well educated—all in the strength and prime of manhood. The average age was 44 years. Samuel Adams, 58; John Hancock, 39; R. H. Lee, 44; Benjamin Harrison, 36; John Adams, 40; Thomas Jefferson, 33; Benjamin Franklin, 70; Roger Sherman, 55; R. R. Livingston, 29;

"And for the support of this Declaration, with a firm reliance on the protection of divine Providence, we mutually pledge to each other our lives, our fortunes, and our sacred honor."

Faith in God

And that brings me to the second principle that actuated the lives of the fathers who founded our Constitution—faith in God.

During the critical time when the representatives of the colonies were trying to frame the Constitution, Benjamin Franklin arose and stated his faith in an overruling Providence, and in the power of prayer, and then said:

I have lived, sir, a long time, and the longer I live, the more convincing proofs I see of this truth: That God governs in the affairs of men. And if a sparrow cannot fall to the ground without his notice, is it probable that an empire can rise without his aid?

We have been assured, sir, in the sacred writings, that "except the Lord build the house they labor in vain that build it." I firmly believe this; and I also believe that without his concurring aid we shall succeed in this political building no better than the builders of Babel. We shall be divided by our little partial local interests; our projects will be confounded, and we ourselves shall become a reproach and byword down to future ages. And, what is worse, mankind may hereafter from this unfortunate instance, despair of establishing governments by human wisdom and leave it to chance, war, and conquest.

I therefore beg leave to move that henceforth prayers imploring the assistance of heaven, and its blessings on our deliberations, be held in this assembly every morning before we proceed to business, and that one or more of the clergy of this city be requested to officiate in that service.

In his farewell address Washington said:

"Of all the dispositions of habits which lead to political prosperity, religion and morality are indispensable supports." Stating that neither property nor reputation nor life is secure when people are not sincerely religious.

Actuated by these two fundamental and eternal principles—*the free agency of the individual,* and *faith in an overruling Providence,* those fifty-six men who signed the Declaration of Independence, those who drew up the Constitution of the United States gave to the world a concept of government which, if applied, will strike from the arms of down-trodden humanity the shackles of tyranny and give hope, ambition, and freedom to the teeming millions throughout the world.

Recently Graham Patterson gave an urgent warning to all Americans to be on guard against the scheming of those who would take from us the freedom so dearly bought. In this warning he quotes Edward F. Hutton as follows:

Why do we enjoy the highest level of personal freedom the world has ever known? Why do we have the finest system of free education anywhere to be found? Why is it that staples here are

luxuries in other lands? Why is our standard of living the envy of
everyone everywhere? Why have we come to own 60% of the earth's
modern industrial plant capacity?

Why do our people possess more autos, more radios, more wash-
ing machines, more of so many things, than the people of any other
country?

After all, we are plain ordinary human beings. Why then do
we have so many more of God's blessings? One impelling reason I
think lies in the simple fact that we believe in the rights of man and
have lived under a government of laws as distinguished from a government of men. We enjoyed the safeguards of the Constitution and
the Bill of Rights, whose word, until recently, we believed was immutable and inalienable. The protection, the confidence, the assurance provided by the Bill of Rights opened up the faucets of human
ambition and let loose an avalanche of new incentives. Men free to
inquire, to reject, to choose, to risk and to create!

Till 20 years ago the Bill of Rights, generator of the genius of
America, was taken for granted. For two decades now it has been
under attack . . . by those who assert, though without proof, that
they can improve upon our system of government. The plan seems
to be to impose upon the people political control of the daily activities. Under communism you lose your liberties immediately and
perhaps your life. Under socialism, you lose your liberties a little
more slowly but just as surely.

Today the Bill of Rights is in jeopardy. If it could speak, I believe it would have this to say: I am your Bill of Rights. Don't take
me for granted. As man brought me to life, I can be slain by men,
and will be slain unless you, the plain people of America, organize
to defend me.

I am freedom of religion, freedom of speech, freedom of the
press, freedom of assembly. I am privacy and sanctity of your home.
I am your guarantee of trial by jury, and I am the custodian who
guards your property rights. I am your signed lease to spiritual, mental and physical freedom.

My existence depends on how vigilantly you watch those who
administer your government. Put every law proposed in Washington
into the crucible of my ten commandments. Your question must
always be: "Not what does a law give me, but what does it take
away from me?"

We, the plain, humble, God-fearing people, made this republic
what it is. Let us unite our voice in defense of the Constitution and
Bill of Rights.

The First Harvest Festival

The first harvest festival in the Rocky Mountains occurred August 10, 1848. It preceded the arrival of President Brigham Young and the twenty-five hundred or three thousand people who accompanied him in the month of September.

The most pressing problem of the pioneers was to provide food and clothing. Much of this at first was obtained by trading. Some of it was obtained by negotiations with fur-traders. In a letter signed by General Rich to one of these companies is itemized a list of things needed by the Colonists. Among the articles required were: "Sugar, coffee, tea, bleached and unbleached domestic cotton cloth, cotton drillings, unbleached and colored calico, broadcloth, cashmeres, full cloths, satinets, moleskin, blankets, iron, steel, powder, hardware, leather, and such like articles."

It is well-known that one of the first tasks undertaken by the settlers was to plant potatoes.

In October of 1847, a 5000-acre tract, known as the Big Field, was fenced, and 2000 acres of it plowed and seeded to fall wheat, and in the early spring of 1848, the rest was sown to cereal and corn. That spring there was plenty of moisture, and everything looked promising, so the settlers looked forward to a bounteous harvest in August. But their hearts fell when two killing frosts in the month of May, blighted, and in some instances killed, their grain and many vegetables. Then in the latter part of that month the crickets came. These are described by Anson Call as about one and one half inches in length when full grown, heavy and clumsy in their movements, with no better power of locomotion than hopping a foot or two at a time. "The Cricket has an eagle eye, a staring appearance, and suggests the idea that it may be the habitation of a vindictive little demon."

"Every day," says Sarah Rich, "women and children went into the fields with tin pans, sticks, bells, and anything that would make a noise, to scare them away; while the men folks dug ditches, filled them with water, and then drove the crickets into the trenches."

All their efforts, however, were in vain to stem the tide of these devastating creatures. Finally the settlers gave up, and began to appeal to God for succor and help. The story of their salvation is now epic. The crops in the Big Field were saved.

In appreciation and thanksgiving, the saints held the harvest festival. The affair was held in the Bowery, built in the Autumn of 1847 by the returning Mormon Battalion Boys. You and I have seen similar boweries erected on the 24th of July in our country towns in which meeting houses were too small to accommodate the celebrants. It consisted of posts set in the ground in a quadrangle; these were bound together by poles at the top; and the whole was covered with brush, to keep out the sun. Benches were carried from the meeting house and the school house, and people brought chairs with them from their homes. Around this bowery, hoisted on poles, were large sheaves of wheat, rye, barley, and other products of the field. But a most significant feature of these celebrations was the liberty pole. Nearly every private record of that day refers to it. It had more significance than a means of flying an emblem. On the liberty pole on that day was "a white flag, an ear of corn, a sheaf of wheat, rye and oats." I have been informed that at some of the early forts, as was probably the case at this celebration, the liberty pole was a spot on which justice was administered. In December, 1847, the presidency of the Church appointed a committee to work out some rules of conduct with penalties attached. "General Charles C. Rich was chairman of this committee." In his biography appears the following:

First there was a rule requiring that every man able to work must do so. It is necessary, the ordinance read, "for every man in our community to use the utmost exertion to cultivate the earth in order to sustain himself and family." If any man would not work, he was hailed before a judge or judges and pronounced a "vagrant." Thereupon an inventory of all his property was made by proper authorities; this property was administered for the benefit of his family, and the man himself was set to work and his wages given to his dependents. Other laws appertained to theft and robbery, drunkenness, and adultery and fornication. For a violation of any of these rules the last was called into requisition. "A certain number of lashes on the bare back, not exceeding thirty-nine" was the punishment. In all cases, except the infraction of the seventh commandment, a fine might be imposed instead of flogging, which was decreed by the judge at his discretion, and ranged from five dollars in the case of violence to five hundred dollars; for adultery and fornication, both a fine and the lash were meted out to the culprit. Where one had robbed or stolen, he was required to restore four times the amount he had taken, but this did not release him from the strap. It is interesting to note that not a few judges in our time have lamented the disappearance from our penal laws of the lash as a means of punishment. *I have not been able to find, however, that the lash was ever applied during these years in the Mormon commonwealth.*

The following quotation from two diaries will give us graphic description of that celebration. August 10, 1848, a feast in honor of the first harvest in Great Salt Lake City was held in the fort, of which Elder Parley P. Pratt writes as follows:

On the 10th of August we held a public feast under a bowery in the centre of our fort. This was called a harvest feast; we partook freely of a rich variety of bread, beef, butter, cheese, cakes, pastry, green corn, melons, and almost every variety of vegetable. Large sheaves of wheat, rye, barley, oats, and other productions were hoisted on poles for public exhibition, and there was prayer and thanksgiving, congratulations, songs, speeches, music, dancing, smiling faces and merry hearts. In short, it was a great day with the people of these valleys, and long to be remembered by those who had suffered and waited anxiously for the results of a first effort to redeem the interior deserts of America, and to make her hitherto unknown solitudes "blossom as the rose."

*   *   *   *   *

Sister Melissa I. Lambson, in writing from Great Salt Lake Valley about the harvest feast, says:

I must tell you something about our feast. Long before harvest many were out of bread, so since we had plenty we had a large bowery built and all gathered together; a liberty pole was raised. There was firing of cannons, band of music, a number of cheers and the harvest song sung, prayer by Brother Parley P. Pratt, speaking by several, the ground cleared by Brother Grant for tables. He called for good dishes of corn, beans, beef, squashes, beets, carrots, cucumbers, water, buttermilk, etc.; all made ready, the bugle sounded, a blessing was asked by Brother Taylor. When done eating the bugle sounded again, the table was taken away and dancing commenced. On the liberty pole was a white flag, an ear of corn, a sheaf of wheat, rye, and oats.

The harvest song referred to is as follows:

Let us join in the dance, let us join in the song,
To thee, O Jehovah, new praises belong,
All honor, all glory, we render to thee;
Thy cause is triumphant, thy people are free.

The Gentile oppressed us, the heathen with rage
Combined all their forces our hosts to engage,
They plundered and drove us full many a day;
They kill'd the chief shepherds, the sheep went away
Afar in the desert and mountains to roam,
Without any harvest, without any home.

There, hungry and thirsty, and weary and worn,
They seemed quite forsaken, and weary and worn,
But lo! in the mountains new sheepfolds appear!
And a harvest of plenty, our spirits to cheer.
This beautiful vale is a refuge from wo,
A retreat for the Saints, while the scourges o'er flow.

Let us join in the dance, let us join in the song,
To thee, O Jehovah, new praises belong,
All honor, all glory, we render to thee,
Thy cause is triumphant, Thy people are free!

Though storms of commotion distress every realm,
And dire revolution the nations o'erwhelm;
Though Babylon trembles and thrones cease to be,
Yet here in the mountains thy people are free.
The states of Columbia to atoms may rend,
And the mob, all triumphant, bring peace to end,—
The 'Star Spangled Banner' for ever be furled,
And the chains of a tyrant encircle the world.

Yet we'll join in the dance, and we'll join in the song,
To thee, O Jehovah, new praises belong,
All honor, all glory, we render to thee;
For here in the mountains thy people are free.

TWO GUIDING PRINCIPLES OF THE PURITANS

For all that God in mercy sends:
For health and strength, for home and friends,
For comfort in the time of need,
For every kindly word and deed,
For happy thoughts and pleasant talk,
For guidance in our daily walk,
For all these things give thanks.

For beauty in this world of ours,
For verdant grass and lovely flowers,
For song of birds, for hum of bees,
For the refreshing summer breeze,
For hill and plain, for streams and wood,
For the great ocean's mighty flood,
For all these things give thanks.

For the sweet sleep that comes at night,
For the returning mornin's light,
For the bright sun which shines on high,
For stars that glitter in the sky—
For these and everything we see,
O Lord, our hearts we lift to Thee,
And give Thee hearty thanks.

                                        Ellen Isabella T.

Thanksgiving Day is a religious festival in the United States, celebrated in New England, as you know, from the first settlement by the Pilgrims.

Thanksgiving

The term "Pilgrim" is applied here in America to those who first settled at Plymouth, Massachusetts, in the month of November 1620. I think it was on the 9th of November. The Pilgrims who landed on that bleak New England shore at Cape Cod were Separatists. They were not the Puritans—the Puritans settled in Massachusetts. But the Separatists, whom we designate now as Pilgrims, settled at Plymouth.

Origin of Thanksgiving

Thanksgiving Day originated one year later—1621— when Governor Bradford appointed the day for public praise and prayer after the first harvest. This is what one account gives of that first thanksgiving:

"In the fall of 1621 the first harvest of the colonists was gathered. The 'corn' yielded well, and the 'barley' was 'indifferently good,' but the peas were a failure, owing to drought and late spring. Encouraged with the harvest of their fruits, but needing more eatables for feasting, the leaders sent four huntsmen for food of the forest, and at their return, 'after a special manner,' the Pilgrims rejoiced together, feasting King Massasoit and ninety men for three days, and partaking of venison, wild turkeys, water fowl, and other delicacies for which New England was then famous."

The first Thanksgiving was but a formal manifestation of the spirit of praise and thanksgiving that actuated the hearts of the pilgrims during that first terrible winter in the new country.

To recall the circumstances of that first terrible winter may serve as a means of increasing our spirit of thanksgiving for what we possess, and awaken a sense of true gratitude for our present surroundings, and for the privilege of living in this age.

History tells us that of the 102 immigrants that landed on the bleak, rocky coast of Cape Cod in the winter of 1620, nearly half died before the following winter barely set in. In December six died; January, eight; February, seventeen; March, thirteen—a total of 44 in four months. Today in our comfortable homes, surrounded with peace and plenty, it is well for us to pause and try to imagine the suffering of the survivors both from destitution and inclement weather. One account tells us that the most of the brave people were not inured to hardships; among them were delicately nurtured men and women. They staked and laid out two rows of huts for the nineteen families that composed the colony; but within the first year they had to make seven times more graves for the dead than houses for the living. Notwithstanding all their trials and hardships, these brave founders of a great and glorious race had so much to be thankful for that they had to appoint "an especial day on which to give special thanks for all their mercies."

May I say here that our attention was called last evening, or the night before, to the fact that the Indians are suffering from want of the necessities of life. Sister McKay and I have driven through the Navajo Indian Reservation, and we have seen the condition of those who live in the hogans. They are not wickiups; they are just little

round adobe houses, or huts. Some of these Indians will
not survive this winter. I think it is well for us on this
Thanksgiving Day to recall the fact that it was the Indians
who kept the Pilgrims from starving that first winter. The
Pilgrims had insufficient food. They saw some mounds
into which they dug and found corn, and they appropriated
it to their own use. They reported it, however, to King
Massasoit, and told him that as soon as they learned to
whom the corn belonged, they would recompense them
for it.

Today we should not only express our thanks in words
and in song, but have in our hearts a deep gratitude for
the integrity, fortitude, and faith of the Pilgrims.

I think I would call your attention to only two of their
virtues, two guiding principles which I shall emphasize
with a view of applying them to our lives.

Two Guiding Principles

As we read the history of the New England fathers, we
cannot help but be impressed with their many sterling
virtues, nor can we shut our eyes to their weaknesses. Today I wish to express gratitude for their strength of character and for the attributes of true greatness which they
exemplified. First, you students know that they chose the
right with invincible resolution. Second, they resisted the
sorest temptations from within and from without. Third,
they bore the heaviest burdens cheerfully. Fourth, they
were most fearless under menace and frowns, and Fifth,
their reliance upon God and truth was most unfailing.
These traits, says Channing, are the marks of true greatness.

As I say, I am going to emphasize only two of their
virtues—*faith and their love of freedom.*

Governor Bradford, I think the day after they landed,
probably the 11th of November, gave an address to that
little company. I think they were still on board the Mayflower, for you know they drew up a plan of government

by which they were to be guided after they landed. Note the concluding paragraph:

"May not and ought not the children of these fathers rightly say, Our fathers were Englishmen which came over this great ocean, and were ready to perish in this wilderness; but they cried unto the Lord, and he heard their voice, and looked on their adversities."

Faith in God was real to them—not just a mere essence.

Right in this connection may I call your attention to the first official proclamation of a Thanksgiving Day in this country. It was signed by George Washington. Note, too, how that element of divine faith is emphasized:

Whereas, it is the duty of all Nations to acknowledge the Providence of Almighty God, to obey his Will, to be grateful for his Benefits, and humbly to implore his Protection and Favour; and whereas both houses of Congress have by their joint Committee, requested me "To recommend to the People of the United States, a Day of Public Thanksgiving and Prayer, to be observed by acknowledging with grateful Hearts the many Signal Favours of Almighty God, especially by affording them an opportunity peaceably to establish a Form of Government for their safety and Happiness."

Now, therefore, I do recommend and assign Thursday and the twenty-sixth Day of November, next, to be devoted by the People of these States, to the Service of that great and glorious Being, who is the beneficient Author of all the good that was, that is, or that will be: That we may then all unite in rendering unto him our sincere and humble thanks for his kind Care and Protection of the People of this Country previous to their becoming a Nation; —for the signal and manifold Mercies and the favourable Interpositions of his Providence in the Course and Conclusion of the late War; —for the great Degree of Tranquility, Union, and Plenty which we have since enjoyed; for the peaceable and rational Manner in which we have been enabled to establish Constitutions of Government for our Safety and Happiness, and particularly the national one now lately instituted; —for the civil and religious Liberty with which we are blessed, and the means we have of acquiring and diffusing useful knowledge; —and in general, for all the great and various Favours which he hath been pleased to confer upon us. And Also, that we may then unite in most humbly offering our Prayers and supplications to the great Lord and Ruler of Nations, and beseech him to pardon our National and other Transgressions; —to enable us all whether in public or private Stations, to perform our several and relative Duties properly and punctually; —to render our national Government a Blessing to all the people, by constantly being a government of wise, just, and Constitutional Laws, directly and faithfully obeyed; —to protect and guide all Sovereigns and nations (especially such as have shown kindness to us) and to bless them with good Government, Peace, and concord; —to promote the Knowledge and practice of true Religion, and Virtue, and the increase of Science among them and us; —and generally to grant unto all mankind such a Degree of temporal Prosperity as he alone knows to be best.

Given under my hand at the City of New York, the third Day of October, in the Year of our Lord, One Thousand Seven Hundred and Eighty nine.

Here may I make an application of this principle of faith and belief in God to our present conditions today. You brethren and sisters know what the Lord has said regarding the perpetuation of this great country—that its perpetuity, its stability depends upon that principle of faith exemplified by the Pilgrims.

Wherefore, this land is consecrated unto him whom he shall bring. And if it so be that they shall serve him according to the commandments which he hath given, it shall be a land of liberty unto them; wherefore, they shall never be brought down into captivity; if so, it shall be because of iniquity; for if iniquity shall abound cursed shall be the land for their sakes, but unto the righteous it shall be blessed forever.

Wherefore, I, Lehi, have obtained a promise, that inasmuch as those whom the Lord God shall bring out of the land of Jerusalem shall keep his commandments, they shall prosper upon the face of this land; and they shall be kept from all other nations, that they may possess this land unto themselves. And if it so be that they shall keep his commandments they shall be blessed upon the face of this land, and there shall be none to molest them, nor to take away the land of their inheritance; and they shall dwell safely forever.

We read further down—

But behold, when the time cometh that they shall dwindle in unbelief, after they have received so great blessings from the hand of the Lord—having a knowledge of the creation of the earth, and all men, knowing the great and marvelous works of the Lord from the creation of the world; having power given them to do all things by faith; having all the commandments from the beginning, and having been brought by his infinite goodness into this precious land of promise—behold, I say, if the day shall come that they will reject the Holy One of Israel, the true Messiah, their Redeemer and their God, behold, the judgments of him that is just shall rest upon them. (2 Nephi 1:7-10.)

So the perpetuity of this land and nation depend upon faith. I pause to point out the fact that any power or any influence that will destroy directly or indirectly this principle of faith in God is an enemy to your constitution and to mine. There is an influence that will undermine the very basic structure of this great nation. Now, I am going to be specific, because I know young men and women are being influenced.

The government of Russia rejects God. It takes its place on the side of Atheism, and answers with disbelief, should one ask what he thinks about God: "I have no need for such an hypothesis." Communists seek to eradicate from the minds of millions, naturally deeply religious, all belief in God, all interest in Church or its activities, all hope, aspiration, and faith outside the political doctrine of a few who have seized the national power. Now you see why I want to emphasize this dominant trait of the pilgrim fathers—Faith. We can govern ourselves accordingly. We should love the stars and stripes, and accept the constitution of these United States as divine. Don't you hesitate to stand on the right side.

Now just a word about that second dominant trait—the love of freedom. Now let's go back again to these Pilgrims, away back at the beginning of the century—1604-5-6. Shakespeare was writing his plays at that time. There were at least four classes or parties in England—(1) The Catholics who remained true to Rome, (2) Members of the English Church who had drawn away from the Catholics.

(3) The Puritans who, as I say, were the founders of the Massachusetts Colony, and (4) The Separatists, the founders of the Plymouth Colonies. The Puritans and Separatists withdrew from the English Church, because they thought the English Church had not gone far enough from the Catholic Church. The persecution of these sects or groups was very intense, particularly under James the First who is described as "the greatest pedant that ever sat upon the English throne." He was "arbitrary, capricious, tyrannical, and unprincipled, he trampled upon the most solemn oaths, and seemed never better pleased than when torturing or anathematizing the victims of his vengeance. Hence at Hampton Court Conference, at the close of the second day, speaking of the Puritans, he said: 'I shall make them conform themselves, or I will harry them out of the land, or else do worse.' "

There is tyranny for you!

Finally he issued a proclamation, July 16, 1604, ordering the Puritan Clergy to conform before the last of November, or to dispose of themselves and families in some other way, as "unfit for their obstinacy and contempt to occupy places."

Well, the Separatists waited awhile, and finally one group under a man by the name of Robinson took a boat to Holland where they might worship free of this autocracy. The others were harried and persecuted. There was one group at Scrooby and one at Gainsborough. So after much suffering they finally decided to go because they couldn't stand it any longer. Accordingly, one group, under Robinson as I have already told you, settled in Holland, and then the others decided that they would have to go.

They endured persecution, were driven from their homes, their leaders were imprisoned. Finally, they said they would leave Holland. The King said they couldn't leave—that "It is conformity we demand." So they schemed to leave by night, and they hired a ship wholly to themselves, and made agreement with the master to be ready

at a certain day, and take them and their goods on board
at a convenient place. After long waiting and large expenses, they were finally taken on board at night only to
learn that they had been betrayed. Governor Bradford
in his account says: "But when he had them and their goods
aboard, he betrayed them, having beforehand plotted with
the searchers and other officers so to do who took them,
and put them into open boats, and there rifled and ran-
sacked them, searching them to their shirts for money, yea
even the women further than became modesty; and then
carried them back into the town and made them a spectacle
and wonder to the multitude, which came flocking on all
sides to behold them."

I think it is well for us to picture their plight three
hundred years ago.

Well, later, they got a Dutchman who said "I will take
you over." He made an appointment to take them in at a
place a good distance from any town. The women and
children with the goods were sent to the place in a small
barke, which they had hired and the men were to meet them
by land. They were there a day before the ship came, and
the sea being rough, and the women very sick, asked the
seamen to put into a creek that was nearby where they lay
on the ground at lowwater. The next morning the ship
came, but they couldn't move because the tide was out. In
the meantime the ship master sent his boat out to the men
and got them aboard the ship. Just as they got aboard, the
master of the boat saw horsemen with guns and other
weapons coming toward them, and he knew what it meant—
the officers had found them. So, Governor Bradford, says:
"The Dutchman seeing this, swore his country's oath,
'sacramente,' and having the wind fair," sailed away with
the husbands aboard, and the women and children left
stranded. Imagine their deplorable state! They had nothing with them excepting the shirts on their back, and their
wives and children left helpless. They should have made
the trip in seven days, but they were out fourteen days be-

cause of a terrible storm which threatened to engulf them. Governor Bradford gives his account of this storm:

And afterward endured a fearful storm at sea, being 14 days or more before they arrived at their port in seven, whereof they neither saw sun, moon, nor stars, and were driven near the coast of Norway; the mariners themselves often despairing of life; and once with shrieks and cries gave over all, as if the ship had been founded in the sea, and they sinking without recovery. But when man's hope and help wholly failed, the Lord's power and mercy appeared in their recovery; for the ship rose again, and gave the mariners courage again to manage her. And if modesty would suffer me, I might declare with what fervent prayers they cried unto the Lord in this great distress, (especially some of them), even without any great distraction, when the water ran in their mouths and ears; and the mariners cried out We sinke, we sinke; they cried (if not with miraculous, yet with a great height or degree of divine faith), Yet Lord thou canst save, yet Lord thou canst save; with such other expressions as I will forbear. Upon which the ship did not only recover, but shortly after the violence of the storm began to abate, and the Lord filled their afflicted minds with such comforts as every one cannot understand, and in the end brought them to their desired Haven, where the people came flocking admiring their deliverance, the storm having been so long and sore, in which much hurt had been done, as yet masters friends related unto him in their congratulations.

This will remind you of Paul on his way to Rome.

Now, that is what the Pilgrims suffered and endured for the love of freedom. It is merely an illustration. I know that they became just as guilty of intolerance as those who had persecuted them, but that only reflects upon their clear sense of justice, and it does not lessen in any way the heroism in their defense of freedom.

Conditions in U.S. That Threaten Freedom

Will you tell me—is there an enemy today in our country that threatens our freedom in this country? I am not very much worried about our leaders hastening war. I think our men who are guiding the destiny of the nation at the present are just as eager for peace as you and I. Have you ever talked to a man or woman, or to a veteran, who really wants war? Now it may be that war will come. If wolves come to my door and threaten to take the lives of my loved ones, I would fight, and if human wolves attack this great country, we shall fight, but we are not going to attack any other country. So I am not going to say anything about that. But there is another element, and it is the conflict between capital and labor. A few years ago capital said— Get as much as you can and pay as little. That is wrong. Labor had to fight. But what of today? Labor says—Do as little as you can and get as much as you can. And that is wrong. We see in that condition a threat to the freedom to work. It is a God-given right to work. Our attention has been called to an article in the New York Times. It contains a laborer, a father of five children. An employee for twenty-three years of the National Silver Warehouse Company. He belonged to local Union 65, CIO. This union recently authorized an assessment equal to one week's wages to set up a $500,000 strike fund. This workman refused to make the payment. Maybe his children needed the groceries a week's wage would buy. The union forced his reluctant employer to fire him, although he was "an excellent and reliable worker."

Commenting upon this a leading figure of our nation says: "The greatest of all civil rights is the right to live. But men can live only if they work. All other rights mean little if the right to work is not enforced." He continued:

Does this man have the right to work? If he is too poor to kick in with a week's wage, does he have to give up a job with 23 years' seniority? Do he and his family have to go on relief? Do I and other taxpayers have to support them?

Do you think a union should have the power to follow this man into the ballot box and force him to mark his ballot as it desires? If not, what difference is there in principle between doing that and forcing him to kick in a week's wage to be used in a political campaign against his will? Or if he refuses, as he did, to be forced to lose his job and his children's bread?

That is the element that I see is threatening the freedom, not of religious worship, against which the Pilgrims fought, but against man's right to live, the right to choose whether he joins the union or not. Here in Utah it is time for us to take the proper stand, and to safeguard our rights as given in the Constitution of the United States. We can find faults. We need to find the right way.

I suggest a share in the profits. That is what should be done. Let the men who work share in the profits of their labor. A share in the profits is being carried on by a little firm in this city. There are thirteen employees in this little organization the manager says:

We decided upon a simple division of profits: 1/3 to capital and 2/3 divided equally among workers and management. If the profits for half a year were $21,000, Capital would get $7,000, and the workers (if there were 13, and counting management as I) would get $14,000, or $1,000 each, paid in cash. Of course an audited and certified copy of our half-yearly balance sheet is posted on the wall for workers to study, giving them complete confidence.

There are no strikes in that place!

I was happy when we were visiting the three million dollar plant of the Thermoid Rubber Company to have the president of that establishment say: "That is just what we are going to do. The workers will share in the profits, and will be amply paid for what they do, and will share with us."

This is the answer. Faith—faith in God, in Jesus Christ, and to us in the restoration of the Gospel of Jesus Christ. A love of freedom to worship and to work, to think, to live. To feel a sense of possession of what we have is ours, and no autocracy or government will say we will take that. I like the spirit that a man's home is his castle—for him, his wife and his children. I am thankful for our government, grateful for the Church, grateful for friends, for men and women whom we can trust this Thanksgiving Day. It is a glorious morning. Grateful for the nation, for the Church, for every individual who lives under that flag.

I am sorry for the information that has come to us concerning the Indians from whom we have taken this land. Let us help them, and the Church has already planned to send help to them. Today a truckload is on its way. We are not waiting for bureaus and regulations. We are going to help those little kiddies who are hungry. I am grateful for a Church that will do this. And so, in conclusion, let us all unite and say:

We thank Thee, O Father, for all that is bright—
The gleam of the day and the stars of the night,
The flowers of our youth and the fruits of our prime,
And the blessings that march down the pathway of time.

We thank Thee, O Father, for all that is drear—
The sob of the tempest, the flow of the tear;
For never in blindness, and never in vain,
Thy mercy permitted a sorrow or pain.

We thank Thee, O Father of all, for the power
Of aiding each other in life's darkest hour;
The generous heart and the bountiful hand
And all the soul-help that sad souls understand.

We thank thee, O Father, for days yet to be;
For hopes that our future will call us to Thee.
Let all our eternity form, through Thy love
A heart of Thanksgiving in the mansions above.
                                                        (Will Carleton)

God grant that this prayer will be in each heart this day throughout this entire land.

Christmas

"And there were in the same country shepherds abiding in the field, keeping watch over their flock by night.

And lo, the angel of the Lord came upon them, and the glory of the Lord shone round about them: and they were sore afraid.

"And the angel said unto them, Fear not: for, behold, I bring you good tidings of great joy, which shall be to all people.

"For unto you is born this day in the city of David a Savior, which is Christ the Lord."

Such is part of the first glorious Christmas message!

Salt Lake City this Christmas Eve is brilliant with light radiating from a million electric lamps.

Christmas Eve in Bethlehem two thousand years ago was dark, excepting perhaps for a few torches seen here and there.

Yet in that humble though historic town was heralded the first Christmas story and in it the Light of the world was born.

How different the world conditions then from what they are tonight—no railroad, no auto, no steamboat, no radio, and a man would have been considered "beside himself" had he even mentioned the possibility of carrying passengers in an air transport, or of hearing a voice on the opposite side of the earth.

Yes, in material things, in science and invention, the world has made marvelous progress, but what about its advancement in the true values of life—those, for example, proclaimed by the heavenly hosts—belief in and reverence for Deity—peace—brotherhood.

I like to think that man has made advancement in these fundamental matters though he lags, far, far behind his phenomenal material and scientific accomplishments.

The announcement of the first Christmas is the sweetest story ever told—the sweetest story because of the eternal principles enunciated—the "glad tidings of great joy"—were to be "unto all people." The Light of the world was to shine in every heart.

Incidents associated with the birth of the Babe of Bethlehem beautifully illustrate this fact. When the weary, travel-worn couple, Joseph and Mary, entered their old home-town of *Bet Lahm*, they anticipated securing comfortable lodgings, but "there was no room for them in the Inn." Only mothers can realize Mary's keen disappointment and fearful anxiety as she and Joseph left the Inn and again entered the darkness to seek lodgings elsewhere. The city was crowded, but among the throngs there were no friends to help, no familiar faces to alleviate their heavy feelings of loneliness—an expectant mother in need of the best, the most comfortable of accommodations, yet not an open door, not even a couch on which to rest!

Well, to quote a modern writer, Herbert Spough: "Providence has a way of overruling the best laid plans of men, and turning their errors to fit the greater, divine plan. The hour has struck for the advent of the world Deliverer, and the Lord of all is ushered into the world in a stable.

"How the guiding hand of the Ruler of worlds directed the stage setting of this greatest of world dramas time has borne testimony."

Humble shepherds informed by revelation said: "Let us now go even unto Bethlehem and see this thing which has come to pass, which the Lord hath made known unto us, . . . and they found Mary, and Joseph, and the babe lying in a manger."

Wise men from the east, were guided to him through the channel of learning—"and when they were come into the house (not the manger) they saw the young child with Mary, his mother, and fell down and worshipped him: and when they had opened their treasures they offered unto him gifts: gold and frankincense and myrrh."

When, after eight days, Mary, in conformity with the Mosaic law, took her child to the Temple, Simeon, a "just and devout" man, receiving witness by the Holy Ghost, recognized the babe as "the Lord's Christ." Taking him in his arms, he blessed God and said: "Lord, now lettest thou thy servant depart in peace, according to thy word: for mine eyes have seen thy salvation."

Thus was it shown even on the first Christmas that all people—the humble, the learned, the rich, the great— who sincerely seek the Christ will find him and become of one mind in a divine brotherhood of which the Lord is the acknowledged head.

Racial and social barriers, economic differences are overcome in the presence of Christ. Even hatred and bitterness, enmity and strife give way to the spirit of good will.

A striking illustration of this fact occurred in Flanders Field in World War I. On December 24, Britains and Germans had fought as only hated foes can fight, and as a result comrades had been wounded and others stilled in death.

When, next morning (December 25th) the sun shone in the trenches, someone cried to the enemy: "This is Christmas Day!" Then followed an exchange of greetings —cautiously, even suspiciously at first. In a few moments bayonets and bombs were laid aside, and between the trenches foes fraternized for a brief period as friends. For a few hours the spirit of Christmas entered their hearts, and they acted as sensible human beings.

If such could prevail for a day on the battle field, surely it is not inconceivable that Christian men can some day make such relationships permanent in the daily affairs of life.

Jesus knew no nationality; neither was he a respecter of persons. "Moses was a Hebrew; Socrates, an Athenian, Buddha, a Hindu; Mohammed, an Arab; Gladstone, an Englishman; Luther, a German; and Lincoln, an American; but Jesus belongs to us all. He is the universal man—the one perfect character."

As he said on the shores of Galilee, so he says to all people in this day: "Come unto me, all ye that labour and are heavy laden, and I will give you rest."

"Take my yoke upon you, and learn of me; for I am meek, and lowly in heart: and ye shall find rest unto your souls."

This Christmas Eve, as darkness envelopes the earth, each of you will retire with absolute confidence that the night will pass and on Christmas morning the earth will be filled again with the light of day. Of this you have not a shadow of doubt.

This old world is enveloped in the darkness of bigotry, intolerance, disbelief in God, and suspicion of fellowmen resulting in ill will and discord. For four thousand years and more the human race has groped in this darkness vainly seeking a light that would dispel it. Blindly have they brought upon themselves the evils of antagonism, the misery of contention, the bitterness of strife, and the horrors of war.

As absolute as the certainty that you have in your hearts that tonight will be followed by dawn tomorrow morning, so is my assurance that Jesus Christ is the Savior of mankind, the Light that will dispel the darkness of the

world, through the Gospel restored by direct revelation
to the Prophet Joseph Smith.

> O Living Christ who still
> Dost all our burdens share
> Come now and dwell within the hearts
> Of all men everywhere.

For this I earnestly pray in his name whose birth the Christian world commemorates.

INDEX

article on lawlessness, 33; fosters religion, 305.

Subversive teachings and pernicious ideas, counteracting, 204.

Suspicion and lack of trust, man must win victory over, 190.

Sutherland, statement on BYU by Chief Justice, 244.

Swearing, boyhood lesson in, 310; an evil in the L.D.S home, 313.

T.

Tabernacle Choir members, lauds, 147.

Taylor, John, incarcerated in Carthage Jail, 167; quoted on organization of Church, 178; song "Go ye messengers of glory," 179.

Taxes, the burden of, 17.

Teacher efficiency depends on personality, preparation, presentation, and prayer, 40; enables child to live well, 229.

Teachers can succeed where parents fail, 43; need for, who are loyal and noble in character, 74; characteristics of good, 75; the, responsibility, 227; young girls as, 366.

Teaching, next to parenthood as greatest responsibility, 229; second realm of women, 362.

Temper, control one's, 29; does he have mastery of, 378.

Temperance a spiritual gift, 30; church attitude toward, unmistakable, 193.

Tempers, control of, 154.

Temple marriage contributes to permanency, 186; 325; significance of, 372; what about marriage in, 380; basically appealing, 381.

Temporary in Latter-day Saint home, nothing, 358.

Temptation from within and without, resisting, 31.

Temptations, five of most common, 96.

Ten Commandments the fundamental law of humanity, 358.

Ten contributing factors to a happy home, 291.

Tennyson, Lord, quoted on war-

drums, 188; quoted on "mother", 250, 251.

Tenth load of hay, lesson of the, 308.

Test, man's earthly existence a, 30.

Testimony of God as Father and Christ as the Savior, 31; relates, which came to father in Scotland, 215; of Job, 242.

Thanksgiving, origin of, 409; account of first, 409; first, proclamation by George Washington, 412.

"This is the Place" monument dedicatory services, 170.

Thoreau quoted on "kind of ballot", 210.

Thought on character, effect of, 86.

Thoughts lead to right actions, right, 18; harbored determine destiny, 143; are seeds of acts, 206; "for a summer day", 276.

Tithing, the best sermon on, 308.

Tobacco condemned as not good for man, 193.

Tomb, the first empty, 390.

Tongues, experience with gift of, 244.

Traitor, man who violates temple covenants is a, 324.

Trusted greater than to be loved, to be, 176.

Truth is duty of every Latter-day Saint, to learn, 197; joy in awakening love for, 223; revelation defines, 240; age-old conflict between, and error, 320.

Truths, need of anchor to fixed principles and, 17.

U.

Unbroken home is Christ's ideal pertaining to marriage, 182.

Unchastity is dominant world evil, 11; a common temptation, 96; dominent evil of the day, 320.

Unclean tabernacles, Christ's spirit will not dwell in, 143.

Unfaithfulness a condition of broken home, 182.

Unhappniess springs from nonconformity, 37.

United Nations Charter for Christ, no room in, 159.